Projection
and Re-Collection
in Jungian Psychology

THE REALITY OF THE PSYCHE SERIES

Projection
and Re-Collection
in Jungian Psychology

Reflections of the Soul

Marie-Louise von Franz

Translated by William H. Kennedy

Open Court
La Salle & London

OPEN COURT and the above logo are registered in the U.S.
Patent and Trademark Office.

Originally published as *Spiegelungen der Seele: Projektion und
innere Sammlung.* ©Kreuz Verlag, Stuttgart, 1978.

Published in a clothbound edition, 1980
First paperback printing 1985
Second printing 1986
Third printing 1987
Fourth printing 1988

Printed and bound in the United States of America.

Library of Congress Catalogue Number 80-52471

ISBN 0-87548-417-4

Contents

Foreword

The part played by projection in practical psychotherapy having interested me for a long time, I finally made up my mind to investigate it. As I began to look into the subject more closely, it became clear to me that the word *projection* does, to be sure, describe a set of facts that in practice are easily enough demonstrated, but at the same time this concept leads into borderline areas where there are still unsolved problems. For some of these problems I am unable to suggest solutions; the purpose of this work is therefore limited to an attempt to shed some light on those questions that are still open. A study of these problems brings us up against a mysterious quality of human consciousness, that of *mirroring* the world. If nothing but epistemological considerations were involved, perhaps we could let the matter drop; but the phenomenon of projection is also an eminently *moral* and practical problem, which I have therefore tried, by circumambulation, to clarify a bit, with special attention to the theory of demons in antiquity. Given the demons in our present world, perhaps one or more readers will be induced to reflect seriously on these matters, which in my opinion we all need to do.

1

Definition of Projection

Projection in Everyday Life

Carl Gustav Jung borrowed the term *projection* from Sigmund Freud;[1] but as a result of his different view of the unconscious, Jung gave that concept a quite separate, new interpretation. He used the word to describe a psychological fact that can be observed everywhere in the everyday life of human beings, namely, that in our ideas about other people and situations we are often liable to make misjudgments that we later have to correct, having acquired better insight. In such cases most people acknowledge their mistake and let the matter drop, without bothering to ask themselves where the false judgment or the incorrect idea came from. The psychologist, however, cannot avoid this question, because to a quite special degree he must concern himself with correcting such misjudgments, since even with his usual neurotic patients he has to battle with these "crazy" ideas that impede the patients' adaptation. When he has to deal with pathological delusions, or indeed with whole delusory systems, as for example paranoia, then the question of where such mistaken ideas come from becomes especially acute, because, as is well known, delusory systems are by no means easily dissolved through improved insight; on the contrary, one often has the impression that the patient will cling to them with every fiber of his being. In such cases the question of the origin of the morbid complex of ideas becomes unavoidable.

It occurred to Freud, in the first instance, that the true and false impressions received by a child in his earliest experience of his parents and siblings play a role in later projections. For example, a child who has experienced his father or mother in a specifically negative form tends to *project* the same father- or mother-image onto older men or women he meets in later life, so that an unprejudiced experience of the relevant persons is no longer possible for him. Such a negative reaction lives on, stored up in the depths of the psyche, and is "projected" onto outer objects at a suitable opportunity.

To be more precise, what is projected is not only a *memory-image,* as one might at first conclude, but rather a sum of characteristic qualities *that constitutes a part of the person observed.* [2] If a son, for example, experiences his father as tyrannical, in later life he will, in many cases, not only project the quality of tyranny onto authority figures and father figures, such as his doctor, his superiors, and the state, *but he will also behave just as tyrannically himself—though unconsciously.* Nowadays there is no longer any need to look for proof of this. One sees everywhere that it is precisely the antiauthoritarian way. "Tyrannical" is thus not only a memory-image of the father, which is true or false to reality, but at the same time an image for a very real characteristic of the person in whom the projection originates, of which he himself is, however, unaware.

The difference between projection and common error is that an error can be corrected, without difficulty, by better information and then dissolve like morning fog in the sunlight.[3] In the case of a projection, on the other hand, the subject doing the projecting defends himself, in most cases strenuously, against correction, or, if he accepts correction, he then falls into a depression. He consequently appears to be diminished or disillusioned, because the psychic energy that was invested in the projection has not flowed back to the subject but has been cut off.

Thus Jung defined projection as an unconscious, that is, unperceived and unintentional, transfer of subjective psychic elements onto an outer object.[4] One sees in this object something that is not there, or, if there, only to a small degree. Seldom, if ever, is nothing of what is projected present in the object. Jung speaks therefore of a "hook" in the object on which one hangs a projection as one hangs a coat on a coat hook. We can take as an example the above-mentioned antiauthoritarian "projector." He will scarcely be able to hang his image of the tyrant onto a gentle, modest worm of a man. If, however, he has to deal with someone who shows even a relatively slight manifestation of self-assertiveness or power, the image of the tyrant lying dormant in him will immediately attach itself to the other person. The projection has taken place; the projector is utterly convinced that he has to deal with a tyrant. A mistaken judgment of this kind can then be corrected only with the greatest difficulty. Social workers, educators, and therapists could tell many a tale on this theme; every day they have to struggle with projections, generally those of parental images.

It is, however, not only a person's negative conscious qualities that are projected outward in this way but in equal measure his positive ones. The projection of the latter then brings about an excessive, delusory, inappropriate overvaluation and admiration of the object.

To the disinterested observer it seems simple and obvious at first that in this or that case there is a projection. But if one considers the case more deeply, it turns out that it is not such a simple matter. It may be that the observer's judgment is mistaken, that the projector "was right." In general, the practical criterion is common sense, the reasonable collective judgment of the environment. If someone who suffers from paranoid delusions[5] informs the police that he is being persecuted by such and such a person, this report will be investigated by so-called objective methods and it will then be decided whether the complaint has substance or not. In the latter case the plaintiff will be turned over to a psychiatrist and not prosecuted for slander. But we know that the matter is this simple only in flagrant cases, that there are borderline areas where the question of accountability arises and it becomes difficult to determine whether the projector was intentionally guilty of slander or a victim of delusions of persecution. It is also possible for a person to infect others with his paranoid idea and for a sizable group to take up the erroneous judgment, until another group finally sets the matter straight. Witch-hunts, as examples of negative projections, or the veneration of Hitler as a savior-hero, as an example of positive projections, bear eloquent witness to the existence of the phenomenon of collective contagion. In such cases nothing can lead the projecting parties to a clearer insight; even the soberest factual evidence will be emotionally dismissed.

Therefore the judgment of a community or of a society cannot always prevent the projection process and the mistaken judgments, errors, and lies that accompany it, because whole groups can project collectively, so that their mistaken judgment passes officially for the acceptable description of reality. Thus all the conceptions current in intercultural psychiatry come into play when, for example, it is a matter of distinguishing between a mass psychosis and a religious movement; the latter will usually seem to the outsider to be a mass psychosis, whereas to the insider it will be experienced as a "redemptive movement."[6]

Under the impression that each person's inner image of reality represents for him, in an absolute sense, *the* actual state of affairs, certain existentially oriented therapists try to deny altogether the evidence for projection. According to their view, each human being is hopelessly imprisoned in *his* image of reality.[7] In his novel *The Stranger,* Camus graphically depicts the tragedy of this situation.

Several representatives of an ethnologically oriented psychiatry have come to similar conclusions. According to them, distinctions between the normal and the abnormal depend upon the entire cultural and religious structure of a society and are therefore inaccessible to any general judgment whatever.[8]

In contrast to this view, W. M. Pfeiffer has rightly emphasized, in his outstanding work *Transkulturelle Psychiatrie,* that clear cases of pronounced mental illness which we diagnose as pathological are also recognized as pathological by *all* peoples known to us; their interpretation differs only with the culture. Indeed, the "norm" for normality cannot be pinned down statistically, because this involves the capacity for "adapting to the greatest possible number of life situations in an appropriate manner." Psychically conditioned morbid symptoms in a reaction are, above all, "ego–alienation" and "behavior that accords only with one's own laws."[9] Religious ecstasy and pathological possession, according to Pfeiffer, can be differentiated by European investigators, even in the case of other peoples, and here the "trivial, the nonsensical, and deviation from the traditional context" are the characteristic features of the pathological.[10]

Existentialist and sociological views that deny the explicitly pathological suffer from the fact that they do not take into consideration the manifestations of the unconscious in human beings, especially dreams. They therefore overlook a fundamental phenomenon, namely, the fact that the same unconscious from which the projections emanate also strives, in certain phases of inner development, to correct them, and that thus, in addition to the commonsense judgment of the collectivity, there is an *inner* factor in the individual himself that tends to correct his image of reality from time to time. The present work will concern itself more closely with this complicated state of affairs. First, however, it should be borne in mind that the sociological denial of the fact of projection is correct to the extent that a projection cannot be unambiguously established by the judgment of an outside observer and cannot in any case be communicated to the presumably projecting fellowman. The one says, "It is so"; the other, "It is not so"—and with that the discussion comes to an end.

To understand this, we must take a further look at the concept of *projection,* as Jung used this term. He writes:

> Just as we tend to assume that the world is as we see it, we naïvely suppose that people are as we imagine them to be. In this latter case, unfortunately, there is no scientific test that would prove the discrepancy between perception and reality. Although the possibility of gross deception is infinitely greater here than in our perception of the physical world, we still go on naïvely projecting our own psychology into our fellow human beings. In this way everyone creates for himself a series of more or less imaginary relationships based essentially on projection.[11]

In these imaginary relationships the other person becomes an *image* or a *carrier of symbols.* Although *all* the contents of the unconscious are in this fashion projected onto the environment, we can recognize them as projections only when we gain enough insight to see that they are *images* of peculiarities that are part of our own makeup; otherwise we are naïvely convinced that these peculiarities belong to the object.

Unless we are possessed of an unusual degree of self-awareness, we shall never see through our projections but must always succumb to them, because the mind in its natural state presupposes the existence of such projections.

. . . In a comparatively primitive person this creates that characteristic relationship to the object which Lévy-Bruhl has fittingly called "mystic identity" or "participation mystique."[12]

Jung calls this *the archaic identity of subject and object.* The need for the dissolution of this identity arises at the moment *when it becomes disturbing, that is, when the absence of the projected content substantially interferes with adaptation, so that the integration of the projected content into the subject is desirable.*

The archaic identity of subject and object is, in its specific form, dominant in children and primitives, among others. Whenever it prevails, the unconscious is merged with the outer world. In such a case it is not yet possible to speak of an ego-environment relation, because an ego, as we understand it, hardly exists. The consciousness of the child, like that of the primitive, is more like an *"immersion in a stream of events in which the outer and the inner world are not differentiated, or very indistinctly so."*[13] The unconscious, as we know it today, has become perceptible only through the differentiation of consciousness. With the primitive the inner is also, in infinitely greater measure, the outer, and vice versa. This immersion in a stream of events in which inner and outer are not clearly distinguished is nevertheless, to a large extent, still a normal condition with us, too, a condition that is interrupted only from time to time to the extent that the reflecting consciousness and a certain ego-continuity intervene.

The less pronounced yet definitely present discrimination of outer from inner world in the case of the child can perhaps best be observed in his play with dolls. On the one hand, the child treats the outer doll as animate, in accordance with an inner image of a mother-child relationship, but, on the other hand, he shows just as clearly, in his behavior, that somewhere he also "knows" that the doll is inanimate. By contrast, many adults can no longer join unaffectedly in play of this kind, because their conviction that the doll is inanimate and the mother–child game is "only fantasy" (therefore only inner) hinders them in acting out the game. We would have to go back rather far, as far back perhaps as our animal ancestors, before we reached the point where inner and outer were *completely* undifferentiated. But the archaic identity of subject and object still lives at the very bottom of our psyche, and it is only above that layer that relatively clearer, more distinct discriminations between subject and object are, in many degrees, built up. This lower or more primitive layer should, however, not be regarded as lesser in *value;* on the contrary, if we must form a value judgment, it is there that the real secret of all life-intensity and cultural creativity lies. It is simply the normal condition that produces all our affective "magic" ties to people and objects. As Jung emphasizes:

> Thus every normal person of our time, who is not reflective beyond the average, is bound to his environment by a whole system of projections. So long as all goes well, he is totally unaware of the compulsive, i.e., "magical" or "mystical," character of these relationships. . . . So long as the libido can use these projections as agreeable and convenient bridges to the world, they will alleviate life in a positive way. But as soon as the libido wants to strike out on another path, and for this purpose begins running back along the previous bridges of projection, they will work as the greatest hindrances it is possible to imagine, for they effectively prevent any real detachment from the former object. We then witness the characteristic phenomenon of a person trying to devalue the former object as much as possible in order to detach his libido from it.[14] But as the previous identity is due to the projection of subjective contents, complete and final detachment can only take place when the imago that mirrored itself in the object is restored, together with its meaning, to the subject. This restoration is achieved through conscious recognition of the projected content, that is, by acknowledging the "symbolic value" of the object.[15]

Therefore, although the original identity of subject and object represents a normal condition, nature has developed, apparently as a result of certain *disturbances* in the adaptation to the inner and/or outer world, a more continuous ego-consciousness in the human being, which forces a sharper differentiation between subject and object, and thus insight into certain projections. Primarily this means simply that something hitherto perceived as outer is now recognized as belonging to one's own inner world. But our mentality is still today so primitive, as Jung emphasizes, "that only certain functions and areas have outgrown the primary mystic identity with the object. Primitive man has a minimum of self-awareness combined with a maximum of attachment to the object; hence the object can exercise a direct magical compulsion upon him. . . . Self-awareness gradually developed out of this initial state of identity and went hand in hand with the differentiation of subject and object. . . . But as everyone knows, our self-awareness is still a long way behind our actual knowledge."[16] To be precise, we could in practice speak of a projection only *"when the need to dissolve the identity with the object has already arisen,"* or, in other words, when the identity begins to have a disturbing effect and exerts a negative influence on the adaptation to the outer world. At this point the identity of the inner image with the outer object becomes perceptible and the object of criticism, whether it be our own or that of other people.[17]

The Five Stages
in the Withdrawal of Projections

The process of gaining insight into a projection takes place in several stages.[18] As an example Jung refers to the case of a Nigerian soldier who heard a voice calling to him from a tree, whereupon he tried to break out of the barracks in order to go to the tree. When interrogated, the soldier stated that everyone who bore the name of this tree heard its voice from time to time. To us this is a case of the above-mentioned archaic identity, because, for the soldier, the tree and the voice were obviously identical.[19] A separation of the idea of the tree from that of the voice or of a tree-demon (as the ethnologist might put it, in this case) is actually a secondary phenomenon, corresponding to the next stage of consciousness, since a *differentiation* has now taken place. A third stage would arise with the need for a *moral evaluation* of the phenomenon of the voice, which would be seen as the manifestation of an evil or of a good spirit. A fourth stage would go still one step further in the process of elucidation. At this stage the existence of spirits would be denied altogether and the experience written off as an *illusion*. At the next, or fifth stage, one would have to reflect on how such an overpowering, extremely real, and awesome experience could suddenly become nothing but self-deception. Even if one must perhaps assume that trees do not talk in human speech and that no spirit inhabits the tree itself or even that, looked at objectively, no "spirit" at all was heard by the soldier, this perception of a spirit must nevertheless have been a phenomenon pushing upward out of his unconscious, whose *psychic* existence cannot be denied unless one denies the reality of the psyche altogether. If we do not do this, today we would describe the spirit in the tree as a projection, which does not, however, imply an illusion but rather a psychic reality of the highest order. The distinction, too, as to whether this spirit was good or evil then becomes relevant again and highly important. In the case of the Nigerian soldier, punishment hinged on whether, in our language, he had unconsciously wished to desert or had experienced a "spiritual call"—the same problem, therefore, that our courts today *mutatis mutandis* have to deal with under the rubric "Refusal to serve for reasons of conscience."

If one recognizes the *psychic* reality of the voice the soldier heard, one has to investigate where and how this unconscious content belongs to him. If it proves impossible to locate the utterances of this content in the subjective environment of the experiencing subject (for example, that the soldier had heard in this voice a wish to desert that could be shown to be *his own* wish), then outer "suitable" objects must be considered as possible causes of the voice, and the cycle starts all over again. If, on the other hand, it could be shown that the spirit was part of the soldier's own psychology, then the task of *moral integration* of this content arises, through which the "good" or "evil" aspect could be understood as the subject's own unconscious tendency and could be integrated into his life. In the present case the unconscious attempt to break out might perhaps in the end prove to be in no way evil. If the integration of such a content occurs successfully, then, as we know today, the experience of a spirit calling out of a tree is not repeated; if the content is *not* integrated, then the same or similar phenomena will occur in another context.

What is known as integration in modern psychology is thus a remarkable and complicated process, in which a hitherto unconscious psychic content is brought repeatedly into the view of the conscious ego and recognized as belonging to its own personality. In the process this content is changed in its functioning and effects. What integration means in *practice* is illustrated by this Chinese ghost story:

> A young man who had been called up for military service was on the way to report for duty. One night, having found no other shelter, he lay down to sleep in an old half-ruined temple. As it grew dark he suddenly saw a ghostly pale, eerie woman with a rope in her hand, sneaking away. He followed her without being noticed and observed her disappear into the house of a poor peasant. In the house a young woman, dissolved in tears, was sitting at the bedside of a small child. The ghost sat on the roof-beam above her, dangling the rope in such a way that it kept making the movements of a hanging. The young woman succumbed to the suggestion, climbed on a chair, and prepared to hang herself. The soldier broke in through the window, seized the rope, and warned the young

woman: "Take good care of your child; we have only *one* life to lose!" On his way back to the temple the ghost appeared and demanded her rope, but the soldier wrapped it around his arm and tried to frighten the ghost away. A struggle followed. Inadvertently the soldier struck his own nose with his fist and blood flowed. "Because ghosts cannot endure the sight of human blood," the ghost stopped fighting and disappeared. The soldier then went on his way, to report for service. Later, the rope could be seen on the soldier's naked arm, "because it had grown onto the arm and surrounded it in the form of a ring of red flesh."[20]

According to a belief prevalent in China, the spirits of women who have hanged themselves from grief over their unhappy lives cannot move on into the kingdom of the dead until they have brought about the suicide of another woman; that was why the evil female spirit had tried to move the young mother to suicide. It is well known that suicide can be contagious, as cases of mass suicide in schools and prisons especially attest. They come from a kind of chain reaction, for which the rope carried by the ghost is an appropriate symbol. In this story it looks at first as though the soldier had become involved with the ghost and her problem only by chance. If, however, we take into consideration the fact that this young man was on his way to military service, which meant giving up for years any possibility of having a wife and children, then from the psychological point of view it is not merely an accident that he was confronted with the weeping young woman. Something in him was surely also concerned with the problem of death. Interestingly enough, it was the soldier's act of *inadvertently hitting his own nose*, thereby causing blood to flow, that frightened the ghost away. Blood symbolizes everywhere the emotional part of the human psyche. *His own effective participation* and the blow against himself that this involved conquered the ghost. The fateful rope then became a part of the soldier himself; it literally became integrated into him, not as a sign of shame but rather as a badge of honor. What had been an objective concatenation of destructive tendencies became a part of his own being and was thereby robbed of its destructive power. The evil spirit herself, however, was not liquidated but only disappeared from the human field of vision.

This last-mentioned fact corresponds exactly to an experience with which we are familiar: unconscious contents can scarcely ever be integrated into the subject in their entirety. The process appears to be more like that of peeling an onion—one or more layers of an unconscious complex can, indeed, be integrated by the conscious personality but not the core itself. However, the core falls back into the unconscious in a condition of latency and is no longer an immediate problem. A resolution does *not* result, though, if further meaningful but unconscious contents remain attached to the bearer of the projection.[21] In this case the *whole* content of the projected image will not become conscious. This is in fact generally the case with archetypal contents, because such contents cannot be integrated by ego-consciousness.[22] Consequently a phenomenon occurs that could be described as *the wanderings of projections:* the unconscious content is in part recognized as subjective and thereby differentiated from the object in which it hitherto appeared as a projection; its still-unrecognized aspect, however, appears again projected onto another object after a period of latency in the unconscious. Or it may appear in another medium, which now becomes the new bearer of the projection.[23] If one wants to prevent such a renewal of the projection, the content must be recognized as *psychically real,* though not as a part of the subject but rather as an *autonomous power.*

Jung once compared the ego-complex to a man who sails out in his boat (the philosophical or religious ideas behind his conscious view of the world) onto the sea of the unconscious to go fishing. He must take care not to haul more fish (that is, more unconscious contents) from the sea into his boat than the boat can carry, or it will sink. This explains why people with weak egos often defend themselves so desperately against any and every insight into their negative projections—they cannot bear the weight, the moral pressure, that results from such insight. The projection of positive qualities can, to be sure, be dissolved with less resistance in most cases, but if a person is weak he flies away, blown up like a balloon, from the solid ground of reality; he suffers an inflation and thus also lapses into unconsciousness.[24] The withdrawal and integration of projections is therefore a delicate problem that, in treatment, demands great sensitivity of feeling on the part of the therapist. He must constantly keep asking himself whether the analysand's ego is strong enough to hold up under the impact of insight into a projection. As mentioned above, apparently a human being can almost never assimilate the archetypal core of all personal complexes; this is why there are ghost stories all over the world in which the spirit, after the completion of certain tasks, disappears, appeased, into the Beyond. So the spirit lives on, but his efforts toward the more drastic forms of harassing human beings cease. If we could see through all our projections down to the last traces, our personality would be extended to cosmic dimensions. But this is a subject that will be treated later.

A Norwegian story, "The Comrade," illustrates the same problem as the Chinese fairy tale.

A peasant lad who had dreamed of a beautiful princess sets out, with what little he has inherited, to look for this beautiful being. On his way, before the door of a church, he comes across a corpse frozen in a block of ice that is spit at by every passerby. He learns that the corpse is that of a wine-dealer who had diluted his wine with water. The pastor has refused him a Christian burial. The lad feels pity for the sinner and gives all he has for his burial. When he goes on his way, an unknown man joins him as a "traveling companion" and offers to win for him the beautiful princess, who is bewitched by a troll. After many battles and much hardship and toil, all of which the companion undergoes as a stand-in for the hero, the princess is won. A year later, the companion reveals that he is the dead wine-dealer and that that was his way of rendering thanks, "but now he must go away forever, because the bells of heaven are calling."[25]

In a German parallel,[26] the dead man is not a sinner but simply so poor that no one will bury him. In this story the hero also donates all his money to have the man buried. The latter, too, as a companion experienced in magic, helps the hero to find and redeem the princess he desires. At the end, he says, "Now I am leaving you and the world. I believe that I have paid my debt to you. May your life be a good and a happy one." After which he, too, disappears.

In these examples the ghost of the one who has died escapes into the Beyond after having expressed gratitude to the hero for his compassionate act. What had been wrong is expiated; as in the Chinese fairy tale, no further aspect of this figure is assimilated.

The poor sinner whose debt the hero pays is, psychologically understood, that component of the human psyche which Jung has described as the shadow, that is, the inferior, all-too-human side of each of us that we are so especially ready to project and then "spit at." The hero feels sorry for him and takes upon himself the price of his guilt. Through this act he gains a helper with magic powers for every emergency. It is the hero's *sympathetic response* to the other's need that effects the bond.

Jung distinguished between two kinds of projection, the active and the passive. Our example illustrates a passive projection, that is, an act of sympathetic feeling, which serves to bring the object (in this case, the dead man) into an intimate relation with the subject (the hero). "In order to establish this relationship, the subject detaches a content—a feeling, for instance—from himself, lodges it in the object, thereby animating it, and in this way draws the object into the sphere of the subject."[27] As a result of his empathetic compassion, the hero gains the magically gifted comrade as companion in his personal enterprise. In the end all compassion is grounded in this kind of unconscious identity with the other.[28] This forms the basis of all our unconscious collectivism and also of all conscious social attitudes, even in their most sublime forms, as with us it has found its highest expression in the ideal of Christian love for one's neighbor. When unconscious identity operates negatively it causes us, naïvely and thoughtlessly, to take for granted that the other is like us and that what is valid for us is also valid for him, so that we feel justified in "improving" him, that is, in raping him psychologically. This is the origin of active projection.

The negative aspect of identity is especially clear in pathological cases, as, for example, in paranoid delusions of reference, where it is assumed as self-evident that one's own subjective content is to be found in the other person. This assumption is at the same time an act of judgment, whose basic aim is a separation of subject from object.[29] If this judgment is taken as absolutely valid, it can lead to the total isolation of the subject, because all criticism of the validity of this judgment by other people is rejected.[30]

Passive projection—that is, unconscious empathy—is part of the psychological principle of Eros and forms the basis of all social relations; active projection, on the other hand, belongs to the realm of Logos, since it is concerned with an act of recognition or judgment, by means of which we make a distinction between ourselves and the—itself unknown—object. Both principles can in practice flow into and out of each other.

The projections of our fellow beings onto ourselves are by no means harmless affairs that disturb nothing but the adaptation of the people from whom they issue; they also substantially affect the person onto whom the projection falls. The projections of parents onto their children are especially influential, because children and young people are very suggestible, for their ego-consciousness is still weak.

As this is a common situation it is frequently pictured in

myths and fairy tales. In Grimms' fairy tale "The Six Swans," the witchlike stepmother throws a garment over her stepsons, thereby transforming them into swans. This can be taken quite literally as projection: the mother, being negatively disposed to the children, sees in them not their own human nature but rather throws over them the projection of something (bird-image) existing in her, namely, her own unconscious, neglected spiritual side. One comes across this quite often in everyday life, when a mother, out of laziness or for other reasons, neglects her own spiritual development. To compensate, she expects the achievement from her son or sons and "bewitches" them into something that is alien to their nature. The sons, for instance, may have to pursue an ambitious academic career in order to satisfy the mother's unconscious expectation—in the fairy tale just mentioned, they become birds, that is, rootless, dehumanized spirit-beings.

The release of the bewitched beings in the fairy tale occurs when the loving sister (or sometimes the bride) sews a shirt of starlike flowers for the bewitched and throws it over them, whereby the birds once again assume human form. This, too, is a projection, albeit one that fits the object, which indeed actually makes it possible for him to appear in his true nature. Many people are, in fact, brought back to themselves through the loving appreciation of another person. The teacher or the therapist who gives credit, so to speak, to his pupil or patient through the expectation of positive results can often nurture a blossoming of the other's real personality and gifts. Perhaps it is not important that it is a projection; it operates like a bridge across which the other can come into himself. That is why the phenomenon of countertransference is so important in psychotherapy, and not just as a disadvantage to be combatted; it can carry the other like a magic carpet and guide him to his goal. *One day,* though, this projection naturally falls away, and then it must be proven whether the other can remain himself even without such help. This transition can be managed with the necessary wisdom, through careful attention to the dreams of both parties.

Whenever parents fail to live their inner wholeness and fail to realize substantial components of themselves, the weight of these parts falls onto the children in the form of a projection and endangers them. This is recognized even in folklore sayings, such as "Parson's children and the miller's calf seldom, if ever, turn out well." Clergymen are often forced by public opinion to live better or more Christian lives than they would if they lived the reality of their own natures. In cases where they identify with their social role, thus repressing the shadow, the latter falls over the children like a garment of an evil witch. The children find themselves driven by a dark compulsion to live out everything the parents have repressed.

The miller's calf, though, presents a slightly different problem. In the eyes of country people the miller is traditionally seen as a man who does not work but grows rich through a *technical trick:* he lets water do the work for him. He is the first technocrat. His calf—that is, his instinctual animal sphere—naturally suffers from this.

In past generations, as Freud was the first to recognize, the repression of sexual impulses had a conspicuously destructive effect. Through this repression many fathers and mothers either forced their children into an uninhibited acting out of sexuality or—in the case of children who unconsciously defended themselves against this projection—made it impossible for them to approach the sexual area of life, because this image had been corrupted or distorted for them by their parents' projections. This situation is pictured in many myths in which a parent shuts the son or daughter into a tower or a glass mountain or a glass coffin, or, through a curse, turns him or her into an animal. In families, projections play the greatest and most disastrous role. But they also play an active part in all other social groups, not least in politics, where certain shadow projections onto the opponent can be shown on both sides in almost all emotionally loaded conflicts.

The reason it is so difficult to acquire insight into one's own shadow is that inferior personality traits are mostly of an *emotional* nature. Emotions and affects are to a large extent relatively autonomous; they possess consciousness and can only with great difficulty be controlled. Projections coupled with emotions isolate the human being from his surroundings and put him into an autoerotic or autistic state.[31] If it is not only his own shadow that stands behind the projections but also the contra-sexual components of the personality, or perhaps still deeper archetypal contents, then insight into the projections in which these are involved is accompanied by almost insuperable difficulties. The father and mother divinities of all religions, for instance, are now often found to be lurking behind a not particularly unusual projection of a father- or mother-imago, and these give to the parental images a wholly inappropriate power over the individual. Or else it is a matter not of collective religious images or ideas but rather of modern variations of these, such as materialism, communism, socialism, fascism, liberalism, intellectualism, and so on—ideas by which people are completely "possessed" and for which they can fight with murderous emotions.[32] "Sacred" convictions are in this sense always suspect, unless they exist together with tolerance and a due regard for purely human considerations.

Projection and Projectile

The archaic identity of subject and object, which is the basis of the phenomenon of projection, persists subliminally, as mentioned above, even in highly cultivated men and women. *In the unconscious the inner world and the outer world are not differentiated.* Only that which has become a content of consciousness is described as an inner or an outer phenomenon, that is, either as an introspectively perceived condition, like the welling up of an emotion, or as an "outer" event or object. Everything else, of which we are not conscious, remains, as before, an undifferentiated part of the occurrences of life. This is why, as we said at the outset, one cannot speak of projection in the strict sense until a disturbance arises that necessitates the revision of a merely assumed perception or of a judgment that has been accepted without reflection. This disturbance finds expression as doubt or uncertainty or in a tendency to defend the previous judgment in an unrealistic way— precisely because its credibility is already undermined from within or without.

Since projection is a preconscious, involuntary process, independent of consciousness, it is to be expected that the process itself will be depicted in products of the unconscious, such as dreams, waking fantasies, and mythological traditions. This aspect will therefore be given special attention in what follows, so that the still-open question of exactly *where* projections come from may perhaps be somewhat clarified.

Whenever projection takes place, there is first of all a "sender" and a "receiver." Interestingly enough, the motif of the sender (of the figure from whom magical effects emanate) is central to many myths, but even more frequently the motif of the one who is "hit" is at the core of the myth, which may often deal with the question of defense against such effects. These will be considered here, because this is an aspect of projection that seldom receives much attention in therapy at present.

One of the oldest ways of symbolizing projection is by means of projectiles, especially the magic arrow or shot that harms other people. The oldest explanation for the causes of illness—to be found almost everywhere in the world—is of a projectile that affects its target for good or ill.[33] It is generally believed that such a projectile is shot by a god, spirit, demon, or some other mythological being, or by an evil person, and that it hits people, and perhaps animals as well, causing them to fall ill. One is reminded of the original relation between the German *Krankheit* (illness) and *kränken* (to hurt or wound).[34] Whether the archer who shoots the arrow should be regarded as inner or outer is a question better left until the material at hand has been examined more closely. Lauri Honko, in his book *Krankheitsprojektile,* has supplied an abundant collection of documentary evidence, to which we shall refer.[35]

In ancient Judaism there is the idea that God (also the devil, in the New Testament) and/or evil human beings send forth harmful arrows. In Psalm 91 there is the passage: "You will not fear the terror of the night, nor the arrow that flies by day, nor the pestilence that stalks in darkness, nor the destruction that wastes at noonday." Job's plague was also caused by Yahweh's arrows: "For the arrows of the Almighty are in me; my spirit drinks their poison; the terrors of God are arrayed against me" (Job 6:4).[36]

But the evil, harmful words of human beings are also described as arrows. Deceitful men "bend their tongue like a bow; falsehood and not truth has grown strong in the land. . . . Their tongue is a deadly arrow; it speaks deceitfully" (Jeremiah 9:3, 8). They "aim bitter words like arrows, shooting from ambush at the blameless" (Psalm 64:3–4).

That these quotations refer to affective, calumnious activities of human beings and that such activities, as we learn from practical psychological experience, are triggered by negative projections is clear enough. As soon as a person projects a bit of his shadow onto another human being he is incited to this kind of rancorous speech. The words (barbs, punches!) that hit the other person like projectiles symbolize the negative flow of energy directed against the other by the one who is projecting. When one becomes the target of another person's negative projection, one often experiences that hatred almost physically as a projectile.

It is more difficult to understand the arrows of a god, or of God, as representing projections, and yet the dispatch of arrows bringing sickness or death is ascribed to divine figures with special frequency. In ancient Vedic literature the god Rudra sends death and illness with his arrows, as we read in the *Rig-Veda.*

> To Rudra I bring thee songs, whose bow is firm and
> strong, . . . with swiftly flying shafts . . . armed with sharp-
> pointed weapons: may he hear our call.
>
> He through his lordship thinks on beings of the earth, on
> heavenly beings. . . . heal all sickness. . . . Thou very gracious
> God, hast thousand medicines: inflict no evil on our sons or
> progeny.[37]

Rudra's arrows could produce fever, coughing, malignant
tumors, and stabbing pains! Whereas today all these illnesses
are considered to be physical, the word *arrowhead* or *arrow-
point* was also used in the *Rig-Veda* to indicate the cause of
purely psychic disturbances. The Indic word *salya* means "arrowhead," "thorn," "splinter"; in one text it is said of the
doctor who removes such an object from the body of a
patient that he is "like a judge who in a trial pulls out the
thorn of injustice." Here the arrow is something *like a bad affect*
that has led to illness out of *uncertainty* about the justice of a
situation.

Today we know that sharp, jabbing forms in the drawings
of patients indicate *evil, wounding, destructive impulses* that
stand in the way of a synthesis of the personality.[38] When
in mythological representations arrows of this kind are sent
by gods (not by evil humans), these destructive impulses,
regarded psychologically, are produced by unconscious archetypal contents. Spears and arrowheads are symbolic expressions of "direction," the directedness of psychic energy,
as has been established in countless drawings by patients.[39]

In the mythology of classic antiquity, Apollo and Artemis
were especially noted for sending death and disease via their
arrows. Thus Apollo sent a plague to the army attacking
Troy (*Iliad* I, 43ff), because Agamemnon had insulted one of
his priests. In Roman renderings, Apollo and Mars dispatch
arrows of disease. Arrows from a god, however, produce not
only sickness and death; sudden seizures of passionate love
also come from the arrows of the god Eros (Cupid, Amor).
Suddenly falling passionately in love is also experienced as

rather like a sickness, in that one pines away or languishes. In Indian mythology the love-god Kama is armed with bow and arrow, and Buddha describes the erotic wish as an arrow: "But if those sensual pleasures fail the person who desires and wishes for them, he will suffer, pierced by the arrow of pain."[40]

In late antiquity the suspicion had already arisen that certain gods might have something to do with the way in which emotions work in human beings, a view that was especially furthered by astrological speculations. Thus Saturn has something to do with a melancholy turn of mind, Mars with aggression and initiative, Venus and Cupid with love and sexuality—all states of mind or moods that strike people suddenly and overwhelmingly and for a time can subjugate the conscious ego. The symbol of the arrow is a visual expression of being suddenly "hit" by a mood or an emotion that often strikes one like lightning out of a blue sky.

The gods are representations of certain natural constants of the unconscious psyche, of the ways in which the emotional and imaginative elements of the personality behave. As is well known, Jung described these constants as archetypes. These are innate irrepresentable structures that always and everywhere on suitable occasions produce similar thoughts, mythological images, feelings, and emotions in human beings, parallel to the instincts, those impulses to action that are characteristic of the human species. These archetypal symbol-forms were in principle assumed to exist in a visible material or invisible spiritual outer world, but the notion that they issued from an inner psychic space unknown to man gradually took hold in late antiquity. This led to an interesting new conception of human personality that Isodor, the son of the Gnostic Basilides, handed down to us—namely, that the human being, or alternatively his ego, also possesses a *prosphyes psyche,* a soul that has "grown onto" him and belongs to a species of animal souls, like those of wolves, monkeys, and lions. These represent affective states that seduce a

man into evil deeds against his will.[41] The Gnostic Valen-
tinus, on the other hand, suspected that such "appendages"
(prosartemata) might also consist of invading spirits.[42] These
spirits *(pneumata)* seduce the human being into indecent desires by bewildering him or confusing him with images of
lust, as with a "fog of evil." While the animal souls tend to
depict the more instinctual aspect of the unconscious, those of
the spirits and the gods appear to represent the more archetypal, that is, the more *spiritual,* contents of the unconscious,
although the two realms overlap a good deal as to their significance, which is not surprising in view of the close relationship of spirit and instinct (which will be discussed below).

When an archetype is immediately and intensively constellated, the experience is like being hit by a projectile sent by an
overpowering being that transfixes us and brings us into its
power. At the same time we are assailed by fantasies and imaginary images experienced either as proceeding directly from
the inner world (for example, as an obsessive idea) or, more
often, as caused by an outer object. An attack of aggressive
hatred, for example, is felt by us as coming not from Mars
but rather from an "evil adversary" who "deserves" to be
hated (shadow projection), erotic passion not from Cupid
but from a woman who arouses this passion in a man (anima
projection). *Ultimately, however, it appears that projections always originate in the archetypes and in unconscious complexes.*[43]

Dreams can substantiate this even more precisely. Thus a
woman dreamed that an unknown figure said to her, "You
have romantic, dreamy blue eyes." The dream-figure had
such eyes, while the dreamer herself has lively grey-green
eyes. One must conclude from this that the dream-figure
projects onto the dreamer's ego a quality that belongs to the
unknown figure and not to the ego-complex. The unknown
dream-figure, however, would be an as yet unconscious partial personality (a complex) of the dreamer, of whose existence she has hitherto known nothing. Nor, apparently, does
the dream-figure know herself, and she therefore projects her

own image onto the dreamer's ego, probably with the intention of inducing the ego to see herself as dreamily romantic and thus to identify with the complex. Presumably this happens in the interest of integration.

When other people project positive or negative qualities onto us, this often produces a certain ego-insecurity. We no longer know whether we really have such splendid or such ugly traits or not, especially since there is almost always a "hook" on which the projection is hung. If in addition our own unconscious complexes can cast such projections onto our ego, as the above dream shows, this can lead to a further source of mistaken judgments by the ego about itself. Sometimes it really seems as if bewildering imaginary images were buzzing all around one, as Democritus once expressed it. As he saw it, the outer world is filled not only with atoms but also with animated images, which he called *demons* or spiritual principles.[44] These *eidola,* or *dianoetikai phantasiai,* can harm us or help us; they appear with special clarity in dreams but also float around us during the day as fantasy images. Only a subtle spirit, says Democritus, can tell them apart, whereas ordinary human beings confuse these fantasy images with concretely perceived objects.[45]

Small wonder, then, that one needs a long process of maturing and a good bit of self-knowledge before coming to a relatively constant ego-identity and a moderate, level-headed estimate of oneself. The attribution of a psychic content in another person's imagination to one's own being, or its rejection as the other's projection, is an occasion not only for critical thinking but also for a feeling evaluation; it can therefore never be managed purely intellectually.

Subjective Level and Objective Level

The same problem of correct attribution of psychic elements arises in the interpretation of dream images, because in dreams, as apparently in the unconscious in general, inner and outer are not separated. With dream figures and with objects appearing in dreams we therefore have to decide in each case whether to regard them as symbols of the dreamer's unconscious psychic aspects that belong to his personality (interpretation on the subjective level) or as information that throws light on outer occurrences and persons (interpretation on the objective level).[46] In general, one can use the rule of thumb that dream figures and objects pictured in a dream in a way that diverges sharply from the person or object as seen in reality are more likely to lend themselves to interpretation on the subjective level than those that appear to reflect outer objects with relative exactitude. But this rule is by no means infallible. If, for example, a man dreams of his wife in the guise of a witchlike monster, is this an objective insight into a side of his wife that until now he has been unaware of, or does it represent an ugly side of his own feeling-life that he is projecting onto his wife? In such a situation one can hardly avoid taking into account the judgment of others in interpreting the dream. If those in the immediate environment regard the wife as an evil witch and the dreamer as blind to her faults, the therapist will lean strongly toward an interpretation on the objective level. If, on the other hand, the wife passes in general as a person of integrity, the therapist is likely to prefer an interpretation on the subjective level. If at the same time we also keep in mind the psychological fact that there is always a "hook" for every projection, we have to ask: Is the image, when interpreted on the objective level, an exaggeration or not? *Exaggeration indicates, in most cases, an interpretation on the subjective level.*[47]

The presence or absence of exaggeration, however, can often be determined only through a feeling evaluation, which in dream interpretation demands a high degree of sensitivity to nuance and atmosphere.[48] It is, moreover, important to differentiate, as Jung emphasizes, between a quality or property that is really present in the object and the *value* or *meaning* this object possesses for the dreamer, that is, for the energy invested in the assessment.[49] It can happen, too, that the other genuinely possesses the qualities of character or the momentary attitude that the projector thinks he sees in him, so that in this way he actually attracts the projection directly to himself. This is especially likely when the bearer is unconscious of the quality. It will then affect the unconscious of the other, thus attracting his projection. This explains why projections so often attract counterprojections, a fact now well known as a result of the much-discussed problem of transference and countertransference in therapy.[50]

If a particular quality is obviously present in another person, one must remember that the outwardly perceived quality is also present in the subject, where it forms part of the object-image.[51] This is an image existing independently of and yet based on all perception[52] whose relative autonomy remains unconscious so long as it appears to coincide with the actual behavior of the outer object.[53] As a result, however, the outer object or the person onto whom something is projected has thus received an exaggerated value and is able to produce an unmediated psychic effect upon us. This can be seen most clearly in cases where the mental image of a long-dead father or mother continues to exert a magical power over the children, because the object-imago, the image of the parents, has lived on as actively as ever. This kind of overvaluation of an outer object can seriously damage the development of a human life. Nothing but a step forward along the road to self-knowledge through discrimination and individual differentiation will lead one out of this situation.[54] The inner mental image, the object-imago, must be recognized as an *inner* factor; this is the only way in which the value or the energy invested in the image can flow back to the individual, who has need of it for his development.[55] This difficult moral task makes it impossible for any relatively conscious person to want to improve other people and the world.

Jung often maintained that if one had in himself only 3

percent of all the evil one sees in the other fellow or projects onto him, and the other fellow possessed in fact the other 97 percent, it would still be wiser to look one's own 3 percent in the eye, because, as is well known, it is only in oneself that one can change anything, almost never in others.

Nevertheless, experience has shown that dreams often warn the dreamer in a very realistic way against outer dangers, so that a persistent interpretation of all dreams on the subjective level must definitely be avoided. Jung reported a case of a neurotic young man whose fiancée appeared in his dreams in a highly ambiguous light. Investigations revealed that she lived as a prostitute. The dreamer had had no suspicion of this.[56] It would not have been advisable, for the good of the dreamer, to interpret these dreams only on the subjective level, because they obviously were trying to warn him against a commitment to the actual woman. Of course, he too must have had a sort of "prostitute" in himself; it was nevertheless obviously very important that he detach himself from his fiancée in outer reality. This approach turned out to have been correct, for his hysterical symptom disappeared as soon as he broke his engagement. If his unconscious had been pointing to realization on the subjective level, the pains would not have abated after a separation and it would have been necessary to ask where in his life the dreamer was prostituting himself with his own feelings. Recognizing when and which dream images point inward and which point outward is a delicate and uncertain matter. It is perhaps worthwhile, therefore, to turn back once again to some ethnological material, in order to look more closely at the empirical aspects.

Possession and Loss of Soul

Belief in the so-called sickness projectiles discussed above is found, according to Lauri Honko, everywhere on the American mainland (except in southern Alaska) and in particular in

Boothia, Melville, Quebec, and southern Argentina,[57] as well as in Australia, Melanesia, and Indonesia. It is also widespread in Europe and is found sporadically in Africa. In Asia, however, it is almost unknown, except in northern Siberia, the Chukotski Peninsula, and here and there in the south. In high cultures like those of Egypt, the Near East, and India, it was also known at one time but was gradually replaced by the belief that disease is caused by an "invading spirit," a view also dominant in Africa and China. In the cultures of the Incas and the Aztecs, too, the "projectile explanation" of disease appears to have been current at one time. It was later replaced by the view that disease was the consequence of breaking a tabu. Wherever sickness is explained as the result of the invasion of the patient by a spirit, the most frequent form of therapy consists in transferring the spirit either to the healer, who spits it out and annihilates it, or onto an animal, which is sacrificed as soon as it is seized by the spirit. A special case is that of possession, in which the invading spirit can speak through the patient's mouth; this conception is used especially in explaining mental disease.[58] It is not always a matter of evil spirits who cause disease; divine revelations and the utterances of spirits in shamanistic séances come into expression in the same way.

In the Bible, Jesus heals diseases by driving out evil spirits (Matthew 8:16, 10:8; Mark 1:34, 39, 5:8–10; Luke 6:18), and this procedure has been known all over Europe since the earliest times. The ceremony of healing in such cases consists in driving out the evil spirits, as the exorcist still does today in the Catholic Church.[59]

From the psychological point of view it is clear that in all these cases the "spirit" is regarded as not belonging to the personality of the sufferer. He belongs to an "objective" outer world that is somewhere, visibly or invisibly, present, as is likewise the case with the "good" spirits who manifest themselves through revelations in visions, dreams, or shamanistic séances.

Another, diametrically opposed, conception is also wide-spread, according to which the "soul," a substance necessary to a human being's survival and health, has gotten lost: the phenomenon of "loss of soul."[60] The soul can be lost in sleep, by being suddenly awakened, by fright or sneezing, but especially often by being stolen by an evil spirit. Above all, there is the fear that someone who has died may take the soul of someone close to him along with him into the realm of the dead. In such cases the patient sickens hopelessly and goes along, unless someone with a knowledge of healing finds his lost soul in time and is able to return it to its rightful owner. This understanding of sickness is dominant in arctic and sub-arctic shamanistic cultures but is also found sporadically in America, Africa, Indonesia, and Oceania. There is also evidence of it in Europe.[61]

Both "loss of soul" and an "invading spirit" can also be observed today as psychological phenomena in the everyday lives of the human beings around us. "Loss of soul" appears in the form of a sudden onset of apathy and listlessness; the joy has gone out of life, initiative is crippled, one feels empty, everything seems pointless.[62] Close observation, especially of dreams, will reveal that a large part of the psychic energy has flowed off into the unconscious and is therefore no longer at the disposal of the ego. This quantum of energy is in most cases attracted by an unconscious complex that is thereby heavily charged (corresponding to the belief that the soul has been taken by a spirit or by the ghost of a person who has died—that is, by the complex). If one perseveres long enough in this condition, in most cases the complex that was activated by the energy attracted to it appears in consciousness; an intense new interest in life emerges, an interest that now strives in a direction different from the previous one. In very many endogenous depressions one can observe beneath the crippling stagnation of the personality an especially intense desire of some sort (power, love, expansion compulsion, aggression, and so on), which the depressed patient, however, does not, for a variety of reasons, dare to allow to come to the surface; in this respect he is like the fabled fox who finds the grapes too sour.

Seen psychologically, the "invading spirit" presents a rather different picture. In this case it is a question of relatively sudden psychic alterations in the personality, brought about by an autonomous complex breaking through from the unconscious. Although such an invasion of the personality appears to happen suddenly, one can nevertheless quite often observe it in process of constellation, well in advance, with the aid of the patient's dreams and fantasies,[63] until one day it reaches the threshold of consciousness.

Both of these age-old ideas of "loss of soul" and of the "invading spirit" are therefore, like the idea of the projectile, closely bound up with the phenomenon of projection. To the extent that, in projection, a piece of one's own personality is transferred to or relocated in an outer object, it is at the same time a loss of soul. Lovers, for example, so often feel listless, ailing, when they are separated from the beloved object; their soul is where the beloved is and they feel truly alive only when they are near him or her. It is even possible for one's own intelligence to be projected in this fashion. According to a traditional report, a pupil of Socrates by the name of Aristides could philosophize very well as long as he had a corner of Socrates' toga in his hand, but when he was away from the master his gift for philosophical argument disappeared completely.[64]

The experience of the actively invading spirit is like being pierced by an arrow or being struck by lightning,[65] and, indeed, sudden projections are often so described. Thus, for example, Charles Baudelaire:

> Amid the deafening traffic of the town,
> Tall, slender, in deep mourning, with majesty,
> A woman passed, raising, with dignity
> In her poised hand, the flounces of her gown;

Graceful, noble, with a statue's form.
And I drank, trembling as a madman thrills,
From her eyes, ashen sky where brooded storm,
The softness that fascinates, the pleasure that kills.

A flash . . . then night!—O lovely fugitive,
I am suddenly reborn from your swift glance;
Shall I never see you till eternity?

Somewhere, far off! too late! *never, perchance!*
Neither knows where the other goes or lives;
We might have loved, and you knew this might be![66]

The lightning symbolizes the impact of sudden passion, whether for good or for ill.

It is not only in connection with love that such sudden seizures occur. If one is living in a group, suddenly, as if "ridden by the devil," one can let loose all kinds of pernicious nonsense at which later, in a sober mood, one can only wonder. In such a case it may be that one's own shadow side has acted as a hook and attracted the negative projections of the others or of another, and one unexpectedly becomes the "black sheep" or the butt of all jokes, which is a sign that the shadows so suddenly discharged by others have taken possession of one and alienated the ego by forcing it into a collective role. As soon as one is separated from the group or from the person exerting the negative influence, everything falls back into place and one awakens as from a bad dream. In the case of a powerful love projection (that is, a projection of the inner partner-images of animus and anima), a double process sometimes takes place and one experiences it both as being struck by an arrow (invasion by a complex) and as loss of soul, as utter dependence on the presence of the other. Inwardly one feels as if invaded by a passionate disquiet and fantasy activity, and at the same time as if one's own life has flowed out to the other in the outer world. This explains a curious mythological motif that has so far gone unexplained. For the most part we assume that when a man falls in love with a woman as a result of a sudden anima projection, he looks upon *her* as the sender of love's arrow, not the god Amor. In antiquity, however, such a man felt that he had been shot by the god Eros or hit by the *mater saeva cupidinum,* that is, by Venus. The flare-up of or invasion by passion is separately experienced as something inner, while the lost soul-fragment is considered as something different, attached to the outer figure.

When an archetypal structure remains latent in the unconscious, it is recognizable. But when it is activated, it often appears in double form: on the one hand, as an inwardly experienced flare-up of emotions and affects and, on the other, as a fascinating image that is, however, regarded as belonging to the outer object. Still, this duality is a special case and need not always appear. Psychic powers are often also experienced as a pure inner image. In this event the doubling, alternatively the projection of the image onto an outer object, does not take place and the image itself is directly perceived within. This can be shown, for example, in visions handed down to us by historical tradition.[67] Thus a Christian visionary in a trance will see an unknown man who heals him and conclude that it was Christ. Such visions are often associated with the feeling of being struck by a ray of light and set afire, with the sufferer caused great torment.[68] This recalls the motif of the passion projectile, which we met earlier. The visionary Marina de Escobar reports on the way her kidney-stone colics came about. She saw an ugly devil who approached her, swept up the dust in her room, and forced her to swallow it. Then he placed a pan full of live coals under her back. From the dust and the coals five small stones were formed in her body and these tortured her for months until, in agony, she was able to discharge them.[69] One is reminded of the old belief in disease projectiles.

Few genuinely believing Christians would regard such inwardly seen figures as endopsychic, belonging to the subject, nor as the projection of a psychic content. Yet the phenomena are quite unmistakably similar to those mentioned above.

One suspects that in many cases Freud is right when he assumes that the phenomenon of projection onto outer objects is connected with the fact that our attention in general is directed more toward the outer world and that we are therefore inclined to overlook inner psychic events. Introverted and introspective people can, however, perceive events in the inner world directly, without the detour of a projection onto an outer object. If such people are inclined by temperament and general outlook to regard endopsychic phenomena as real in their own right, this would also naturally be an important consideration. In the cultural history of the West, at least until the time of the Enlightenment, these experiences were held to be actual and real, though for the most part they were not thought of as being subjective in character but rather as phenomena from a "Beyond," a "spirit world" or a "metaphysical religious" realm of invisible, transsubjective objective reality. In modern depth psychology it was in some quarters (but only in some!) that this field of experience began for the first time to be understood as endopsychic, that is, as belonging to the unconscious psyche of a human being. That even today this is by no means a generally accepted view is illustrated in the essay by Pastor Friedrich Jussel in which he describes in detail an exorcism that he himself carried out.[70] Jussel regards it as entirely self-evident that the evil spirits he successfully expelled from a young girl were not part of the girl's psyche. His essay comes immediately after a paper by the psychologist Wulf Wunneberg in which it is taken for granted with equal conviction that the demons are complexes, that is, "split-off parts of (the girl's) own psyche which have been repressed from consciousness."[71] In view of the uncertainties in such a situation, it would be worthwhile to go back and take a look at certain features of the historical context that might shed some light on it.

2

The Withdrawal
of Projections
in Religious Hermeneutics

The Approach of the Gods to Men

The five stages in the withdrawal of a projection, as described in the preceding chapter, not only may be demonstrated in the single, individual case but run like a red thread throughout the history of spiritual development in our culture. Following this thread, one sees that many great historical conflicts have originated because men whose religious ideas express different stages of development fail to communicate with one another. Today the problem is charged with affect, as, for

example, in the discussion between theologians and representatives of depth psychology. The latter frequently look upon
certain religious images and ideas as projections (the Freudian
school altogether, the Jungian school in part), whereas most
theologians attribute a "metaphysical" reality to the objects
of their reverence and are reluctant to accept religious images
and ideas as "nothing but" projections. This modern problem, however, has a long history. A short sketch follows,
therefore, in which I shall limit myself to antiquity and the
Middle Ages, periods for which, it seems to me, we have a
better perspective, as we are too close to recent times.[1]

In the Greek world of antiquity, before the period of relatively reliable records, the original mythical psychic condition of archaic identity prevailed, as it did everywhere, a
condition in which inner psychic factors were not differentiated from outer natural facts. The whole world was alive with
demons and spirits, or, in other words, single components of
the human psyche were for the most part unreflected and
were seen out there in nature where the human being was
confronted with them as parts of an objective "world."[2] Encounter with these factors meant working magic or being
worked upon by it, whether for good or for ill.

At about the time historical records began, we can recognize the emergence of the second stage, in which natural objects are partially differentiated from the mythical beings that
animate them. Poseidon and Nereus and his tribe *dominate* the
sea, to be sure, but they are no longer simply identical with it.
Hamadryads and nymphs live in trees and fields; the higher
gods inhabit Olympus or live in the depths of the earth. But
though their will is revealed in the humming of bees in Del-
phi or in the rustling of oaks in Dodona, they themselves
have their own existence. Even moral distinctions (third
stage) have already begun to be made. Human beings judge
the deeds of the gods and permit themselves moral criticisms.
Naturally, this is true only of a small circle of the educated;
the masses remain true to the older beliefs.

With the beginning of pre-Socratic natural philosophy, the mythical-religious world picture of educated Hellenes was fundamentally altered. The divine was now sought in a *world principle (arché)* (later in several) that was presented either as material (water, fire, air, and so on) or as an abstract spiritual principle (in the form of numbers), as the infinite, as a psychic vortex, or as *"das Sein an sich"* (existence).

The gods hitherto revered were either reinterpreted as this new world principle or as existing alongside it (Plato), or their existence was denied. This rationalistic attitude became increasingly widespread with the coming of the Sophists. It culminated in the teaching of Euhemeros, who saw in the gods nothing but dead, deified, historical personalities.

This initial appearance of a certain rationalism in Greek natural philosophy means psychologically, as Jung explained, *an intensive emphasis on human consciousness* that sought to assert itself against the boundlessness and dissolution of the mythical psychic state. Scrutinized, *"I* interpret," *"I* construe," or *"I* understand" is seen to be an apotropaism. An apotropaic character clings to all knowing in any case; knowledge is magic power that we need in order to protect ourselves against the strangeness of the unknown. The human being feels more at home in an "explained" world.

The ideas and views of the first natural philosophers of course seem to us today to be mythical projections too, but at that time they passed for *the* new truth and the gods of the previous age were strenuously criticized. Xenophanes of Kolophon (second half of the sixth century B.C.) says angrily: "Homer and Hesiod have attributed to the gods everything which, among men, means disgrace and dishonor: stealing, adultery, and mutual betrayal. Mortals imagine that the gods were born and that their appearance and voice and form is like to their own."[3]

A somewhat younger contemporary, Theagenes of Rhegion, tried to rescue the "old truth" by conceiving it as "allegorical" (today we would say "symbolic") and tried to translate the old myths into the new philosophical language. Thus he actually became the father of hermeneutics.[4] According to him, either the gods are *symbols of material objects* (Apollo, Helios, Hephaistos, for example, stand for fire, Hera for air, and so on) or they mean *psychic qualities and states in human beings.* (This is the beginning of the fifth stage.) Athena symbolized insight; Ares, insensate passion; Aphrodite, carnal desire; Hermes, reason. But all these states of mind (which we today regard as endopsychic) were still understood as "outer," that is, as objectively present powers. Air, according to Philodemos, is an all-pervading capacity for thought, "which can also be called Zeus."[5] Plato ridiculed these attempts at interpretation as "sophistical,"[6] while Aristotle tried to replace such half-mythical ideas with more precise philosophical concepts.[7] Democritus (circa 470–360 B.C.) went farthest in conceiving the old gods as concrete "images" that, flowing out of the ether, the fire of the heavens, pervaded the whole world.[8] Objects, plants, animals, he says, can also radiate such images. These images then frequently attract to themselves mirror-images from psychic movements, thoughts, passions, and characteristic properties of other men, invade our dreams, and influence us in this way.[9] Their effects can be benevolent or maleficent.[10] Envious men can send out images filled with their sender's envy, thereby damaging others both physically and psychically.[11] (Here the disease projectiles come up again!) Positive images are at work in poetic inspiration. The images of gods, finally, are "symbols" or speaking images that issue from the living creative world substance itself.[12]

Insofar as these interpretations draw no demarcation between material and psychic world substances, they restore in part the first stage of archaic identity, alongside the emergence of the fifth stage. This seems to correspond to a general psychological law: *The statement of the new truth reveals the previous conceptions as "projections" and tries to draw them into the psychic inner world, and at the same time it announces a new*

myth, which now passes for the finally discovered "absolute" truth.
The new outlook, which is evident here and there in the
theories of pre-Socratic natural philosophy and was given its
clearest and most significant formulation by Democritus, became generally dominant in the Stoic formulations. Zeno of
Citium (circa 336–264 B.C.), the founder of the Stoa, interpreted the Greek gods either as physical facts or as psychological powers; thus the Dioscuri, for example, stood for right
speaking and a stimulus to the nobler feelings,[13] the god Eros
for fiery "pathos" (affect, emotion, and so on).[14] Cleanthes of
Assos (circa 331–233 B.C.) went so far as to interpret whole
myths, like the Hercules saga, in this way. The gods, he said,
are *rationes informatae in animis hominum* (innately formed
concepts or imprints in the human soul), mythical *schemata*
or "holy designations" of a cosmic mystery.[15] The Stoic
Chrysippus interprets the god Ares[16] as the wrathful, aggressive element in man,[17] Athena as reasoning thought, and so
on. All these gods are taken to be *logoi spermatikoi,* creative
primordial ideas in the divine pneuma that pervades the
whole universe.[18]

Through such interpretations of the myths and of the figures of the gods, the Stoa brought about an enormously significant cultural achievement, because it succeeded in linking
the old myths to the new religious consciousness of the time
so that they were not rationalistically devalued. In this way
the Stoics laid the cornerstone on which the edifice of the
religious syncretism of late antiquity was erected. They produced comprehensive concepts by means of which the gods
of different peoples could be recognized, as through a *tertium
comparationis,* so that, for example, a figure like Aphrodite
could be equated with the Babylonian Astarte or the Egyptian Isis.

The fourth stage, in which the reality that had hitherto
been believed is explained as nonexistent, could be described
as the stage of apotropaic reflection. In contrast to this, the
fifth stage of reinterpretation represents an act of *assimilation*

through reflection, through which the psychic energy of the projected content flows back to man and raises the level of his consciousness, as this was achieved for the first time in the Stoic interpretation of myths.

Allegory in the Gnosis and in Early Christianity

The same spirit of symbolic interpretation of myths continued to live on in the Gnosis. The bridge from the Stoa to the Christian Gnosis was created by the Biblical exegesis of Aristobulus, of Numenius, and, above all, of Philo of Alexandria (c. 20 B.C.–c. A.D. 45), whose work exerted a decisive influence on the allegorical exegesis of the Church Fathers.[19] Philo and his forerunners not only "cleared up" the whole Greco-Roman Olympus; they went further to interpret the mythological motifs of the Old Testament as *typoi* (prefigurations).

While the concept "allegory" seems to have first appeared during the first century before Christ, Plato often made use of the concept of hyponoia (deeper or underlying thought),[20] an expression also used by Plutarch, Clement of Alexandria, and Origen. Following an exactly definable (so-called *diaeretic*) procedure, certain texts of the Old Testament, starting from the concrete statement, are related to an "other" set of facts. The relation between the scriptural text and this "other" was called a *symbolon*.[21] Philo justified a certain number of his interpretations by saying that God had communicated them directly to his soul,[22] others by the logical consistency resulting from a comparison of the images.[23] The *tertium comparationis* used is in most cases from the realm of the psyche or from that of Platonic ideas.[24] The two realms thus brought together are body and psyche, or the physical world and the world of ideas. Through this method of interpretation, a certain number of myths that hitherto had been understood as concrete descriptions of the outer world were brought into *the realm of the psyche,* although they were still by no means thought of as belonging to the subject but rather were understood as a kind of world soul or psyche, whose existence was "nonsubjective."

With the coming of Christianity there occurred something completely unprecedented that put a stop to the development of the old hermeneutics and at the same time made a new beginning: the doctrine of the *historically real* Christ-figure. It is as if the whole mythical heaven full of gods had come down into one human being and as if the Gnostic *pleroma,* the primordial mythical world, had now been incarnated on earth. It was concentrated in the *one man,* Christ, in whom it took historical shape. Christ clothed himself, as it were, in all the earlier images and assimilated them into his own image. *"Figuris vestitur typos portat . . . thesaurus eius absconditus et vilis est, ubi autem aperitur mirum visu"* ("He is clothed in figures, he is the bearer of types. . . . His treasure is hidden and of small account, but where it is laid open, it is wonderful to look upon.")[25] Or: "Because the creatures were weary of bearing the prefigurations of his [Christ's] glory, he disburdened them of those prefigurations, even as he had disburdened the womb that bore him."[26] The advance of rational ego-consciousness that had taken place in the previous centuries was thereby overcome and compensated by a new myth. But in Christ the whole primordial mythical world took on real form and definition, and this new myth would dominate our spiritual world for almost two thousand years.

It was not long, however, before the problem of the interpretation of myth was posed in a new form: in the confrontation of the Church Fathers with the Greek spirit of pagan antiquity. The polemic of Origen against Celsus, a neo-Platonic advocate of paganism, is an especially illuminating example. In about A.D. 178, Celsus defended the traditional philosophic culture of late antiquity against the Christians, whom he regarded as destructive and revolutionary, and based his argument on an interesting view of the philosophy of history.[27] The truth (his writing was entitled *Alethes logos — The True Logos*) of the old culture, which he spoke up for, is based on traditional usage and customs *(nomos),* on the one hand, and on its meaning *(logos),* on the other. A hidden, divine meaning, he said, is revealed by the course of history.[28] The true origin of all cultural tradition lies with the "divinely inspired poets, wise men, and philosophers of the past" who, inspired by a divine spirit, spoke the truth in enigmatic images. These images are not rationally comprehensible (that is, with the help of the philosophic spirit), but the intellect helps the philosopher rise to the heights from which the gods look down and to the realm of the eternal ideas, where he can then find the true meanings of the image-filled sayings of the wise men of old. Even the half-animal gods of the Egyptians, the symbolic proceedings and ideas of the mysteries, and the myths of all peoples are expressions of such "eternal ideas."[29] The quarrel between Zeus and Hera, for example, in the course of which Zeus ties up his wife (*Iliad* I, 590ff), was, according to Celsus, an indication of how God had "bound matter together in orderly wise" at the beginning of the world.[30] All the many and varied divine figures, myths, and initiations and other ceremonies of the mysteries could be related to the hidden oneness behind all of them through this labor of allegorical interpretation. This method served, as Andresen puts it, "as a lens which gathered up the many diverse radiations of historical tradition into a focal point."[31] It was through the wise men, the poets, and the philosophers of the past that the divine Logos of history itself revealed the rationality of its tremendous store of mythical ideas and images.[32] Celsus sought by means of allegory to reconcile his unwavering loyalty to tradition with his need for philosophic rationality. "It transforms the old into the eternally new and makes of words and writing the bearer of the creative spirit . . . with its help the Logos of history is revealed as the unending metamorphosis of the spirit."[33]

Typos in Origen
and the Early Middle Ages

Although Origen made a passionate effort in *Contra Celsum* (written ca. A.D. 248) to confute these views, his attitude toward allegory is in fact quite similar to that of Celsus himself. In justifying his interpretations Origen leans heavily on the Apostle Paul (Galatians 4:21), but his method (not the content) is in every way the same as that employed by his pagan opponent.[34] He stresses the fact that in both Greek and Judaeo-Christian tradition there are many things that cannot be proven to be historical facts. Those who hold these tales to be of little value but who do not wish on this account to risk deception can decide which they may simply believe, which they should interpret allegorically by examining the motives of those who thought them up, and to which they must deny credence as being chronicled merely for the advantage of certain people.[35] Origen repeatedly distinguishes these three kinds of text from one another: concrete historical description, images which make sense, and empty tales.[36] As to the first two forms, he says, the level of education of the hearer must be taken into account; while the uneducated man conceives everything concretistically, the educated man tries constantly to improve his understanding of the "deeper meaning."[37] It is for this reason that there are three degrees of understanding Scripture. The highest is "the word of wisdom" *(sophia),* the second "the word of knowledge" *(theoria),* the third "faith" *(pistis).*[38] There are many symbols in the Old and New Testaments, for example, the opening up of heaven *(Ezekiel)* or the appearance of the Holy Ghost as a dove, that according to Origen can be interpreted only in the symbolic manner. He refers to the fact that many people had prophetic sight in dreams and suspects that something similar could also happen in the waking state: "How, then, should it be inconceivable that that same power which influences the soul in dreams could also in the waking state communicate through (second) sight knowledge which would be useful to him who receives it or to people who hear of it later?"[39] There is, he thought, a certain "general divine knowledge that only the blessed know how to come by"; from this knowledge issues the allegorical understanding of Scripture.[40]

If we think about these interpretative efforts from our modern psychological standpoint, it is immediately noticeable that the source of *true insight,* with Origen as with many of his contemporaries, is relocated in a metaphysical world that is understood as the world of Platonic ideas or as the godhead itself is understood, in contrast to the "empty tales" that issue from the mere subjective intention of an author. This metaphysical reality was also understood by Origen as a kind of *subtle body* permeating the whole world. Many miracles recorded in Holy Scripture took place only in that sphere of psychic reality inhabited by the subtle body, not in the concrete here and now.[41] *"Jesus appeared namely in the middle ground between created and uncreated things."* The special merit of the Christian reports, in contrast with the pagan, lies not in their different form[42] but rather in the higher moral effect that proceeded from Christ and became visible in the way in which Jesus and many of his followers lived their lives, as well as in the miracles of healing, especially in the healing of psychic illnesses.[43]

According to Origen, however, the sole correct interpreter of the allegorical sections of Holy Scripture is the pneumatic man who has been informed by the Holy Ghost, the "spirit of truth."[44] Origen based his view that much in Scripture might be symbolically interpreted on the text from Psalm 78:2: "I will open my mouth in a parable; I will utter dark sayings from of old."

Origen, like Celsus, sees single events in the course of history as allegories, *eikones* of God's transactions. The visible world points beyond itself to the invisible principle through which alone it can be completely understood, and this principle is revealed in the *alethes logos* (the truth) of Scripture.[45] In

Origen's view, however, this course of history is goal-directed, either in linear fashion or spirally, while Celsus understands it more as cyclical. Origen interprets long passages of Jewish law in this sense.[46] Those things prescribed by the law, when taken literally as among the Jews, are, as it were, but the reflection and the shadow of the true law of Jesus, which concerns "the things of heaven," since the law "contains many things which must be explained and expounded after the fashion of the spirit."[47] Not only the law but long passages throughout the Old Testament were in this way understood *sub umbra,* that is, as hints of, or allusions to, the revealed truth of the New Testament *("quod lucet in Veteri Testamento, hoc fulget in Novo").*[48] Thus Gideon's fleece, for example, is a symbol of the Virgin Mary, onto which the dew, that is, the Holy Ghost, flowed down; the serpent that Moses hung from a staff in the desert is a prefiguration of the Crucified One. In the light of the prophecy of Christ as the one "true Logos," all Old Testament prefigurations, or *typoi,* are for the first time recognizable in their genuine significance.[49] In this sense everything in the Bible refers, as allegory, or even as mystery or sacrament, to the gradual revelation of the Spirit.[50]

As Henri de Lubac makes clear in his excellent book *Exégèse médiévale: Les quatre sens de l'Ecriture,*[51] four aspects of Biblical exegesis gradually crystallized out in the Middle Ages: (1) the historical-concrete interpretation, which treats Scripture as a factual report; (2) the allegorical, which works out its basic dogmatic content; (3) the tropological, or moral, which derives rules of conduct; and (4) the anagogic, which says in images, "Hither everything is going and what we may hope for."

Again and again Holy Scripture as a whole is referred to by the Church Fathers in images that, taken psychologically, we would today regard as symbols of the unconscious: as spring, labyrinth, endless sea, unfathomable heaven, impenetrable abyss, or as a wild and untamed stream from which we can draw new life eternally but whose final mysteries remain forever unattainable for us.[52] "This is that river that has its source in the place of blessedness and divides into the four rivers of Paradise. . . . Thus there are also four procedures *(regulae)* or ways of interpreting the meaning *(sensus)* of Scripture: historical . . . allegorical . . . tropological . . . anagogic. . . . *On these four wheels moves (volvitur) the whole of Holy Scripture.*"[53] The same quaternity of interpretative procedures was also seen in the four Evangelists and in the four Fathers of Theology: Gregory (Luke), Ambrose (lion), Hieronymus or Jerome (ox), and Augustine (eagle).[54] Jerome (Hieronymus) is the historian; Gregory, the moralist; Ambrose, the dogmatist; and Augustine, the eagle "that rises up to the height of mystical speculation."[55]

This fourfold exegesis corresponds quite amazingly to the theory of the four basic functions of consciousness that Jung developed, purely empirically, through observation of his patients and with no knowledge of the above methods of interpretation. According to his description, the functions of consciousness, reduced to their simplest formulation, may be divided as follows:

1. The sensation function, which ascertains facts, that is, sees, hears, smells, and so on, what is

2. Thinking, which brings what has been perceived into logical connection

3. Feeling, which evaluates what has been perceived, in the sense of pleasant-unpleasant, to be admitted–to be rejected, better-worse

4. Intuition, which represents a kind of faculty of divining and orients us as to whence what has been perceived came and anticipates whither it goes[56]

The historical interpretation of Scripture corresponds to sensation insofar as it regards Scripture as a report of concrete facts; the *sensus allegoricus,* which de Lubac calls *"le nerf de la construction doctrinaire,"*[57] is concerned with the theological-dogmatic classification of the scriptural text; the *sensus tropologicus* corresponds to feeling, to moral evaluation; and the *sensus anagogicus* is equivalent to intuition, which, "like an eagle flying heavenwards," circles round what is hoped for, the future, what is to be speculatively surmised.

In the Middle Ages, Holy Scripture was looked upon as a unit, as a *mysterium,* which makes clear to us the reality of the Christ. When this mystery, in itself inconceivable, rotates by means of the four wheels of the four scriptural exegeses, it draws nearer to our understanding. But our understanding can never explain Scripture "exhaustively," for "the purport of the divine word is of infinite diversity," as John Scotus Erigena puts it.[58]

Signs of Schism in the Second Millennium

When we examine the Christian interpretation of images, what strikes us at once is that fact that the opposition, light-dark, is polarized in all these images. The metaphysical split in the god-image of Christianity, which sees God as the *summum bonum* and excludes evil from the image, ascribing it either to man or to the devil, runs through the whole field of ontology. Just as Christ represents the incarnation of the good God, so the Antichrist represents the power of evil. Hence *all images* can refer, at one and the same time, either to Christ or to the devil. This is most conspicuous in the comparatively schematic work of interpreters like Rhabanus Maurus, Vincent de Beauvais, and Honorius of Autun. Fire, for instance, can mean either the hell of the passions or inspiration through the Holy Ghost; the raven is a symbol of the devil or of deeper thoughts directed toward God; the dove symbolizes erotic lust (Venus!) or the Holy Ghost; the lion, which "sees what he devours," is Satan or Christ, "who wakes us with his roaring," and so on. Around the year 1000, when the world did not come to an end—an event many had been waiting for—a spiritual transformation began to become visible, a transformation characterized, on the one hand, by a more widespread and more conspicuous interest in the natural sciences and, on the other, by a new and less concrete kind of belief in the truths revealed by the Bible; both were associated with an increasingly rational attitude toward matters of faith. As early as the brief heyday of Charlemagne's reign there had been impulses here and there to combat the all too great naïve concretism of popular piety (the stage of archaic identity within the new myth),[59] impulses that later, with Bishop Claudius of Turin, almost led to the destruction of all ecclesiastical symbolism; at the same time the transcendence of Christian teaching was more and more emphasized.[60] By the ninth century, Agobard of Lyon was combating the uncritical search for miracles by his contemporaries and recommending the use of reason in religious matters.[61] John Scotus Erigena also believed that revelation did not stand in contradiction to reason-knowledge.[62] For the thinking man, in his opinion, the history of God's action as related in the Bible represents mysteries that must, at least in part, be interpreted, because those parts of the story that are sensorily perceivable are transitory and only that which is spiritual and invisible will remain for all eternity.[63] *Theology therefore is a kind of poetic art* that transforms Holy Scripture in the interest of a full comprehension of those things that are intelligible and thus leads us out of our imperfect childishness by reducing that which is outwardly perceptible in Holy Scripture. It is in this fashion that belief must be enlightened by knowledge.[64] The Ascension of Christ, for example, is for John Scotus Erigena a purely "parabolic" event, not a concrete historical fact but an event in the realm of human consciousness.[65]

As a result of attacks by those who could no longer accept certain passages in Holy Scripture literally and concretely (fourth stage), the kind of symbolic-psychological interpretation that had been supported by John Scotus Erigena gained ground. Thus for Abelard, the ascension of Jesus is a symbol for the soul's ascent to heaven, brought about by Jesus, and at the same time for the appearance of this ascent on the horizon of human consciousness. Only the common people, in accord with their understanding of things, must be encouraged to go on taking such passages concretely.[66]

We are not concerned here with particulars of the struggle between reason and authority or between knowledge and faith. The psychological aspect of this conflict can be clearly recognized in the attempt at rational criticism of concretistic belief in favor of "intelligible" belief, which then, in its moral aspect, becomes psychological interpretation.

The tendency to seek the symbolic-psychological meaning in Scripture was seen most strikingly in some of the heretical movements of the time. The neo-Manichaean Catharists, who had been coming increasingly to the fore since the year 1000, taught, for example, that their members, filled with the Holy Spirit, were the first to be able to understand Holy Scripture and to reveal its hidden spiritual meaning.[67] They denied most of the concrete assertions of the Evangelists concerning the life of Christ: his birth from a virgin, the fact of his burial, his resurrection.[68] The heretic Girard di Monteforte (near Turin) even interpreted God as the primordially existing mind, or spirit, of man (!) and the Son as the spirit *(animus)* of man (!) beloved by God, but the Holy Spirit as the understanding of Scripture.[69] A certain rationalistic, enlightening tendency can be recognized in such views, but also elements of the fifth stage, of the withdrawal into the subjective-psychic realm of what has hitherto been projected outward.[70] In the case of the Albigensians a moral criticism of Christ himself even began to set in, which led to a belief in two Christ-figures—an evil, earthly, visible son of Joseph, and a good figure, born in the new, invisible Bethlehem and crucified but who possessed only an apparent body and who had appeared to the Apostle Paul as pure spirit.[71] Even among the "Brethren of the Free Spirit" one finds a withdrawal of the divine into the inner psychic realm, which evidently led to dangerous inflations among those called "Perfect."[72] They taught that human beings might be so closely bound to God that they could become identical with Him. Such people were without sin through all eternity and could create more than God Himself;[73] indeed, they could surpass even the merits of Christ.[74] As for Holy Scripture, people were to attend more to their own inner promptings and to the imaginings of the heart than to the teaching of the Gospels.

One of the most significant figures in all these movements is that of Abbot Joachim da Fiore (died ca. 1202). According to him, time in this world is divided into three main periods that correspond to the three persons of the Holy Trinity. The first era is that of the Father, of those who marry, and of obedience to the law; the second era is that of the clergy and of the struggles with passion; and the third is that of the Holy Ghost and of the monks who are "called to the freedom of contemplation."[75]

In this latter era love will prevail and—insofar as Holy Scripture is concerned—the *spiritualis intellectus;* the letter withers and the Spirit begins to work.[76] Joachim interpreted the stories of Job, Tobias, Judith, and Esther in this spirit,[77] that is, historically, in regard to both Christ and the coming age of the Holy Ghost.[78] For Joachim this latest age of the Holy Ghost is an age not so much of inner psychic events as of a *new myth* struggling to be realized in the world. Success was denied to the announcement of this new myth and, historically, the struggles in the direction of a rational resolution of the Christian myth at first won the upper hand.

The few examples cited here thus produce a complex picture. First, certain rationalistic elements are unmistakable, standing in opposition to an overly concrete understanding of the Christian myth, elements that today are for the most part looked upon as precursors of the Reformation. Second, there emerge attempts to expand the Christian myth with the help of the inspiration of the Holy Spirit, without dismissing him in a rationalistic spirit. And third, there are clear indications of a tendency to deal, by means of symbolic interpretation, with what is no longer concretely believable and to understand it as a purely inner psychic happening in the experiencing subject.

During the course of the succeeding centuries the "rationalistic" tendency (fourth stage) became more and more the dominant one.[79] The Reformation, which sought to compensate this tendency by going back to a rigorous Christianity that saw the Bible as historical truth, was not in a position to stop this process, which signalized its victory with the enthronement of *la Déessée Raison* (the Goddess Reason) during the French Revolution and which since then has conquered the most important fields of European thought. In a way this rationalistic tendency reached its zenith with the Communist view of religion as "the opium of the people" and, *mutatis mutandis,* with the Freudian interpretation of religion as an illusion rooted in purely subjective complexes explicable in terms of the "family romance." In Protestant theology Bultmann's "demythologizing" of the Christian religion belongs to the same stage, for the logical consequence of this development is that only the reverend theologian decides, out of his own mental processes, what is to be believed and what not.[80]

In the Catholic Church the tendency either to read Holy Scripture with rigid dogmatism or to judge it rationalistically prevailed down to the end of the eighteenth century. Then gradually literary textual criticism and historical criticism were permitted.[81] Today the exegetes are trying to arrive at the meaning of Holy Scripture from every direction, from one of which comes the occasional insistence that symbolic language must be used for interpretation, so that in one Congress report even the words of a Freudian analyst were included. In general, however, it is the linguistic and (antipsychological) structuralist systems that are broadly represented; the prevalent tendency seems to be to allow different methods simultaneously, in order to arrive at the meaning of

Scripture[82] and to unite researchers into a kind of ecclesia of research,[83] and thus overcome "the alienation of modern man from Biblical language."[84] A kind of instinctive or emotional understanding, born of the faith, is the basis of this generally rationalistic chaos of various methods within the Catholic world, a feeling born of faith that prevents the different attempts at interpretation from falling into confusion. Still, a certain rationalistic corrosion of the myth seems to be gaining ground, even in Catholicism.

In the face of these tendencies, almost all of which belong to the fourth stage of projection-withdrawal, Jung can be understood as the initiator and advocate of the fifth stage. Going ahead consistently from the fourth stage he put the question: "If all these assertions concerning the faith are, taken concretely, no longer credible, then where did the projection come from?" Through the investigation of the dreams of his patients he discovered that these contents go on appearing and operating, producing living effects in the inner psychic world, quite untroubled by the dreamer's rationalistic conscious judgments. But, according to Jung, these symbolic religious experiences do not spring from personally acquired complexes but rather from a much deeper, generally human unconscious psychic matrix that, as is well known, he called the collective unconscious, and also the "objective psyche." This discovery, however, raises once again the problem of the extent to which the contents of the collective unconscious may be described as subjective, as belonging to the subject. In Jung's view many elements of faith, to be sure, can no longer be regarded as metaphysical realities, but on the other hand they are not simply subjective contents either. Moreover, Jung stressed that he definitely believed in the possibility of the metaphysical reality of religious contents, although there is no possibility of investigating such contents psychologically. What we observe in the field of unconscious psychological experience and can investigate empirically is always psychic.

3

Projection and Scientific Hypotheses

The First Principle

It is perhaps clear from the preceding chapter that projection plays an important role in the field of higher religious ideas. Two questions, nevertheless, remain unanswered: Where can the line be drawn between what is transsubjective and what is not? What is psychic and what is metapsychic? *Transsubjective* and *transpsychic* are not interchangeable, although many authors carelessly use the two words as if they had the same meaning. For Jung the collective unconscious is indeed transsubjective but it is *not* metapsychic. The collective unconscious, a reality that comprehends in the widest sense everything that is psychic, in all probability exists, but everything we can say about it is of necessity psychic—received through the filter of the psyche.

In Western cultural history the transpsychic has been described sometimes as "spirit," sometimes as "matter." Theologians and philosophers are more concerned with the former, physicists with the latter. During the course of history almost as many contradictory statements have been made about matter as about religious ideas, and today we can no longer avoid seeing in many of these statements the projection of psychic contents. In the development of the natural sciences the human spirit proceeded less conservatively than in theology. When a statement in the realm of religion was no longer regarded as absolutely valid, theologians, as was clearly implied in the preceding chapter, often attempted to keep it alive and include it within the new truth by means of a new interpretation. In the natural sciences, however, such "outdated" statements were for the most part simply dropped; they were rationalistically invalidated in line with the fourth stage and it did not occur to anyone to ask, "Where did this error in which we believed for such a long time come from?" Today, however, a few historians of science have been struck by the fact that certain basic themes or primordial images occur and recur as dominants, that, though transformed, never quite disappear. And what was once regarded as the opposition between spirit and matter turns up again in contemporary physics as a discussion of the relation between consciousness (or "mind") and matter. In the past there was yet a third term, the idea of a "world-soul," which occupied an intermediate position between mind and matter.

The split between mind—or spirit—and matter can be traced back to pre-Socratic natural philosophy, which for the first time tried to free mankind from a polytheistic-mythical picture of the world. The new dominant principle was thought of either as matter and a material primary world element (water, fire, air, atoms) or as a mental (spiritual) principle (numbers, Platonic ideas, spiritual vortex, and so on). Consequently when the old images of the gods came to be reinterpreted, they were seen in part as psychological powers—love, aggression, reason, and the like—and in part, too, as material powers (the heat of the sun, fire, water, and so on); thus another dualism of *mind* (psyche)[1] and *matter* resulted. The materialistic interpretation was called *logos physikos,* the theological *logos theologikos;* the former was scientific, the latter religious-metaphysical.[2] The two realms, psyche and spirit, which stand in opposition to matter, frequently overlap among different authors. The world principle that was called "spirit" or "mind" has in general more to do with the ordering dynamic, with the principle of thought (ideas) and with the source of inspiration; the collective psyche (world-soul), on the other hand, has more to do with man's moods and humors and affective states *(pathe),* such as wrath, love, longing, and instinctuality.

The modern student of these early philosophical systems cannot avoid noticing that they leave us in the dark on the question of whether these mental principles or states of mind were imagined as belonging to the individual subject or as transsubjective general principles. As a rule, however, the latter was nearly always the case. "Big" thoughts and feelings were "influences" of the gods on the subject, who was gripped or possessed by them; such thoughts and feelings had little or nothing to do with the subjective, personal being.

What we would describe today as psychic elements belonging to the individual subject were projected, at least in part, onto an object, which is where even today many biologists are still looking for it—namely, the human body. In the Homeric age the soul of the individual human being was apparently situated in the *phrenes,* which in classical time was usually understood as the diaphragm but which in Homer more likely meant the lungs.[3] From this source sprang the *thymos* (character, attitude, mind), with which a man could carry on an inner dialogue, just as he could with his heart, the seat of his feelings.[4] Contents that today we should regard as pure mental ideas also sometimes came from this region; such ideas, however, were never abstract, that is, "detached," but still directly accompanied by an emotion and a tendency to act. Onians therefore refers to them correctly as "ideo-motor."[5] All these impulses were felt in the *phrenes* or in the heart, occasionally in the liver. If the *phrenes* were filled with fluid, madness, drunkenness, or forgetfulness ensued.[6] For a detailed account of this manner of thinking, the reader is referred to the outstanding work by R. B. Onians, *The Origin of European Thought.* In other cultures still other bodily organs were taken to be the seat of the soul. Incidentally, the bodily seat of the soul seems to have moved slowly upward, from the kidneys to the belly, to the chest, to the larynx, and finally to the head, which even today many people think of as the "seat of the soul."

There were thus two realms in which psychic powers were thought to be located: an immaterial or subtly material cosmic world-soul, from which they "flowed into" the human being, and a specified part of the human body. The latter, to be sure, was more personal and closer to the subject but still not yet identical with the ego, since Odysseus could converse with his *phrenes* or with his heart, as with a partner.

If we look back at the scientific-mythological world principles that Greek natural philosophy understood as the ground of being, we are struck by the fact that most of them represent the intuitive-visual pre-stage of what has developed into today's scientific hypotheses or thought-models. Because the forms, as they became outworn, were still not recognized as projections, these archetypal basic images have consistently conformed to the law of the *wandering* of unintegrated projections.

The Infinite Sphere
as God, Cosmos, and Soul

One primordial image in particular has survived in scientific tradition for a greater length of time than most, one that has appeared as a visual image of God, of existence, of the cosmos, of space-time, and of the particle: the image of a circle or of the "sphere whose center is everywhere and whose circumference is nowhere." Over the centuries this image has undergone many transformations, until finally it was understood more and more as the image of an endopsychic reality in the human being. Dieter Mahnke's work *Unendliche Sphäre und Allmittelpunkt* provides a comprehensive study of the history of this symbol; in the main I rely on it here.

An early Orphic hymn had already described Zeus as a "royal body in which everything here circulates," a description that may have influenced Plato and Plotinus.[7] And although Anaximander described the ground of all being as *apeiron* ("boundless"), it was for him at the same time an encircling of separate existences, not yet, however, explicitly spherical.[8] Parmenides was the first to describe the *One* explicitly as a geometrical sphere,[9] and Empedocles was unambiguous in his description of cosmic reality as an infinite sphere:[10] "Sphairos, the spherical, above the everywhere prevailing solitude, filled with happy pride."[11] For Plato, the cosmos is a spherical, blessed god, a reflection of his eternal primordial image. Plotinus took over this idea and elaborated on it.[12] The eternal primordial image is a mental sphere *(sphaira noete),* the model for the visible sphere of heaven created by God. This purely spiritual sphere is without extension in space, so that one can say of God either that he is the All-embracing One or equally that he lives "down in the depths."[13] With his energy, however, he flows throughout the whole world as a kind of omnipresence.[14] On the one hand, as Mahnke has shown, this image of Plotinus was passed on via ben-Gabirol's *Fons vitae* and via an anonymous

57

Liber XXIV philosophorum to Alain de Lille (d. 1203),[15] though not as a god-image in ben-Gabirol but rather as an image of the first primordial spirit emanating from God, with whom God accomplished the creation. On the other hand, and more significantly, the same Neoplatonic cultural inheritance was passed on via Dionysius Areopagitica to John Scotus Erigena and from there to medieval theology.[16] For Scotus Erigena, God is, to be sure, infinite and without dimension, but he can be figuratively described as the "place, time, and circumference" of everything.[17] Temporally, in him, beginning, middle, and end are one, coinciding in an indivisible, eternal point, as it were; and, spatially, periphery and center are also one *("manet in se ipso universaliter et simpliciter")*. God is "everywhere whole"—whole in each individual and at the same time whole in himself.[18]

The image of the divine sphere is also to be found in the works of the mystics, Seuse, Tauler, Ruysbroeck, and Meister Eckhart.[19] In the *unio mystica* of the soul with God, man, in spite of his creaturely finitude, has his share in the infinity of this infinite sphere. "Here sinks, here drowns the spirit in the bottomless sea of the godhead. It can say, In me God, outside of me God, around me and around God, everything is God, I know nothing but God" (Tauler).[20] For Meister Eckhart God is "an infinite spiritual sphere, whose center and circumference is everywhere."[21]

Johannes Kepler, drawing on the writings of Nicholas of Cusa, later made use of the same image. The primordial image of the world, he writes, is God himself, "to whom no other figure is so like as the surface of a sphere."[22] God is, so to speak, the point of origin at the center of this sphere; the Son is the universal revelation of the onefoldedness of this point; the Holy Ghost, finally, is the "identity of the space between." The finite world is created to accord with this divine primordial image, which is why geometry is a divine art. The human spirit also possesses the same spherical form; it stands between the divine spirit and the physical world, like the circular line between the surface of a sphere and the plane from which it cuts a piece.[23]

For Isaac Newton, too, three-dimensional space is still *"tamquam effectus emanativus Dei."* The omnipresence of God thus became, so to speak, the primordial image of a physical field.[24] Newton writes: "God is eternal, infinite, omnipotent and omniscient, that is, He exists from eternity to eternity, is everywhere present, governs everything and knows everything that happens and that can happen. Inasmuch as He exists forever and is everywhere present, He establishes space, eternity and infinity."[25] Newton distinguishes, further, an "absolute true mathematical time" that flows constantly into itself, from a relative, apparently ordinary time that is the measure of duration. In the same way "absolute space" for him is always in itself the same, while measurable, relative space is the measure for whatever moves. Absolute time and absolute space are the "primary loci of all things and themselves immovable." In them God's omnipresence becomes manifest. Physics is, therefore, a special kind of theology.[26] Geometry, too, is a divine art, because the law of the creation of the world is revealed, so to speak, in its axiomatic structure.[27]

In the general theory of relativity accepted today, space and time are regarded as a four-dimensional metric field that determines the distance between closely adjacent points. The metric components attributed to the field have absolute meaning, that is, one cannot speak of them without taking into account the presence of matter.[28] "We know, therefore," writes Markus Fierz, "that in one quite essential respect space is still what it was in the beginning, the all-embracing, in which everything moves and acts. And when nowadays Pascual Jordan . . . wants to conceive of space as a metric manifold in which new stellar worlds are always being spontaneously produced, we can see that the thought of actually identifying it with the old Creative Spirit has not yet quite faded away."[29] It is in our time, of course, that purely mathematical concepts and symbols have become the most highly respected representations of reality and have pushed aside the more visually representable earlier ideas.

In Einstein's theory not only does the same primordial image turn up in modified form, but it is also closely joined to the idea of matter. According to Einstein, matter would be an excited state of a "dynamic geometry."[30] The superspace of this dynamic geometry contains "wormholes" in which the electric lines of force are, so to speak, caught in the topology of superspace.[31] This is a true manifold whose configuration, which is temporally always just instantaneous, is a 3-geometry. Superspace itself, however, has no 4-geometry (the concept space-time completely loses its validity in this domain);[32] Wheeler compares it to an undulating foam-carpet, shot through with countless "wormholes" in which new bubbles are constantly appearing and disappearing; this carpet is the "dynamic geometry" itself, in which components of the vacuum energy, compensating one another, are to a large extent canceled out.[33] The 3-sphere (S3), the 3-sphere with a handle or wormhole! ($S_2 \times S_1 = W_1$), and the 3-sphere with n wormholes are today regarded as the most acceptable topology for such a superspace.[34]

These conceptual models are new variants of the old paradoxical image of the sphere whose "circumference is nowhere" *(circumferentia nusquam)*. The dualism mentioned at the beginning of the chapter between a physical and a theological interpretation of the sphere-image existed in later centuries, too. Although authors like Weigel, Baader, and Boehme continued to attach importance to the theological meaning of the sphere-image, the age of Newton and Kepler saw the beginning of a process of partial secularization and mathematicization of the image, with the loss of its "mythical" meaning; more and more it became the basis of a purely scientific use of the geometry of the space-structure and the idea of time. The aspect of the symbol of the sphere as a god-image gradually receded into the background.[35]

On the other hand, yet another historical process of transformation in the use of the sphere-image took place: its increasingly *psychological* interpretation. To be sure, the image is still applied almost conventionally by Fichte to the godhead, but at the same time it is also widely used to indicate a *centerpoint of the personality* to be found in the human being, a point Fichte describes as the "productive, creative ego" or as the "absolute ego"[36] (in contrast to the usual, empirical ego). The "infinite ego-substance"is again and again constantly taking on specific form in the accidental ego. The latter, for its part, is always striving to extend itself asymptotically toward that ideal or absolute ego. Hardenberg (Novalis) understands this Fichtean ideal ego more as an image of God within the individual.[37] How closely these ideas approach the Jungian concepts of Self and ego is quite obvious.

Particles, Elements, and Causality

If we attempt to sum up Dieter Mahnke's extensively detailed, here very abridged, account of the tradition of the image of the sphere in the West, it is at once apparent that, up to the end of classical physics, this archetypal image formed the basis of scientific ideas about time and about space as three-dimensionally conceived, as well as the idea of the atom (omnipresent point) and the idea of continuum and discontinuum, and that therefore *all these fundamental scientific hypotheses are, in the end, derived from a mandala-formed God-image.*[38]

The idea of the particle has yet another archetypal background, which overlaps only partially with what has been said of the sphere. The atomic theory of Leucippus and of Democritus was based not on any observation of some way of splitting atoms but rather, as Jung has already emphasized, "on a 'mythological' conception of smallest particles,"[39] the soul-atoms, an idea that can be found, for instance, among the Central Australian aborigines. A further mythological variant of this primordial idea may be found in certain Gnostic systems of late antiquity, according to which the ultimate reality consists of an abundance of light-nuclei or of a totality of seeds containing the potentiality of everything that is or can be *(alles Gewordenen)*. The same idea reappears in later Stoic philosophy. There we learn of certain "fiery sparks" *(igniculi)* in the divine world-permeating fiery ether, and these sparks are also the basis for the *notiones communes* (the collective ideas) of humanity.

Even the obviously "false" theory of the four elements, which enjoyed general recognition from the time of Aristotle up to the end of the Middle Ages, has not died out but, as an archetypal image, has persisted through various transformations. As early as the third century the alchemist Zosimos emphasized that the four elements were not to be understood concretely; they were much more like mysterious "centers" or "principles" in matter. Later they were interpreted as aggregate states: all solid materials were taken as "earth," all fluid as "water," all gases as "air," and everything of a burning or caustic or corrosive nature as "fire." Without entering into details, I would merely like to remind the reader that today one speaks of four natural constants: energy, gravitation, affinity, and weak interaction; that the Minkowski-Einstein model of the world is four-dimensional; and that an S-matrix (mentioned below) is associated with four principles. Whenever physicists attempt to construct a comprehensive model of reality or a thought-model of what they are doing, they return to a *quaternity* of principles, generally without suspecting that Jungian psychology long ago discovered the quaternal structure of consciousness.

As Samburski has demonstrated, the principle of causality also has its roots in ancient images and ideas to which we must attach an archetypal significance. This principle goes back to the Stoic concept of the "iron law of the cosmos" or of "necessity," according to which everything takes its preordained course in conformity with immutable rules.[40] With the coming of Christianity this conception was transferred to the God-image. God then became the One who, so to speak, administers this cosmic law. The alleged absolute validity of causality in the natural sciences, which was first dethroned by the uncertainty principle of quantum physics and had to give way to the idea of statistical probability, stems ultimately from the theological God-image. Descartes, the father of modern thinking about causality, based the validity of the causality principle expressly on his conviction that God would always and absolutely hold himself to his own rules that he had established once and for all. God's veracity and his immutability guarantee the regularity of the physical laws of motion.[41] Each particle of matter, when considered in isolation, never moves in crooked lines or in curves; the reason for this, too, is "the immutability of God and the simplicity of operation whereby He conserves motion in matter."[42] God cannot manifest himself in the material world either irrationally or acausally.[43] When Albert Einstein said emotionally to Niels Bohr that "God does not play with dice," this primordial image is evoked once again, this image of a rational, consistent God who holds himself to his own laws and could produce nothing irrational, accidental, or even anything genuinely new or meaningful. At present the so-called S-matrix theory is a new experiment. It is based on three (plus one) principles: first, that reaction probabilities are independent of displacements of the experimental apparatus and of its orientation in space, as well as of the observer's state of motion; second, that the result of a specific reaction is predictable only in the form of a mathematical probability; and, third, that an elementary particle can originate in one reaction and disappear in another only if the latter reaction occurs after the former. The fourth principle would be that of the singularities or relative nonpredictability of the creation of new particles. These singularities cannot be localized, even though they seem to appear in the context of the principle of causality.[44]

The principle of complementarity introduced into physics by Niels Bohr also has an archetypal background. Although it is not known for sure whether Bohr was influenced by William James or whether the idea came to him quite independently, he later referred frequently to James's assertion that conscious and unconscious are complementary[45] and that therefore not only does a complementary relation exist between the particle and wave theories of light but that such a relation can be shown to exist in many other scientific fields as well. Bohr speaks of a "deep-reaching analogy with the difficulty in the formation of human thoughts, which lies in the differentiation of subject from object." In the principle of complementarity, therefore, he saw a concept of far-reaching general significance, and it was not by chance that he chose as the motto for his coat-of-arms the words *Contraria sunt complementa* when he received the Danish Order of the Elephant in 1947. For his heraldic figure he chose the intertwined Yang and Yin in the Chinese Tai-gi-tu:

In exactly the same way as Jung, Bohr postulated that in any description of life phenomena both a causal and a final method of observation should be applied simultaneously, although the two methods and their relation to each other are complementary.[46]

In recent developments in physics there is an increasing tendency to include the observer's mental presuppositions in the field under examination and to pay more attention to what really happens psychologically when a human being attempts to grasp natural processes experimentally and theoretically. Physicists have of late been much preoccupied with the epistemological foundations of their science. Wolfgang Pauli's way of defining scientific knowledge of the natural world is closer to the Platonic view in that he postulates that the purpose of science is to bring inner images into coincidence with external facts. "The process of understanding nature as well as the happiness that man feels in understanding, that is, in the conscious realization of new knowledge, seems thus to be based on a correspondence, a 'matching' of *inner images preexistent* in the human psyche with external objects and their behavior." This is possible only because "both the soul of the perceiver and that which is recognized by perception are subject to an order thought to be objective."[47]

In contemporary physics it is emphasized again and again that intuitive images have recently tended more and more to disappear; they have been "refined" into purely mathematical formulae. The physicist consciously refrains from visualizing the given material in images, and most physicists today guard against using a visual model of outer reality as anything more than a stopgap,[48] a makeshift, although, in the end, as Rudolf Carnap writes, we may always have to come back to one when we know the facts about matter.[49] Meanwhile the physicist makes use of conceptual structures, that is, of mathematical equation systems from the mathematics of physics.[50]

As I see it, this process of abstraction has unobtrusively led to the unconscious projection of a new God-image, namely, the image of the "divine" number. This reactivation of Pythagorean ideas in modern physics has been noticed and emphasized, especially by Werner Heisenberg.[51] Nowadays, as is well known, the physicist regards *mathematical forms,* not "things," as the smallest building blocks of matter. Heisenberg writes: "If one wishes to give an exact description of the elementary particle—and the emphasis here is on the word *exact*—then the only thing that can be written down as a description is the probability function or statistical matrix. The consequence of this, however, is the recognition that not even the property of 'being' can be attributed, without modification, to the elementary particle. It is a possibility, or a tendency, to be."[52] The mathematical forms that represent the elementary particles had to be solutions to an immutable law for the motion of matter.[53] The basic equation, however, is at bottom a mathematical representation of a whole series of symmetry characteristics.[54] For this, it is necessary that certain transformation groups, which are the simplest mathematical expression for specific symmetries, be invariant. But it turned out that the so-called parity, which had previously been regarded as a law of conservation, is *not* always conserved,[55] and Lee and Yang, the scientists who discovered this, have doubts about the validity of certain other of these mirror symmetries. Thus, the hope that Heisenberg formulates, that all the natural laws of matter could be represented as solutions to a closed mathematical schema, is today once again far from realization.[56]

Since mathematical forms appear to be the hitherto single knowable aspect of that unknown Something that we call matter, we have now to ask what these forms are based on. When we do so, we discover that the whole structure of mathematics itself and with it all the equations used by the physicist in the investigation of matter are based on an irrational just-so datum, that is, on *the series of natural whole numbers,*[57] and that they are just-so and not otherwise and cannot be derived from anything beyond themselves. So we are again faced with an ancient God-image, that of the Pythagoreans! The projection has secretly wandered once again and has been transformed into a "new myth," the myth of the "divine number."

Energy and Field of Force

In contemporary physics, energy is taken to be the basic substrate of all forms and it is materialized, so to speak, in the great variety of particles that are the basic components of matter. Heisenberg correctly pointed out that this concept is related to Heraclitus's idea of world-fire, but in the latter we have an archetypal idea with much more ancient roots. It goes back to the primitive idea of a magic potency that was thought to be both an objective force in the outer world and a subjective state of intensity in the inner world of the subject.[58] The Dakota Indians, for example, call this force *wakanda;* the sun is *wakanda,* and so are the moon, thunder, lightning, stars, the wind, the shaman, the fetishes, ritual objects, animals, and conspicuous or peculiar objects. The word *wakanda* can mean "secret," "force," "greatness," "holy," "old," "alive," and "immortal." Among the Iroquois the same force is called *oki;* the Algonquins call it *manitu;* and the Yaos, *mulungu. Churinga* has the same meaning for the Australian aborigines and *mana* for the Melanesians.[59] *Mulungu* means the soul of a man or a woman after death, the world of the spirits, the magic power in an object, life and health in the body, the active principle in everything magic, the mysterious, the incomprehensible, the unexpected, and the great spiritual power that creates the world and all its life.[60] This primordial idea of "power" is the name for "a diffuse substance or energy upon the possession of which all exceptional power or ability or fecundity depends."[61] Its personified form, in spirits (animism), represents a further stage of development.[62] As Jung suspected, this primitive idea of *mana* is a pre-stage of our psychological concept of energy, and, in all probability, of the concept of energy in general.[63] In Greek natural philosophy this idea crops up in a form that is further developed conceptually in Heraclitus's idea of world-fire; this is the Logos—the all-directing world mind, identical with the godhead but at the same time also with the material primordial fire that circulates throughout the course of all happening, since it condenses or thins out, grows more intense or less intense, penetrates upward or downward in eternal rhythm: "Fire brings about the death of earth; and air

67

survives the death of fire, water extinguishes air, and earth extinguishes water."[64] "God is day and night, winter and summer, war and peace, satiation and want. He changes in the manner of fire, which, when it is mingled with scents, is named after the odor of one or another particular thing."[65] "This world, as with all things, was made neither by man nor by God, has always been and is and will always be, an eternal living fire, igniting in accordance with measure and extinguished according to measure."[66] In its profoundest depths, the human soul (according to Heraclitus) is connected with this world-encompassing fiery Logos and participates in its meaningfulness. Thus, Heraclitus's image of energy is in the end also a God-image.[67] The Stoics' conception of *pneuma,* too, had much in common with this image; for them the *pneuma* was identical with God. It is clear, then, that there is a God-image in the primordial forms of the concept of energy, as in the concept of space-time and in that of the particle.[68] The Stoic concept of *pneuma,* however, also forms the pre-stage of the idea of a field of force as it was developed in nineteenth-century physics.[69] Even Newton still believed that he could explain gravitation through the action of "subtle spirits," and he rejected every mechanical explanation put forward by the Cartesians, who tried to show that gravitation was effected by the ether.[70]

Henry Moore, Newton's friend, also believed that the movement of things in space is caused by immaterial spiritual essences or stems from spatially extended spirits (in contrast to Descartes' purely mechanistic explanation). Spiritual principles effect the activity and the cohesion of all material particles.[71] This notion is reminiscent, as Samburski points out, of the Faraday hypothesis of fields of force, advanced two centuries later.

The old way of picturing energy lived on in the alchemistic tradition in the idea of Mercurius as a "hidden fire" or a fiery life-breath or a kind of life-spirit inherent in all things, which occasionally was identified with the Holy Ghost.[72] This fire-spirit imagines everything in nature; he is a creation spirit who contains in himself "the images of all creatures."[73] In the alchemical opus he must be liberated from his imprisonment in matter and then he begins to rotate in himself, vortex-fashion; at the same time he reveals himself as an immortal component of the alchemist's psyche. By way of the different stages of the so-called phlogiston theory, this archetypal image gradually developed into the energy concept of modern physics.[74]

There is therefore no concept fundamental to modern physics that is not in one degree or another a differentiated form of some primordial archetypal idea. Samburski, too, stresses that fact.[75] "The study of the ancient Greek theory of matter is particularly gratifying to anyone who believes that he sees an inner logic in the history of natural scientific thought, a power that again and again forces upon the researcher, each time at a different stage in the growth of knowledge, *a small number of images and sequences of ideas.* Our respect is increased when we recognize that through all the differences and beyond every transformation of the Greek cosmos there remains the primordial image that is still the model for our own."[76] Gerald Holton also emphasizes that the natural sciences always circle around the same "themes."

Along with the concepts of time, space, energy, and the field of force, as well as of the particle, there remains finally that of chemical affinity, which has its roots in the primitive idea of sympathy (the sympathy of all things) and in the mythological-alchemistic idea of *coniunctio.* Kekulé's vision of the pairs of dancing atoms, which suggested to him his theory of structure, and his vision of the snake biting its own tail, which gave him the idea of the structure of the benzene ring, show how active and effective such images still are in the background of the consciousness of a modern chemical researcher.[77]

It is worthwhile to read Kekulé's own description. He writes of returning to Clapham (London) after having visited his friend Hugo Müller in Islington and talking about chemistry.

> One fine summer day, I went once again with the last bus. . . . I sank into reverie, and the atoms flickered before my eyes. I had always seen them in motion but I had never succeeded in discerning the way in which they moved. Today I saw how many times two of the smaller ones joined together in pairs; how larger ones embraced two small ones, still larger ones held fast three and even four of the small ones, and how it all rotated in a sort of swirling round-dance. . . . When the conductor called out "Clapham Road," I awoke from my reveries, but I spent a part of the night in putting sketches, at least, of those dream images down on paper. This was the origin of the structure theory.[78]

"It was much the same with the benzene theory." Kekulé describes how, one evening in Ghent, he was making no headway with his work.

> I moved my chair over to the fireplace and fell half-asleep. Once again the atoms fluttered about before my eyes. This time the smaller groups remained modestly in the background. My inner eye . . . now distinguished larger formations of varying shape. Long rows, much more thickly joined together; everything in motion, winding and turning, snake-fashion. But look, what was that? One of the snakes caught hold of its own tail and the whole formation swirled mockingly before my eyes. I awoke as if struck by lightning; this time, too, I spent the rest of the night working out the consequences of the hypothesis.[79]

Experiences of this kind inclined Kekulé to the view that ideas are like "seeds of the life of the mind" that float around in the atmosphere until they "accidentally" find fertile soil in the head of a researcher and take root and grow there.[80] This somewhat primitive explanation calls to mind the Stoic theory of "seminal ideas" that float in the world-*pneuma*.

As soon as an archetypal idea that has been serving as a model no longer coincides with the observed facts of the external world, it is dropped or its origin in the psyche is recognized. This process always coincides, as least as far as I have been able to observe, with the upward thrust of a new thought-model from the unconscious to the threshold of consciousness. This is the origin of that "disturbance of adaptation" which indicates that it is advisable to withdraw the projection.

Whereas the smaller sort of scientific "errors" are usually dropped without much ado as soon as they are seen through, there are others that even in natural science are passionately defended. This makes it clear that, seen from a psychological standpoint, they represent the projection of an especially important unconscious psychic factor that one wishes to preserve at any cost. When it is a question of projected aspects of a *God-image*,[81] as in the case of the world-mandala or the three-dimensionality of space or the concept of energy, the passion with which these concepts are disputed and often fought over, even today, becomes understandable.

Nevertheless we have to proceed from the assumption that all scientific hypotheses and/or explanations will in the end turn out to be projections but that their psychic "nuclear energy" will survive in still another new myth.

If we compare the above brief outline of the history of the development of a few of the concepts used in physics with the history of religious hermeneutics, we see an *apparent* difference in that the third stage in the withdrawal of projections—the stage of moral evaluation—seems to be missing in the natural sciences. Nowadays, a good deal is made of the fact that the concepts of the natural sciences are free of values. In my opinion this is an illusion, arising from the fact that many natural scientists, being thinkers, artificially repress the feeling function in their professional activities. This has led to that overvaluation of reason and of its product, technology, whose destructive consequences, both concrete and *moral,* we are today beginning to see in the form of problems of pollution, disturbances of ecology, and so on.

The battle over the construction of nuclear power plants is also a *moral* problem, however much this fact is beclouded by rational arguments. Euthanasia, abortion—again and again it becomes plain that one cannot get at the heart of the problem by rational means alone, and that the value function, feeling, *must* participate in the discovery of a solution. The omission of the third stage, of the feeling evaluation of scientific models, takes a bitter revenge, since behind these thought-models or dominant images stand the archetypes, which are never morally neutral powers.

A second element that, up to the present, seems to be missing in the history of natural science is the insight that outmoded models originated in the human unconscious; scarcely a thought is given to what they might mean, *psychologically,* once they are no longer fit to serve as a model in describing the outer world. It is only today, when we know that the assumptions of the *observer* decisively precondition the total results, that this question is becoming acute. Recognition of scientific projections has also almost always been occasioned by a disturbance, a pressing need, or an emergency (for example, cancer research or the necessity of finding new sources of energy). In such cases human curiosity is prone to discover new facts that do not fit the old model and force us to think up new hypotheses. Or sometimes a new, more suitable model is born *spontaneously* in the mind of a researcher of genius.

Basically there is not *one* essential scientific idea that is not in the end rooted in primordial archetypal structures. As Jung pointed out and emphasized, the parallelism of theological speculation and the thought-models of physics indicate that they rest, in the last analysis, on the same archetypal foundation, and Jungian psychology itself naturally also rests on the same foundation.[82] In its original form such an archetypal thought, however, was not yet consciously thought; rather it was experienced as the "appearance of a thought," that is, it was a "revelation" from the unconscious. As Jung emphasized, thinking preceded the formation of a consistent ego-consciousness and the ego in primordial times was the object of a kind of unconscious primordial thinking rather than the subject. It is a thinking *preexistent* to ego consciousness that has created the great themes or primordial thoughts of Western natural sciences.

Psyche and Matter

In what are perhaps his most important works, *Psychology and Alchemy* and *Mysterium Coniunctionis,* Jung has shown how important were the psychic contents projected onto matter in the earliest periods of chemistry and physics. Since matter—the material the researcher of the time was studying—was for all practical purposes completely unknown to him, it was especially easy for him to project his unconscious into its darkness.[83] This was naturally a purely involuntary occurrence. "Strictly speaking, projection is never made; it happens, it is simply there. In the darkness of anything external to me I find, without recognizing it as such, an interior or psychic life that is my own."[84] During the course of his experiments the researcher may have had certain psychic experiences that he interpreted as the particular behavior of the chemical process. "Since it was a question of projection, he was naturally unconscious of the fact that the experience had nothing to do with matter itself (that is, with matter as we know it today). He experienced his projection as a property of matter; but what he was in reality experiencing was his own unconscious."[85] However, everything unconscious, insofar as it was activated, was projected into matter; that is, it approached the experimenter from without. The alchemist in this way *"recapitulated the history of man's knowledge of nature.* As we all know, science began with the stars, and mankind discovered in them the dominants of the unconscious, the 'gods,' as well as the curious psychological qualities of the zodiac: a complete projected theory of human character. Astrology is a primordial experience similar to alchemy. Such projections repeat themselves whenever man tries to explore an empty darkness and involuntarily fills it with living form."[86] According to Jung, knowledge may be said to exist, in the final analysis, when the reactions of the psychic system that stream into consciousness (perceptions induced from without or endogenous psychic impulses) are brought into an order that corresponds to the behavior of metapsychic things (inner or outer "realities"). When an order thus created no longer corresponds to the way things behave, it is then recognized as a projection, but until this occurs it appears to us simply as "true knowledge."

Since earliest times, alchemy has always had two faces, "on the one hand the practical chemical work in the laboratory, on the other a psychological process, in part consciously psychic, in part unconsciously projected and seen in the various transformations of matter."[87] Many alchemists themselves half suspected a certain connection and therefore sought, through meditation and by cultivating their own inner life by means of imaginative work, to influence the outer chemical experiment,[88] since for them fantasy was not something shadowy and substanceless but had about it *something half material, half mental* that therefore could definitely influence the concrete materials found in the external world. "But," continues Jung,

> just because of this intermingling of the physical and the psychic, it always remains an obscure point whether the ultimate transformations in the alchemical process are to be sought more in the material or more in the spiritual realm. Actually, however, the question is wrongly put: there was no "either–or" for that age, but there did exist an *intermediate realm* between mind and matter, i.e., a psychic realm of subtle bodies whose characteristic it is to manifest themselves in a mental as well as a material form. This is the only view that makes sense of alchemistic ways of thought, which must otherwise appear nonsensical. Obviously, the existence of this

intermediate realm comes to a sudden stop the moment we try to investigate matter in and for itself, apart from all projection; and it remains non-existent so long as we believe we know anything conclusive about matter or the psyche. But the moment when physics touches on the "untrodden, untreadable regions," and when psychology has at the same time to admit that there are other forms of psychic life besides the acquisitions of personal consciousness—in other words, when psychology too touches on an impenetrable darkness —then the intermediate realm of subtle bodies comes to life again and the physical and the psychic are once more blended in an indissoluble unity. We have come very near to this turning-point today.[89]

Since Jung wrote the above, this trend has become much more visible, as researchers in the natural sciences, especially in physics, have become increasingly conscious of the extent to which the psychological circumstances in which the physicist conducts an experiment influence the result.[90] This has led to a revival of interest in basic research in these fields, to inquiry into thought-models and their origin, although in my view inquiry into the psychological origins of mathematical models is still to a large extent neglected, even though inquiry into precisely this area would be especially significant.[91] Inquiry into the preconscious creative processes in the researcher's unconscious is also still largely ignored. In contrast to this neglect, interest in parapsychological phenomena has livened up considerably (even in the Soviet Union); the object of this interest and research is once again that "intermediate realm of subtle bodies" in which the psychological and the physical can no longer be differentiated.

In order to prevent yet another naïve projection of psychic contents onto external phenomena, without at the same time denying the effectiveness and importance of such contents, Jung created the concept of the *collective unconscious,* which enables an empirical psychology to investigate more closely this intermediate realm of a single reality, or *unus mundus.*

This destroys the illusion of the positivistic natural scientists that we can acquire absolute knowledge of matter[92] and also the illusion of those psychologists who want to have it that the psyche consists of nothing more than the contents of our subjective consciousness.[93] For the concept of the collective unconscious defines that "intermediate realm of subtle bodies" without, however, presuming to say anything definitive about its substance.[94] It is a pure hypothesis. Jung says nothing about the contents of the collective unconscious, which are the province of experience alone.

4

The Hypothesis
of the Collective Unconscious

The Model

With a circumspection characteristic of genius, Jung in his description of the "collective unconscious" brought forth a concept in which the traditions of this idea in cultural history could be united with the empirical findings of contemporary natural science and through which the dualism of matter and mind/psyche may perhaps at the same time be overcome.

From the point of view of cultural history the idea of the collective unconscious is, as we have already indicated, a new formulation of the archetypal conception of a "world-spirit," as it was postulated by the Stoics, or of a "world-soul" that animates the universe and flows from the divine or demonic "in-fluences" (in-flowings) into the human subject. The Gnostic idea of a *prosphyēs psyche* (an "on-grown" soul) was a precursor, in the form of an intuitive hunch, of what today we would call the collective unconscious. The expression "on-grown" is an especially good choice, inasmuch as it can actually be demonstrated that the realization of the objective psyche originated historically in the process, here described, of the gradual withdrawal of projections. In fact, as Jung emphasized, nothing was "thrown out" of the psyche originally; rather, the human psyche as we know it today developed via a long series of *acts of introjection*.[1] It is only later, after a piece of the psyche has been experienced and recognized as an inner factor that one can speak, in the past tense, of a projection, of a transfer of inner elements to things external. "The collective unconscious, as we understand it today, was never a matter of 'psychology,' for before the Christian Church existed there were the antique mysteries, and these reach back into the grey mists of neolithic prehistory. Mankind has never lacked powerful images to lend magical aid against all the uncanny things that live in the depths of the psyche. Always the figures of the unconscious were expressed in protecting and healing images and in this way were expelled from the psyche into space,"[2] into a metaphysical "Beyond" or into occurrences in man's natural environment.

In contrast to his predecessors, however, Jung set the hypothesis of the collective unconscious on the solid ground of reality by demonstrating how it could be investigated empirically, namely, in the dreams of modern men and women. Adolf Bastian had already opened up one possibility of empirical research, that of comparative mythology. But his contemporaries took very little notice of his work. *And yet it is precisely myths and mythical religious systems that are the first and foremost expression of objective psychic processes.*

> Primitive man impresses us so strongly with his subjectivity that we should really have guessed long ago that myths refer to something psychic. His knowledge of nature is essentially the language and outer dress of an unconscious psychic process. But the very fact that this process is unconscious gives us the reason why man has thought of everything except the psyche in his attempts to explain myths. He simply didn't know that the psyche contains all the images that have ever given rise to myths, and that our unconscious is an acting and suffering subject with an inner drama which primitive man rediscovers, by means of analogy, in the processes of nature both great and small.[3]

For some time students of mythology sought to derive the mythological images of primitive cultures from external factors, from the given presence of the sun, moon, vegetation, and so on. Jung refuted this by pointing out that when one refers an imaginary image, or elements of it, to outer objects, this is, after all, a *response made by the psyche* to something external and never an exact, purely photographic, reproduction. Myths are created by the unconscious in very *free* relation to the sense perceptions.[4]

Thanks to Jung, we all possess today, in addition to Bastian's early attempt at a psychic explanation of myths, the further possibility of empirical dream-research, by means of which the *effect* of the archetypes, particularly in individual human beings, can be more accurately observed.

An impression of what the collective unconscious actually is can perhaps best be conveyed visually (see page 80).

Immediately under the field of consciousness of each individual ego is a layer of unconscious psychic contents (E) that have been acquired as a result of the individual's biographical experience: repressed and forgotten material that, when it occurs in dreams, can be understood only by a precise interrogation of the dreamer. Then underneath this layer are

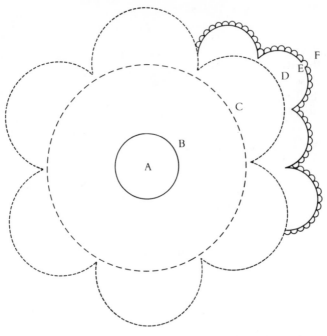

A	Unified layer, *unus mundus*	D	Group or folk unconscious
B	Collective unconscious of mankind	E	Unconscious in the individual
C	Regional unconscious	F	Individual ego

contents (D) that can be common to an entire group (for example, when an individual in *one* company of soldiers seems to be the "company goat," symbolic of the common shadow, or when everybody in the whole group unconsciously sees his own "shadow" in him). The same holds good for larger segments of the population. Next come contents (C) that are common to a country, or more frequently to a geographical region, as when one sees, for example, that certain myths or sagas occur only in certain areas,[5] or that contents, such as the myths of weakening the sun, which appear to belong to great nations or to large areas of the earth, are to be found throughout the East but not in our part of the world.[6] Then

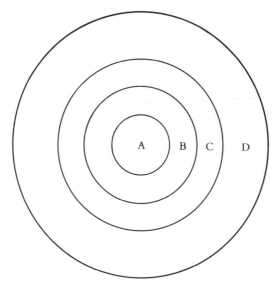

A   Conscious field with ego-center   C   Group unconscious
B   Personal unconscious   D   Collective unconscious

come contents (B) that are known to be present in *all* human beings, like hero myths, beliefs about paradise or about the Beyond, belief in spirits, and so on. This layer of the psyche, from which the most universal human myths come, contains at the same time the basic structure of the human soul. And, finally, there is another level, a unit (A) in which the multiple archetypes appear to be united or integrated into one *single* center. The diagram could just as well be turned inside out, as shown above.

Obviously the transition from one layer to another is extraordinarily fluid. In dreams, for example, one often finds universal mythological symbols mixed with contents stemming from personal experience.

Within the context of his work on the hypothesis of the collective unconscious, the word *symbol* acquired for Jung an entirely new meaning.[7] *Symbolikōs*, in antiquity, meant "figurative, not literal." The expression was almost synonymous in those days with metaphor or allegory and was so used in the early days of Christianity, when the concrete image served to point to the "real" spiritual-psychic meaning. Jung uses the concepts "symbol," "allegory," and "sign" in rather different ways. A sign, for him, is a mark or token of something of a concrete or psychic nature that is generally known; this also applies to allegory, with the difference that half-unconscious mythical associations often surround and cling to allegorical images. Both allegory and sign are to a large extent consciously created or developed. (A good deal that is allegorical, however, is still partly unconscious and is an image whose meaning the interpreter believes he consciously knows and has exhaustively described but which nevertheless contains other aspects still unknown to him. The border between allegory and symbol is therefore often fluid.)

A symbol is an image that *expresses an essential unconscious factor* and therefore refers to something essentially unconscious, unknown, indeed to something that is never *quite* knowable.[8] It is "the sensuously perceptible *expression of an inner experience*."[9] It is in the secondary instance made visible through the fact that it activates and groups the material available for representation. The archetype, in itself unknowable, clothes itself, so to speak, in this material, just as a primitive dancer does with animal hides and masks. In this way a symbol is created whose nucleus is a nonrepresentable, consciousness-transcending archetypal basic structure that emerges from the unconscious at different times and in different places as a structured complex of images and leads to the formation of religious and mythological systems of ideas and representations. "So long as a symbol is a living thing, it is an expression for something that cannot be characterized in any other or better way. The symbol is alive only so long as it is pregnant with meaning. But once its meaning has been born out of it, once that expression is found which formulates the thing sought, expected, or divined even better than the hitherto accepted symbol, then the symbol is *dead,* i.e., it possesses only an historical significance."[10] "A symbol really lives only when it is the best and highest expression for something divined but not yet known to the observer. It then compels his unconscious participation and has a life-giving and life-enhancing effect."[11]

Differentiated and primitive, conscious and unconscious are united in the symbol,[12] as well as all other possible psychic opposites. Whenever such a symbol comes spontaneously to light from the unconscious, it is a content that dominates the whole personality, "forcing the energy of the opposites into a common channel," so that "life can flow on . . . towards new goals."[13] Jung called that unknown activity of the unconscious which produces the real, life-giving symbols the *transcendent function,* because this process facilitates a transition from one attitude to another.[14] A still-living, genuine symbol can thus never be "resolved" (that is, analyzed, understood) by a rational interpretation, but can only be circumscribed and amplified by conscious associations; its nucleus, which is pregnant with meaning, remains unconscious as long as it is living and can only be divined. If one interprets it intellectually one "kills" the symbol, thus preventing any further unfolding of its content. Scientific hypotheses are also always symbols to begin with, to the degree to which they refer to a set of facts of which a number are still unknown; when this set of facts has gradually become sufficiently known, however, the symbolic aspect of the hypothesis has merely historical significance. The more significantly a symbol expresses an unconscious component that is common to a large number of people, the greater its effect on society.

When one reflects on these formulations by Jung, it is easy enough to understand the resistance of the churches to psychological interpretations of their symbols that probe too deeply; the fear that the symbols might thereby be destroyed was well founded. However, the insistence that they should be believed as concrete facts was an unfortunate way out of the dilemma, since it merely fed the rising doubts. The only way out of this impasse, the only way that guarantees that the living quality of religious symbols will not be prematurely extinguished, is through the realization that religious symbols do not refer to material and concrete facts but to a collective-psychic unconscious *reality.*

The Multiple Unity of the Collective Unconscious

The collective unconscious appears at first to be—to put it simply—the sum of archetypal structures that manifest themselves in typical mythological *motifs* in all human beings. Underneath these structures, however, one finds a still deeper layer that has the appearance of a unit. Jung remarks: "Our Western psychology has, in fact, got as far as yoga in that it is able to establish scientifically a deeper layer of unity in the unconscious. The mythological motifs whose presence has been demonstrated by the exploration of the unconscious form in themselves a multiplicity, but this culminates in a concentric or radial order which constitutes the true centre or essence of the collective unconscious."[15] It is the same center that becomes visible in mandala symbols, in those circular, square, and spherical symbols we have already met in the preceding chapters. As this central, unified area of the unconscious is approached, time and space are increasingly relativized.[16] That deepest area of the unconscious that is simply a unit or the center may therefore be understood as an *omnipresent continuum,* "an omnipresence without extension." "When something happens here at point A which touches upon or affects the collective unconscious, it has happened everywhere."[17] As this part of the "objective psyche" "is not limited to the person, it is also not limited to the body."[18] This psyche "behaves as if it were *one* and not as if it were split up into many individuals."[19] The multiplicity of the archetypes seems to be nullified or suspended in it.

It is naturally very tempting to identify the hypothesis of the collective unconscious historically and regressively with the ancient idea of an all-extensive world-soul, a kind of cosmic "subtle body."[20] The empirical findings that could serve as a basis for this are still, in my opinion, a long way from being adequately clarified. Even though phenomena such as psychokinesis and psychophotography appear to indicate the existence of a psychoid (similar to the psychic and also similar to matter) layer of psychic phenomena, these can by no means be identified with other aspects of the collective unconscious with which we are acquainted but look rather more like mere "boundary" phenomena. On the basis of such phenomena we cannot at present attribute to the collective unconscious any of the qualities of the subtle body. It seems far likelier that its omnipresence and timelessness point to some kind of purely transcendental existence. In what follows, therefore, I prefer to remain within the context of what is demonstrable and leave open questions about the essential nature of the collective unconscious.

But we must return to the subject of multiple archetypal structures. In this connection it may be well to emphasize once again that an "archetype in itself" cannot be visualized and that any idea of its reality can be attained only by inference. Just as we conclude that because light shows interference phenomena when it passes through lattice structures, it must therefore have a wavelike character,[21] we are also entitled to conclude that when people of all times and all cultures possess, for example, the collective imagery of a healer-hero, there must be in the human psyche a structured predisposition that motivates the production of a healer-hero fantasy in times of need (and frequently the projection of these fantasies onto suitable or unsuitable concrete persons). The same holds good for the mythologems of the "Great Mother," the "treasure that is hard to attain," the "magical helpful animal," the tree of life, the "mighty" spirits of the dead, and so on. The imagery that arises in any one such local product of the collective imagination—religious, literary, mythological—is naturally only rarely completely identical with that in any other country (when it *is,* the origin is apt to be traditional) but similar only in *structure.* The similarity is sufficient, however, to reveal clearly enough the kinship with the mythologems of other cultures. Even in cases where there is a known tradition that can be historically explained, and this occurs frequently, the effect of the archetype must still be taken into consideration, because there is no other explanation for the fact that certain mythologems spread like wildfire while others remain localized and are seldom or never borrowed. Viewed psychologically, it is noticeable, in cases of widespread dissemination, that an archetypal representation (like a rumor) comes into wide acceptance only when the underlying archetypal structure in the collective unconscious is activated, that is, charged with energy.

Jung surmised that an archetype in its quiet state is not projected.[22] In this state it would have no determinable form but would be, in respect to form, completely undefinable, "with, however, a potential, due to projection, of appearing in definable forms."[23] *Thus, projection is an essential part of the process by which the archetype assumes a determinable shape.* This depends on the activation, that is, on the energic charge of an archetype. Just as there are "excited points" in an electromagnetic field, so it seems that in the "field" of the collective unconscious there are also such "excited points," comparable to single archetypes to the extent that the latter do in fact behave like relatively isolatable nuclei. The points of the electromagnetic field can be charged—to continue the comparison with physics—by the action of external influences, such as the incidence of light and radiation, or by some internal shift of energy within the field itself. An analogous process can be observed in the case of the archetypal structures in the collective unconscious: an external emergency, such as epidemics or famine, can suddenly "charge" the fantasy of a healer-savior, in itself always present in a latent state, in the collective psyche of a group or it can intensify pessimistic fantasies of the end of the world. Internal shifts of energy within the field itself can also occur in the collective unconscious: when, for example, an active-masculine stance and a one-sidedly extroverted attitude toward life, with their corresponding values and ideals, have been dominants in a society for quite a long time, then complementary or even countertendencies may spontaneously be activated and come up from the unconscious, perhaps a tendency toward introversion or toward a more feminine outlook on life. In both cases, whether prompted from without or from within, the law of compensation or complementarity seems to dominate, that is, a tendency to establish balance or wholeness (wholeness achieved by two logically incompatible opposites, in the strict sense of the word *complementarity,* as used in physics).

These self-regulatory processes in the psyche seem to be controlled by the archetype of the Self, the supraordinate center of the collective unconscious, and appear to be independent of ego-consciousness and of the will and all its exertions; they are therefore also to a great extent unpredictable. One usually recognizes their compensatory character only later and marvels at the strange and curious byways and detours by means of which the compensatory function of the unconscious accomplishes its ends.[24] A ray of light, as we know, does not take a direct Euclidean linear path through matter-filled space; it takes the shortest way, which in the case of resistant material does not mean a Euclidean geometrical path but rather a "detour." The same can be demonstrated in the case of a compensatory current of energy flowing from the archetype of the Self.

And now at last we can return to the unresolved questions from the first chapter. We saw there that when a man projects his anima onto a woman and falls in love with her, two currents of energy are set in motion. The lover experiences an affect directly, as if from the impact of an arrowshot, and sees it as coming from the god Eros (Amor, Cupid), a symbol of the Self. Another current of energy "activates" the anima-imago in his unconscious and projects it (throws it forward) onto the outer woman, who in this way becomes forthwith fascinating to the man. The obvious assumption is that the reasons for this detour via the outer object are analogous to the reasons that a ray of light does not follow a direct linear path, namely, because there is "impermeable material" between consciousness and the anima-image in the unconscious that stands in the way of an unmediated psychic perception of the anima-image. We know today that when the person affected opens up a way, through active imagination,[25] to the inner anima-image and comes into direct contact with it, the image that appears externally in projected form begins to fade. The recognition of this phenomenon inclined Freud to the assumption that only repressed material is projected. This is not always true, however, because experience shows just as often—indeed, even more often—that the impermeability is due not to any kind of repression but simply to the fact that in consciousness the *means of reception* necessary to the admission of something new coming from the unconscious *are missing*. This is seen most clearly in cases where a creative inspiration or fantasy is making its way up from the unconscious.

The mathematician Henri Poincaré describes in detail in *Science et méthode* how, through a revelation from the unconscious, he discovered what today are called automorphic functions. It took him a good half hour to write down in logical sequence the vision he had seen in a flash. He declared, rightly, that this vision would have led to nothing if he had not been striving—in vain—for a long time to reach a solution. Through this exertion his consciousness created, as it were, a net to catch the new conception, so that what he had seen could be put in its proper place.

Kekulé's above-mentioned vision of a dancing pair and of a snake biting its own tail, which facilitated the discovery of the ring shape of the benzene molecule, is a similar example. The vision alone would not have led to anything if it had not been preceded by intensive conscious work on chemical research.

In psychological practice one frequently meets with men and women who see themselves as "unrecognized geniuses." I have noticed in such cases that the unconscious does in fact relatively often present genuinely creative impulses and inspirations in dreams. Tragically enough, however, the right conscious attitude is missing. It is too narrowly conventional or the necessary education is lacking, so that what is being revealed from within is falsely evaluated or distorted; it may be, too, that the person concerned is simply lazy and prefers, instead of working at a genuine assimilation of his unconscious intuitions, to proclaim them in an inflated and vague way as "newly discovered truth." The products of such an attitude generally fail to find a publisher and mercifully disappear into the wastepaper basket. Only an inwardly open, "naïve" attitude to the unconscious on the one hand and an honest, conscientious, and painstaking devotion on the part of ego-consciousness on the other can bring the creative contents of the unconscious matrix successfully over the threshold into consciousness. Play, with neither plan nor purpose, is the best precondition.

The Polar Nature of the Collective Unconscious

As we saw in the second chapter, a dualism developed among the religious hermeneuts of the European past. This led to images in the writings of poets and of the Holy Scripture being interpreted as either *physikōs,* in reference to the material cosmos, or *theologikōs,* in reference to a spiritual image of God or to a world-spirit or world-soul. Jung brought this dual aspect to light again in his writings on the collective unconscious and the archetypes, but his interpretation gave it more the meaning of a polarity. He compares the realm of the psychic (ego-consciousness *and* the unconscious) to the light spectrum. At the infrared end, the psychic functions change into the instincts and physiological processes, which take on a more and more compulsive character.[26] At the other, ultraviolet end of the scale are the archetypes, psychic structures that precondition our fantasies and ideas by producing symbolic images. (Consciousness and, with it, freedom of choice and free will prevail only within the middle range.) The *form* and the *meaning* of instincts are represented in the images produced by the archetypes.[27] The archetypes, therefore, are collectively present, unconscious preconditions or innate predispositions that act as regulators and stimulators of creative fantasy activity.[28] Their effect on the human ego is numinous–magical and is felt as something spiritual, even— on the primitive level—as a spirit or spirits.[29]

Archetype and instinct are "the most polar opposites imaginable."[30] This is most clearly illustrated by comparing a man who has fallen under the domination of instinct with one who has been seized by the spirit. Yet extremes can meet and can even change into their former opposites.[31]

At the infrared end of the scale, analytical psychology can extend a hand to students of behavior, because at this pole typical human ways of reacting pass over into the realm of instinctive patterns of behavior, which in their relatively mechanical stereotypes resemble those of animals. It is also at this pole that those psychic patterns of reaction become visible that express themselves in typical moods and actions (instincts) and can be observed statistically from the outside. At the ultraviolet pole, on the other hand, one would look for those phenomena where it is no longer a question of impulses coming from without but rather of inspirations, of being seized by archetypal spiritual insights or images that, just as much as drives and instincts, can overcome the freedom of the individual personality (Paul's vision on the road to Damascus). It is here that one could look for the *alethēs logos* of the ancient hermeneuts, who expressly emphasized that their interpretations come from a "pneumatic inspiration" and are involuntary and impersonal.

The polarization of the psychic middle range, between the two consciousness-transcending poles of matter and psyche, is only a means, however, for our consciousness to describe its psychic experiences a bit more exactly; "outward-material" and "inner-spiritual" are only characteristic labels that tell us nothing about the real nature of what we describe as "matter" nor about what we call "spirit," except that both move and affect us psychologically.

All the stronger instinctive impulses and all creative spiritual experiences and realizations are linked with emotions. *E-motio* of course is what "moves outward." Archetypes, as we have noted, have a "specific charge," that is, they develop *numinous* effects that manifest themselves as affects. These affects lift *one* content, which occupies the forefront of consciousness, into *super*-normal clarity but at the same time darken the rest of the field of consciousness. This brings about a lowering of the orientation to the external world and therewith a relativization of time and space.

It is in the moments when an emotion-charged archetypal content is influencing consciousness with unusual force that so-called synchronistic events often tend to occur; concrete events take place in the individual's outer environment that have a meaningful connection with the inner psychic contents that are constellated at about the same time.[32] An activated archetype behaves rather like a whole "situation," or "like a circumambient atmosphere to which no definite limits can be set, either in space or in time."[33]

Jung conjectured therefore that the two poles of matter and psyche at the deepest level become one, in the sense of the existence of an *unus mundus* in which matter and spirit, outer and inner are no longer separate. In actual psychological experience a distinction between the two realms is unavoidable; in the realm of the deeper layers of the collective unconscious,

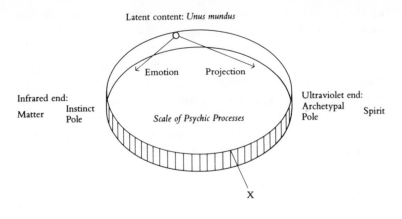

Latent content: *Unus mundus*

Emotion   Projection

Infrared end:
Matter Instinct Pole

Scale of Psychic Processes

Ultraviolet end:
Archetypal Pole Spirit

X

X = The roving light-ray of ego–consciousness

however, no such distinction can be made with a high degree of certainty.[34]

The observation of synchronistic phenomena leads us to surmise that a *latent* unitary reality,[35] which Jung called *unus mundus,* exists beneath the above-described poles of instinct and spirit, or matter and spirit. This is the unitary layer A of the diagram on page 80. The diagram of a kind of scale of psychic occurrences could thus be enlarged, as the above diagram shows.

When the sphere of the *unus mundus* is activated for any reason, its latent energy is expressed in a *double* manifestation: in the realm of what we call matter and can ascertain or establish by means of physiologically mediated sense-perception *and* as image suddenly emerging from the spiritual pole into consciousness and whose meaning is identical with what is observed externally. This dual manifestation recalls the fact, discussed above, that a double phenomenon also becomes evident in the process of projection: the bullet or the arrow of passion (instinct) by which the one who is projecting feels himself directly affected and the image that is thrown outwards and that he thinks he sees externally.

A very serious difficulty with the hypothesis of the collective unconscious arises when we are faced with the problem of *attribution:* that is, to what extent one may or should attribute archetypal manifestations to the unconscious of an individual and to what extent not. In a court of law, as we know, a person shown to be unable to offer conscious resistance to his drives is regarded as not responsible for his actions. The same is also true for compulsions that come from the archetypal pole! If a man is so possessed by a religious idea that he is unable to criticize it morally, he is also considered to be irresponsible. I think of the case of a man who was mentally ill and killed a child because, as he claimed, the Holy Ghost had commanded him to do it. As we have already seen, a problem which even today remains completely open is that of whether evil demons in a person possessed are alien invaders or unconscious components which belong to the person's own psychology. A mistaken judgment in such a case has, however, very serious consequences. "A wrong attribution," as Jung writes, "may bring about dangerous inflations which seem unimportant to the layman only because he has no idea of the inward and outward disasters that may result."[36] "The effect of inflation is that one is not only 'puffed up' but too 'high up.' This may lead to attacks of giddiness, or to a tendency to fall downstairs, to twist one's ankle, to stumble over steps and chairs, and so on,"[37] to say nothing of megalomania or Messianic fantasies. But if one *fails* to attribute to an individual a content that belongs to him, the opposite of an inflation takes place—a loss of soul, as described above, that is, a depressing decrease in the whole individual life-potential; worse, the rejected content turns up again in a new projection in the individual's environment, as one sees in the case of Don Juan, who chases one woman after another in his search for the *one* inner image of woman (anima), only to realize, in the moment of possession, that it is not "there." One sees the same process go on in people who do not realize their shadow and therefore always find their *bête noire* wherever they go;

they then enter into a power struggle that takes its stereo-typed course but never ask themselves, "Why does this al-ways happen to me?"

Such schematic repetitions of situations or exaggerated de-pendencies belong to the kind of disturbances in adaptation, discussed previously, that indicate the desirability of with-drawing the projection. How much one may attribute to the individual as personal and how much one leaves, as "objec-tive psychic," in a realm that is not personal can in many cases be clearly seen only through a thoroughgoing interpretation of the person's dreams, and even then not in every case. Moreover, one should never lose sight of the irrationality of human fate. Jung was once consulted by a patient with a number of different phobias, all of which gradually disap-peared except an insuperable fear of outdoor stairs. Later this person was killed on an outdoor flight of steps by a stray bullet in a street battle. This fear, then, unlike his other phobias, was not a projection; it was a genuine premonition! What may or may not be described as projection is today still very largely a question of judgment and/or of careful assessment, so that in my opinion psychologists should use the greatest caution and discretion in dealing with this concept.

5

The Evil Demons

Exorcism of Devils
or Integration of Complexes?

In psychological treatment, when the point has been reached where the withdrawal of a projection seems due, one is struck by the energy with which some people resist accepting the appropriate insight. Occasionally a patient will see the situation for what it is, with a liberating "Aha!" reaction, and is freed at least momentarily from his wrong attitude; more often, however, there is a strong resistance against the healing insight or a helpless, apathetic perseverance in the disturbed attitude. This can be especially observed in the treatment of paranoia and schizophrenia, which in practice present the greatest difficulties.[1] Deep-seated mendacity, too, often remains therapeutically completely inaccessible. In such cases the autonomy of certain complexes is unusually strong, so that they "possess" the ego, so to speak, like completely independent beings—a psychological fact that found expression in the belief in demons among all peoples in all ages from time immemorial.[2] On the primitive level it is therefore self-evident that "demons," or in our language "complexes," have to be removed from the realm of the subject; integration —that is, a responsible acceptance into the total personality —is attempted only exceptionally, namely, by certain shamans or medicine men who kept a few conquered "demons" near them as "spirit helpers." If we look at the mythological traditions to which this theme is central, we see that a particularly widespread form of liberation from such a complex is represented in the motif of the so-called magic flight, in which a hero or heroine escapes a pursuing demon by tossing behind certain objects that grow into major obstacles for the pursuer and thus contribute to the rescue of the pursued. The following fairy tale from Turkestan, "The Magic Steed," will serve as an example:

> A king has only one daughter. When she comes of marriageable age the king feeds a flea until it becomes as fat as a camel, has its skin removed, makes slippers from the skin, and announces: "I shall give my daughter in marriage to whoever recognizes whose skin this is." Nobody can find the solution until an evil, man-eating Div (demon) learns the secret from a slave, appears at the court as a scurvy beggar, solves the riddle, and demands the daughter. As the king is about to drive him away, the Div threatens the whole realm with disaster. The daughter must therefore go off with him. When she is seeking a horse for herself in the stable, a small magic horse speaks to

her and counsels her to take him, a mirror, a comb, salt, and a
clove and ride away. The Div sets out in pursuit. She throws
the clove behind her. It becomes a thick underbrush of thorns
that delays the Div for a time. Then she throws behind her the
salt, which becomes a desert of sand and salt; then the comb,
which turns into a high mountain; and finally the mirror,
which turns into a torrential river. Thereupon she seeks shelter with a poor brushwood-gatherer and his wife. A king
finds her there and marries her. She bears him male twins. But
in the meantime the Div has again set to work; he threatens
the queen and her children while the king is away hunting.
The little magic horse then decides to fight the Div. At first
they fight on land; then they fall into a river and go on
struggling underwater. The little horse wins the fight, but as
he climbs out of the river he asks to be sacrificed: "Throw my
head aside, arrange my bones according to the four directions,
toss my entrails to the side, and sit with your children under
the ribs." As the queen obeys, golden poplars grow out of the
horse's bones; villages, fields, and meadows from his entrails;
a golden castle from his ribs—and out of his head there
springs a silver-bright little brook. The king finds the queen
in the castle after a long search and they live "from then on
happy and contented in this beautiful kingdom."[3]

At the beginning of the story the old king apparently wants
to keep his daughter with him; he is unwilling to set her free.
Therefore as king he symbolizes a masculine-collective conscious attitude that controls the feminine, the Eros principle,
and holds it prisoner. This calls up the "demon." In the case
of an individual, such a daughter develops a father complex
and a tendency to be dominated by destructive masculine impulses (what Jung calls the negative animus). But the magic
horse, a healthy instinctive tendency to wholeness, prevents
the daughter from falling completely into the possession of
the demon. At first this cannot be accomplished in direct
combat but only through the magic flight. The objects
thrown behind may be understood as sacrificial gifts to the
unconscious: the sacrifice of worldly ornament (clove), van-

ity (mirror and comb), and esprit (salt). All these must be given up in order to prevent possession by the Div. Only later can there be the open battle with the demon and the transformation of the horse into a lasting psychic center—an inner habitation of peace.

For the moment, only the flight motif matters to us, a motif corresponding to a state of affairs often encountered in therapy. In the treatment of such "devilish" states of possession resulting from a negative father complex in a woman, I have often been impressed by the fact that the woman's ego is for a long time not strong enough to confront such an inner devil directly;[4] for the time being nothing but methods of repression or avoidance are possible, literally "flight" through evasive measures. The disturbing factor has to remain outside the circle of the subject's life and can be neither conquered nor integrated. One can only advise the patient to stay away, as far as possible, from situations and areas of concern that could touch the complex. In the event possession has actually taken place, therefore, defensive action and careful avoidance of the complex and of situations that constellate it are indicated. At this stage it is altogether appropriate to think of the complex as a threatening "demon." One can in no way hold the patient responsible for what is happening, but can only help him to follow his healthy instinct (the magic horse) and to avoid everything that might provide an opening for what is destructive. In this situation I think that exorcism can be completely effective for those who are still firmly anchored in the Catholic faith. There are certain dark powers in the inner world that one really can only run away from or keep at a distance in some other way.

In the following fairy tale of the Siberian Yukagir the magic flight takes a different course from that of the above story (and this is a rare exception):

> A lonely girl who has no parents and no husband is able to take care of her house and to water the reindeer with magic

songs. One day half the sky darkens; it is "the evil spirit." One of his lips touches the sky; the other rests on the earth—an open mouth threatening to swallow up everything. The girl escapes in a "magic flight." First she throws behind her a comb, which becomes a forest; next her red handkerchief, which turns into a giant fire. Then she transforms herself successively into a polar bear, a wolverine, a wolf, and a bear, and in the form of the bear runs on. She comes to a tent and falls to earth, fainting from exhaustion. As she recovers, the evil spirit stands before her as a handsome young man, "more beautiful than the sun." With him are his two brothers. The girl chooses the handsome youth as a husband, and they all live together in peace.[5]

In this version of the magic flight, not only does the heroine succeed in escaping but the pursuer also transforms himself on his own, after a time, into her future partner with whom she can share her life. The trouble she goes to in order to avoid being possessed by the negative complex is in itself sufficient to bring out the latter's positive side. In this version the magic flight is followed by a "transformation flight," an equally widespread mythologem.[6] The girl transforms herself successively into four animals. This is identical with the "healthy instinct" embodied in the magic horse in the Turkestan fairy tale. The will to live and to become whole conquers the temptation to fall, fainting, into the jaws of the evil demon, that is, to be "possessed." Whether the pursuer is essentially good or evil is apparently not the main consideration; *it is the state of possession in itself that is destructive.*

The spirit-world of the Yakut, for example, includes both the lower, evil spirits and the higher spirits of light, but possession by the higher spirits leads to madness, just as possession by evil spirits does, and can be cured only by a shaman.[7] The shaman has this power because during his initiation he has overcome his own states of possession. "The shaman," writes Adolf Friedrich, "is the incarnation of that type of religious man who is able to master the spirits who beset him—

that is, his psychic struggles—and who therefore can help others whom the spirits threaten. The person possessed, however, is not able to help himself but is delivered over to the storm of divergent and one-sided powers; he needs the help of an exorcist who can liberate him."[8] Friedrich's description of the spirits as "one-sided" is exactly right, for they are the autonomous complexes that upset the total equilibrium of the personality by compelling one-sidedness. One among other easily recognizable symptoms is the way in which the thoughts and deeds of the possessed person tend to circle, in incredible monomania, around the *one* complex-theme, to the damage of the whole personality.

This peculiar one-sidedness of the autonomous complex is vividly represented in the folklore and myths of many peoples by demons who are often crippled or have only a partially human form: eyes or faces in the wrong place (in the stomach or the genital region) or in the wrong number (like Polyphemus, who had only one eye, or the evil one-eyed or three-eyed creatures in Grimms' fairy tales).[9] Among the polar peoples, spirits often appear who consist only of a head or a skull. The German expression *ver-rückt* (crazy, insane) illustrates this state of affairs impressively: in cases of possession by projected complexes certain psychic components are really *ver-rückt* (displaced, shifted away, moved away) to the wrong place!

Sometimes a person who is otherwise healthy enough will be turned into a demon through being crippled. The Warrau in former British Guiana tell the following story:

> One day two brothers who are hunting in a forest come upon a noisy, festive drinking-party. The elder brother, carried away, joins the party, but the younger one anxiously stays on the sidelines, because he is rightly afraid that this is a party of ghosts, ghosts of rain-frogs that have been transformed into people. The brothers spend the night in hammocks in a hut. The drunken elder brother lets his feet dangle over the fire, and when the younger brother warns him his only reply

is: "Akka, akka!" But he does draw back his legs. Then he dangles them over the fire again and after a while notices that both his feet are charred. Thereupon he takes a knife, hacks off both feet and all the flesh, and sharpens his leg bones into a spear. Lying in his hammock, he uses it for spearing birds as they fly past.

He will not take his eyes off his brother, who finally runs away. The cripple hurries after him on the stumps of his legs. On the way he spears a deer with the spear made from his leg bones, thinking that the deer is his brother. The younger brother hurries back to the tribe and gives the alarm to his people. They lure the cripple from his hammock, surround him, and kill him.[10]

This story is superbly graphic in its portrayal of the way in which a human being is possessed by "spirits" (here they are rain-frogs, that is, nature spirits) and as a result loses his feet, his standpoint on the earth of reality. As a consequence he himself becomes inhuman and demonic and can only call out: "Akka!" like a rain-frog. More and more, too, he wants to "possess" his brother. When the latter runs away, the cripple becomes a murderous foe and has to be eliminated by the community.

Not only people who are bewitched but also people who have been murdered can similarly become demons. The Kaschinaua Indians of South America tell the following story:

A man of the neighboring Kutana tribe treacherously murders a Marinaua and leaves his severed head on a stake in the forest. However, the murdered man's mouth remains open; he blinks his eyes and begins to weep bitterly. A fellow tribesman finds him, and the entire tribe brings the corpse home and mourns the murdered man. They bury the body and take the head along in a basket. The head, however, bites one hole after another in the basket, keeps rolling out of it, and then bites the bearer in the behind. The tribesmen begin to fear that the murdered man perhaps wants to bewitch them, so they leave him and run away. Weeping, the head rolls after them, crying out again and again, "Friends, wait for me!

I want to go home with you!" The people become ever more frightened in their flight and the cries of the pursuing head ever more desperate. When the tribesmen run into their huts and close all the doors, the head cries out, "Friends, you have fear of me and have locked the house so I cannot enter and fetch my things. I will transform myself." The head then ponders for a long time, wondering whether he should transform himself into fruit or into earth or water, or fish, or firewood, etcetera, so that the others might eat him, walk upon him, drink him, and so on. Finally he decides to make of his blood "the way of enemies," that is, the rainbow, and to turn his eyes into stars and his head into the moon. The moon is at once carried up into the sky, borne upward by hawks. "Then all the women began to bleed and their men lay with them. Then the blood ceased to flow and the woman became pregnant. . . . And that is all I remember of the story of the Marinaua who was beheaded by the Kutanaua. There is no more."[11]

This tale illustrates how deeply someone prematurely or violently taken from life longs to remain with his people, which is why the murdered man pursues his friends and haunts them like a demonic ghost. This is a belief we also find in Western documents of antiquity, in which haunting spirits are mainly of those who died prematurely—for example, women who died in childbirth, young men killed in wars, and suicides. These are the unquiet spirits of the underworld; in magic papyri they are always being called upon to work all kinds of harm through magic.[12] It was believed that these spirits were embittered because they were forced to part too early from their lives and consequently became evil, even if as human beings they had been good. The Marinaua's head in our story suddenly began to bite without any apparent conscious wish to turn malevolent. It is important here that the spirit appears as a head (the body does not haunt). The head is the seat of thoughts and aspirations, the spiritual and mental essence of the dead person, but it is also merely a *part* of the whole and therefore uncanny in a way similar to that of the man with the spear of leg bones in the previous story. Demons almost never have a "normal" form; they are always images of disfigured or incomplete human beings and thus are very suitable visual images of the distorting effects of autonomous complexes.

The best analogy of the way in which a demon tends to compel one-sidedness is the way in which the rabies virus works. If this virus touches a peripheral nerve of a person who has been bitten by a rabid dog, it travels, as we know, to precisely that place in the victim's brain from which it can control the whole person. It causes him to reject water so that the virus cannot be spit out of the mouth; it induces him to wander about so that he comes into contact with as many other creatures as possible; and finally it brings about an actual rage to bite so that the virus can be transplanted in a new carrier. When we recall that this virus could so enslave an outstanding man like Kant or Goethe that he could be forced to perform mechanically only what furthered the propagation of the virus . . . ! Autonomous complexes behave in exactly the same way; they can warp or destroy the whole personality. Viruses, we know, are "dead" matter; it is only in a living creature that they acquire a "quasi-life." The same is true of autonomous complexes. They take all the life out of a person; when they have "eaten him up" they become entangled with life in the surrounding environment. That is why, when in the vicinity of people who are possessed, one often experiences a sudden fatigue and an inexplicable feeling of having one's vitality sucked out.

Mythical images of demons are extremely varied; not all demons belong in the same category, nor are they all equally dangerous. The Siberian Yakut have made a classification of demons that is serviceable enough for general use. They distinguish (1) Aji, the spirits of the upper world, (2) Abassy, the spirits of the underworld, (3) Itschi, the spirits of the middle world or the spirits who rule over animals and plants, and (4) the spirits of the dead.

The first two classes of spirits are eternal beings and pre-forms of the gods in the high cultures; psychologically they illustrate in symbols the archetypes of the collective unconscious. Along with the often purely destructive tendency of such spirits there is also the motif of a spirit (especially often from the upper world) who falls in love with a human. The latter is thereby induced to commit suicide in an attack of madness so that he may be united with the beloved in the Beyond. In Greek mythology Daphne's flight from Apollo corresponds to this motif, a flight that, however, does not lead to union in the Beyond apart from the fact that Daphne (laurel) becomes *the* plant of Apollo.

The spirits that rule over animals and plants are probably the oldest forms in which archetypal contents were imagined; among the Bushmen and the Australian aborigines—that is, in cultures that have remained especially close to their origins—they are actual gods. In contrast to the upper and lower spirits, they are localized in the surrounding world of nature and are not separated into "light" and "dark."

The spirits of the dead seem to embody mainly psychic contents, which are closer to the personal realm of the psyche;[13] in the dreams of modern men and women they often appear as projected images (inner *imagines*) of the deceased. Hence Jung, in his early work, assumed that such spirits were nothing more than the embodiment of projected images, approximate representations of the father complex, the mother complex, and so on; "a persistent attachment to the dead makes life seem less worth living, and may even be the cause of psychic illnesses."[14] Jung later revised this opinion and was no longer quite sure that spirits are *only* such personal *imagines,* possessing no separate reality of their own. "This opens up the whole question of the transpsychic reality immediately underlying the psyche."[15] Jung is alluding here to the principle of synchronicity, which will be discussed below.

Many primitive peoples believe that the spirits of the dead gradually become "mightier" than the deceased were during their lifetime and that their images become increasingly actual images of divinities. The above story of the murdered Marinaua whose head became the moon is an example. Psychologically this means simply that the images of the spirits of the dead are gradually assimilated to collective archetypal images. The psychic energy that clings to the memory image of the deceased charges an image in the collective unconscious, which is thereby activated. If such a newly activated content can be translated into communicable language, beneficial creative inspirations may result; it can also lead, however, to morbid disorientation phenomena. Spirits are "either pathological fantasies or new but as yet unknown ideas."[16] As we have seen, this is true of the archetypes in general. Jung emphasized that the demonic works with negative effect mainly at that moment when "an unconscious content of seemingly overwhelming power appears on the threshold of consciousness"; then it will lay hold of the personality in the form of a possession.[17] Before such a content is integrated into consciousness it will always *appear physically,* because it *"forces the subject into its own form."*[18] The negative aspect can be avoided if the man or the woman holds his or her ground against the thrust of the unconscious content and tries to become conscious of its meaning through reflection.[19] *The demonic, therefore, would be the creative* in statu nascendi, *not yet realized, or "made real," by the ego.*

One form of evil that is especially feared is black magic. It comes from a conscious attitude that exalts destructive psychic impulses into the only valid truth. "The means used for this purpose are primitive, fascinating or awe-inspiring ideas and images," which are placed in the service of some antisocial personal goal.[20]

The demonic rests, as Jung emphasizes, "on the unconscious forces of negation and destruction and on the reality of evil. The existence of the daemonic is demonstrated by the fact that black magic is not only possible but uncannily successful, so much so that it is tempting to assume that black magicians are possessed by a daemon."[21] The theory of Albertus Magnus may also be mentioned: "When anyone gives free rein to violent emotion and in this state wishes evil, it will have a magical effect. This is the quintessence of primitive magic and of the corresponding mass phenomena like Nazism, Communism, etc."[22] When in such mass psychoses chaos erupts from the unconscious, it is seeking "new symbolic ideas which will embrace and express not only the previous order but also the essential contents of the disorder"[23]—a creative achievement, therefore, has become a necessity. So we see that demonism and creativity are psychologically very close to each other. Nothing in the human psyche is more destructive than unrealized, unconscious creative impulses. That is why a psychosis can, as a rule, be cured only if the patient can begin some creative activity, some creative shaping of the contents that are disturbing him. And when it is a question of a mass psychosis, nothing but new, creative, "redemptive" archetypal conceptions, brought up from the depths, can stop the development toward a catastrophe.

Many demons are not such radically distorted creatures but rather "mixed" figures that do not occur in nature—centaurs, mermaids, Pegasus, the bird Garuda, and the like.[24] Images of this kind express something supernatural and hence spiritual or mental. *They embody essentially creative fantasies,* which are morally neutral but in general tend to be benevolently disposed to human beings. The centaur Chiron is skilled in the art of healing; Garuda mediates between the gods and men; Pegasus carries the poet up to the heights of spiritual inspiration.

The question that nevertheless keeps recurring is to what extent such beings can be integrated. Perhaps this much can be said: Whenever a demon, for example a "poltergeist," consistently "follows" a man or a woman in spite of a change in place and atmosphere, this "spirit" is at least to a substantial extent subjective; if he disappears with a change of place, the relation to the subject is not of great importance. (It was especially this phenomenon of the place-bound ghost that prompted Jung to correct his earlier view that spirits are simply subjective complexes.) Yet even when a spirit "follows" a human being everywhere, it is sometimes only in part subjective; this "subjective" component attracts, so to speak, the "objective devil": as soon as the former is integrated, the latter withdraws, as we have seen in the case of the suicide demon in the Chinese tale "The Spirits of Those Who Were Hanged."

There are demons in all times and all cultures. Here we shall consider briefly only the specific ancient Mediterranean development of European belief in spirits, in its analogy to and its differences from the examples of the imaginary realm of primitive peoples already discussed.

The Demons of Antiquity

In ancient Egypt there were good spirits and evil ones. The dwarf Bes and the youthful Horus, for example, were positive demons; the evil demons were often referred to as a nameless collective, the "companions of Seth." Similarly with the Devas of Iran. In Mesopotamia and Asia Minor there were also such good and evil demons; the latter, for instance, are spirits of the dead and evil winds that bring sickness, as well as "spies," and "secret agents," whose aim it is to bring harm to human beings.[25]

There were Canaanite and old Judaic demons who were thought to be closely connected with the human psyche, "breath-spirits" that could, when they invaded human beings, produce moods, enigmatic impulses, sudden reactions, and so on, but also a moral standpoint or conviction; the Old Testament contains many references to a spirit of lust or of jealousy, but also to a spirit of insight or understanding. Even bodily functions like smell, speech, sleep, and sexuality have their "spirit."[26]

In pre-Hellenic Greece the demons, as in Egypt, were part of a nameless collectivity. The word *daimon* comes from *daiomai*, which means "divide," "distribute," "allot," "assign," and originally referred to a momentarily perceptible divine activity, such as a startled horse, a failure in work, illnesses, madness, terror in certain natural spots. There are even skills that are in a way demons. The idea of a demon as a person's constant companion emerged in the fifth century B.C. in Hesiod, and in the third century B.C. it spread very widely. Such a demon causes the individual's happiness or unhappiness; as early as the fourth century B.C., sacrifices were made to a good *(agathos)* daimon as house-spirit.

Plato does not use the word *daimon* unambiguously; usually it is synonymous with *theos* (god), sometimes with the nuance of a "near-human" being.[27] In the *Symposium,* Diotima says that Eros is a mighty daimon and "spirits, you know, are halfway between god and man."[28] To Socrates' question, "What powers have they then?" she answers, "They are the envoys and interpreters that ply between heaven and earth, flying upward with our worship and our prayers, and descending with the heavenly answers and commandments, and since they are between the two estates they weld both sides together and merge them into one great whole. They form the medium of the prophetic arts, of the priestly rites of sacrifice, initiation, and incantation, of divination and of sorcery, for the divine will not mingle directly with the human, and it is only through the mediation of the spirit world that man can have any intercourse, whether waking or sleeping, with the gods. . . . There are many spirits, and many kinds of spirits, and Love [Eros] is one of them."[29]

In the Stoa and in Platonism of the middle period the shades of difference between gods and demons were more sharply drawn: the gods are the mighty powers of the universe, remote from men, majestic, for the most part aloof from the suffering and the passions of humanity. The demons, on the other hand, inhabit the intermediate realm between Olympus and mankind, especially the regions of the air and the sublunar world, and there they join the nature spirits in springs and plants and animals. In presenting his late Platonic conception, Apuleius of Madura formulates this as follows: The poets had falsely attributed to the gods what was valid only for the demons; "they exalt and favor certain human beings and they oppress and humble others. They feel therefore compassion, anger, joy, and fear and all the other feelings of human nature . . . all the storms that are so far removed from the tranquility of the heavenly gods. All the gods pass their time in an unchanging spiritual state . . . since nothing is more perfect than a god. . . . All these feelings are suited, however, to the inferior nature of the demons, which have immortality in common with the upper beings and passions with the lower beings. . . . I have therefore called them 'passive,' because they are subject to the same disorders as we are."[30] In a certain sense a man's spirit, his "genius," and his "good spirit" (like Socrates' *daimonion)* are themselves also *daimons* like the other spirits that inhabit the air. After death they become *Lemurs* or *Lares* (house-gods) or, if they were evil, *larvae* (ordinary ghosts).[31]

Apuleius' great model was Plutarch (born A.D. 50), who worked out this world order: At the top of the cosmic order are the visible gods, the celestial bodies that belong to the element fire; beneath them the demons who belong to the air; still lower the spirits of the dead heroes (in water); and finally human beings, animals, and plants with their earth-nature. Our souls can climb upward or downward, according to merit.[32] The demons are not immortal but can live for thousands of years.[33] When they die there are often storms or epidemics of the plague.[34] Evil demons mostly punish transgressions of taboos with incurable madness.[35]

The distinction made in late antiquity between gods, who are remote from all earthly suffering, and demons, who are subject to all the human passions and feelings, seems to me to be very important. The demons are, so to speak, closer to human beings, more subjective-psychological than the gods. Cicero even describes them as *mentes* or *animi*, that is, as "souls."[36] Others call them *potestates,* "powers."[37] The description of demons as "souls" may be found in many earlier authors but especially in later ones, in the Stoa, Poseidonius, Philo, Plutarch, Clement of Alexandria, and others.[38] From the standpoint of Jungian psychology the distinction in antiquity between gods and demons means the following: The gods represent more the archetypal ground-structure of the psyche, which is far removed from consciousness, while the demons are visualizations of the same archetypes, it is true, but in a form nearer to consciousness, which comes closer to the subjective inner experience of humans. It is as if a partial aspect of the archetype were beginning to move closer to the individual, to cling to him and to become a sort of "grown-on soul."

In Neoplatonism we have the following cosmic world-order:[39] The highest god in wise providence ordered all things. A further providence is attributed to the gods who move through the sky, the celestial bodies; they see to the growth of mortal man for the preservation of the species.[40] A third function of providence is entrusted to the daimons, which are the protectors and guardians of special human concerns. Celsus, who was of an academic-Stoic cast of mind, even attributes to them specific functions: they provide the human species with vitally needed water, wine, bread, and air; they bestow fertility in marriage and each one watches over a specific part of the body, which is why they must be appealed to whenever a certain part of the body is in need of healing.[41] They can grant prophecies to men, but in certain circumstances can also bring about physical evil. Such evil can best be healed through public tribute to such a demon.

The Demons in Christianity

Regarding the question of the affiliation of the archetypes to the subject, there was not much change as Christianity spread; instead a much sharper *moral* line of demarcation was drawn[42] (the third stage!). Only Christ, that is, God himself (and certain angels), is positive; certain nature-spirits are neutral though better avoided; but all other daimons are evil. The pagan gods of the earlier age were regarded simply as evil daimons. Furthermore, the Judaic tradition of Satan and the fallen angels was mixed with the picture projected by the Greeks. According to Justin Martyr, the celestial bodies and God's angels possessed a providence over things beneath heaven.[43] (The angels are identical with the "gods" of Plato.)[44] But the cause of everything evil was the fall of certain angels and their intercourse with human females. They try to usurp divine power and they pander especially to sexual passion.[45] Their sin lies not so much in hostility toward God as in disobedience and in deceiving and deluding *(apoplanan)* humanity.[46]

These views went back to the Book of Enoch (around 100 B.C.), in which the story, as we know, is told of certain angels who fell in love with human women and descended from heaven to be with them. Together they gave birth to a destructive race of giants who laid the whole earth to waste. As Jung explained, if looked at psychologically this signifies a precipitate invasion of human consciousness by contents from the collective unconscious. The giants are images of the resultant inflation that leads to a catastrophe for mankind.[47] The fall of the angels, in Jung's words, "enlarged the significance of man to 'gigantic' proportions, which points to an inflation of the cultural consciousness at that period."[48] It was a question of an all-too-rapid growth of knowledge—exactly as is again the case today. This story from the Book of Enoch is once more especially timely, because it is obvious that today, too, such invasions of collective contents from the unconscious occur frequently. This can be illustrated by the account of a dream of an American, unknown to me, which was sent to me just as I was writing the chapter on demons. It runs as follows:

> I am walking with a woman along the Palisades, where one can have a panoramic view of New York City. A man is leading us. New York is a mass of ruins; we know that the world has been destroyed. Fires are burning everywhere, thousands of people are fleeing in all directions in panic, the Hudson River has flooded large sections of the city. It is twilight; fiery balls in the heaven are spinning towards the earth. It is the end of the world. . . . The cause is a race of giants which has come from extraterrestrial space. In the midst of the ruins I see two of them sitting, casually picking up people and eating them by the handfuls, with a nonchalance as though they were eating grapes at the table. The giants have different sizes and shapes. My guide explains that they come from different planets, where they live together in peace and harmony, and that they landed in flying saucers. The fiery balls mean more such landings. In fact our earth had been set up by giants in the very beginning. The earth is, so to speak, their hothouse and now they are coming back to harvest their fruits; there is a definite reason for this, which I will discover later.
>
> I am rescued because I have high blood pressure. That is why I have been chosen to undergo this test; if I pass it I will become a "saver of souls," like my guide. We walk on and suddenly I see before me an enormously high golden throne, on which the king and queen of the giants are sitting. They are the "intelligences" behind the destruction of the planet. To pass my test I have to climb up a stairway to them. It is a very difficult ascent; I am afraid but I know I have to do it; the world and mankind are at stake. I awake bathed in sweat from this dream.

The giants are here modernized to inhabitants of outer space, but it is easy to recognize the same archetypal background. The king and queen represent the divine pair who celebrate the *hieros gamos,* the uniting of the torn-asunder psychic opposites. The divine marriage is an archetypal image intended to heal a deep psychic dissociation.[49] Whenever man's consciousness had become too far removed from its natural basis, such reconciliation rites were instituted for the purpose of healing, and they generally culminated in the motif of the divine marriage. It is the parallels to the Book of Enoch that are of the most interest to us. We are obviously living in a time resembling that of the beginning of the decline of ancient culture and the origins of Christianity—a time of extreme inner and outer crises, a time that presses toward a deep-reaching change.

But let us turn back to the early Christian peoples' theory about demons. The Church Father Athenagoras, in the manner of Euhemeros, conceives many demons as the postmortal souls of important deceased men, like heroes and kings.[50] (This corresponds to a reactivation of the beliefs of primitive peoples concerning the spirits of the dead, but in rationalistic disguise!) In addition to the demons, Athenagoras recognizes a whole crowd of angels who rule over the stars and over everything in the cosmos.[51] In his view Satan, before the fall, was the angel who ruled over all matter, so that after the fall the material world became part of the realm of evil.[52] Satan descended into hell because he had betrayed his office[53] and because he and his followers had been wanton and presumptuous and had succumbed to lust for mortal women.[54]

It is clear that these early Church Fathers did not really want to think of Satan as a force in opposition to God, as this would have meant falling into a dualistic conception of God. God is and remains the One and the Whole, and the evil angels, that is, the demons, are spirits of transgression, of compulsion (sexuality), and of pride (hubris), which *disturb* the harmony of creation and, according to the teaching of Tatian, separate man from his original fellowship with the divine Spirit. It is the task of mankind to rediscover this fellowship.[55] The forces pulling man downward are on the one hand cosmos and matter and on the other the demons. According to Tatian, spirits are not pure spirit but rather a *pneuma* of a subtly material kind.[56] However, because they are "fleshless" they cannot die easily.[57] In Tatian's view, the capital sin of the angels is not sexual lust but their claim to divinity, that is, their power-drive. They attempt to seduce mankind by means of *phantasmata* (false imaginations and delusions) into worshipping them instead of God.[58] This is why the Pauline injunction to "test the spirits" (1 Corinthians 12:10) is so important. According to Theophilus of Antioch, it is not the power-drive but jealousy and bloodthirstiness that are the chief attributes of the evil spirits.[59] After the fall from paradise these spirits usurped divine names and employed magic signs and images of terror in their efforts to seduce mankind. The heathen gods do the same thing, according to Justin Martyr.[60] This view was a continuation, modified, of a pagan tradition. In their day Plutarch and Xenocrates had interpreted a number of heathen cult practices as serving the evil demons, in order to relieve the highest gods of the burden. Justin Martyr expressly places the guilt for the crucifixion of Christ not on the Jews but on the evil demons.[61] It was precisely for this reason that the cross became *the* power that overcomes demons.[62] If the demons occasionally succeed in achieving miraculous healing, this is merely, according to Tatian, in order to attract public honors;[63] the same holds true for mantic proceedings, when for once they speak the truth.

This demand on the part of the demons for public cultic honors is worth a somewhat closer examination, because until the late seventeenth century it even played a role in exorcism. If we accept the interpretation, widely held today, of the word *religio* as a "conscientious consideration of the numinous," then the demons simply want, basically, to be "religiously" taken into account by human beings. We know from the mythically colored Greek historical writings that plague, harvest failures, defeat in war, and so on are often sent by a god who has been inadvertently overlooked in a cultic ceremony. It was for this reason that Artemis sent a lull in the wind as the Greeks were about to set out for Troy, a lull that could be ended only by the sacrifice of Iphigenia. In this respect the demons behave no differently from the gods themselves. Seen psychologically they represent contents of the unconscious that make an unconditional claim on the attention of people; they act like "organs" of the psyche that do not function if not treated with respect.

The picture of the demons as sketched in by the early Church Fathers shows some very complex features: the demons are now fallen angels, now heathen gods or quasi-material nature spirits. They act from sexual lust, the will to power, passionate jealousy, or bloodthirstiness, or out of the desire to be ceremonially or ritually honored. They delude human beings by means of *phantasmata*—delusory images and notions of all kinds—or, in modern terms, through projections. Only Christ and the cross have more power. They alone can hold the demons in check.

The demons were conceived and experienced, as outlined, throughout the Middle Ages and well into the period of Enlightenment, and this view formed the basis for the practice of exorcism in the Catholic Church. During the period of the Enlightenment, however, all these diabolical or demonic powers were declared out of hand to be mere illusion, to be nonexistent, a view that, broadly speaking, even modern psychiatry has retained. But here we find ourselves in the fourth stage of the withdrawal of projections. Only with modern depth psychology has this judgment begun to be revised. Freud and his school assume, even today, that complexes are purely subjective in character. How far this postulate is carried can be illustrated in the recent book by Cecile Ernst on exorcism of the devil.[64] The author states emphatically that she herself does not "believe" in devils and demons. She stresses especially the strong craving for recognition that psychically ill persons have and interprets their statements as hysterical confabulations they use in order to attract the interest of those around them. The extravagant theatrical display of exorcistic rites has a positive effect only because it panders to this hysterical need of the patient for attention and recognition. To me this interpretation seems to oversimplify the facts of the matter quite considerably. We have seen that demons are often regarded as desiring ceremonial honors. When a person who is psychically ill wishes to attract the interest of other people to himself, this desire, in my opinion, belongs more to the complex and not always so much to the patient's ego.[65] Dr. Ernst holds the patient categorically responsible for his behavior. But in my opinion, the patient's responsibility is only *conditional*. In this connection the explanation given in an old text on exorcism from Stans (1729)[66] seems worthy of note. This text emphasizes that a man can be possessed by "devils" when he has surrendered to sinful feelings such as wrath, envy, hatred, lechery, and faintheartedness.[67] This seems to me to be a closer approximation to the true state of affairs: The ego is responsible only to a certain extent for the effect a person has on his environment—namely, for what Jung called the personal shadow of the individual, but not for archetypal psychic factors. Ignoring one's own shadow, though, is often very much like opening a door through which these powers can break in. The question of moral responsibility is therefore extremely subtle and requires different judgments from case to case.

The Problem of the Relation of the Archetypes to the Subject

If we attempt to shed some psychological light on the above briefly outlined development of theories about demons, we have a complex picture to deal with. On the one hand, demons are unambiguously characterized as archetypal powers; on the other hand, the distinction made in late antiquity between demonic intermediate beings and the higher gods remote from men brought with it something like a shading of the archetypal image. It is at once apparent that the instinctive and emotional component of the archetypes has moved nearer to the human, while the spiritual component—the "gods," which are more like the Platonic ideas—remains projected into a transcosmic "metaphysical" space. The suspicion had arisen that the "demons" somehow had something to do with the psychic states of human beings. Yet the gods, ideas, and mathematical structures were felt to be purely extrahuman; they dwelt in the Beyond in eternal tranquility. This corresponds to the psychological fact that "an archetype in its quiescent, unprojected state has no exactly determinable form but is in itself an indefinite structure which can assume definite forms only in projection."[68] The demons, accordingly, are archetypal formations that appear in the field of human projections.

Even during Christian times the conceptions of the demons did not change substantially; the devils, attracted by depravity, can cause a human being to be possessed. On the other hand, Christ, the counterpower, is something objective-metaphysical, except in the case of certain mystics who had a direct experience of the reality of the "inner Christ." The fact that the demons at least were looked upon as being in part "psychic" meant that the archetypes of the collective unconscious began to push their "tip" upward, so to speak, into the subjectively experienced psyche of the individual human being; underneath this tip, however, they possess a base which lies deep in the collective unconscious and even reaches downward or onward into the realm of transpsychic reality.

In the diagram on page 118, the historical concepts are on the left and their psychological equivalents on the right.

It is only in the field of ego-consciousness that a human being is fully responsible for everything he does. The ego's control begins to weaken in the field of "personal, complex-conditioned inferiorities"; but the Christian ethic demands individual ethical responsibility even in this field. What lies

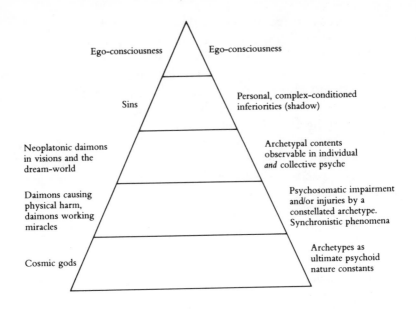

behind and outside this area lies also to a large extent outside conscious control, so that integration—that is, the assimilation of these contents into the conscious personality—is as a rule no longer possible. Jung performed an important service, however, by showing that it is possible to relate to these contents, instead of repressing them, thus neutralizing their negative effects quite considerably. This can be done through the technique of meditation that is called active imagination. In this method the conscious ego permits the unconscious contents to come into the field of consciousness as fantasy-images, as objectively as possible, and then enters into dialogue with them as with an autonomous vis-à-vis.[69] Through this conscious and voluntary attention the demons, if it be a question of demons, receive the respect or "ritual worship" that they demand and that serves to placate them. If the objectives of the ego are at cross-purposes with those of the "daimons," it may be that a compromise which takes the needs of both parties into account can be found.

A classification of the various modern psychotherapeutic methods according to their affinity to exorcism or to the efforts to achieve integration would make an interesting exercise, but it would take us too far afield from the main line of our considerations. Psychopharmacology and behaviorism, at any rate, are purely "exorcistic"; Freudian analysis, as well as group therapy, is closer to the "cathartic" in respect to "honoring" the daimons. As far as I know, the Jungian school is the most unambiguous in its advocacy of integration through insight.

The integration of unconscious contents through active imagination seems to function, however, only when it is a question of the lesser daimons, of the "little devils" that go to make up the personal shadow, but not when it is a question of the *principle* of evil (the *archetype* of evil). Jung makes a special point of this: ". . . it is quite within the bounds of possibility for a man to recognize the relative evil of his nature, but it is a rare and shattering experience for him to gaze into the face of absolute evil."[70] Jung's allusion is to the *archetypal* aspect of evil, the dark side of the God-image or of the Self, whose unfathomable depths exceed by far the evil of the human shadow.[71] *This* inner power, like all the archetypal powers of the unconscious, cannot be integrated by the ego. That is why Jung took issue so sharply in *Aion* with the theological doctrine of the *privatio boni,* the nonsubstantiality of evil. If evil is not part of the image of God, it becomes the burden of the human soul,[72] which means a transgression of human limits.[73] "If," writes Jung, "this paramount power of evil is imputed to the soul, the result can only be a negative inflation—i.e., a daemonic claim to power on the part of the unconscious which makes it all the more formidable."[74] This means a possession by absolute evil, as was foreseen by the Christian world in, for example, the coming of the Antichrist, and as we know it today, day by day, in the incredible cruelty of modern man. Behind this phenomenon stands, in fact, an activation of the dark aspect of the God-image that, in the case of certain weak individuals, can lead to a catastrophic disintegration of the components of the psyche, to panic or some other uncontrollable, hence fateful, emotion. The seat and center of such destructive emotions, existing as a potentiality in every human soul, is the Self, an inner center from which both the greatest creative and the worst destructive effects can issue.[75] The fact that both hell and redemption are aspects of precisely the God-image is, as Jung says, "shattering."[76] "But the same note is struck by Meister Eckhart when he says that, on returning to his true self, he enters an abyss 'deeper than hell itself.' " He brings together into one the innermost thoughts, God and hell. This, comments Jung, "is grounded on the experience that highest and lowest both come from the depths of the soul, and either bring the frail vessel of consciousness to shipwreck or carry it to port, with little or no assistance from us."[77]

According to the Jesuit Picinellus, the destructive aspect of the inner center lies in the tongue (James 3:6: *"Et lingua ignis est, universitas iniquitatis"*). As we have seen, negative projections cause mainly venomous or rancorous speech that strikes others like arrows; the tongue is the instrument for lies and slander—and not alone for such malicious attacks but also for every possible idealistic, intellectualistic nonsense, disseminated as it is by means of slogans like "welfare," "existence," "security," "peace among the peoples of the world," and all the rest. Evil often hides behind idealism—and behind -isms in general, which are as often as not simply labels disguising a very unspiritual doctrinairism.[78] In such cases one "knows" what is right and what is good for other people and, indeed, for mankind. That is the beginning of the end, of the decline. The intellectual schoolmasters of the Kremlin are a classic example of this. The dangers involved in taking this road are very great. It starts with lying, that is, with the projection of the shadow.[79] More human beings are tortured and killed in the name of all these -isms than die as a result of the forces of nature. Behind such -isms are the projections of our own inner unrealized problem of the opposites.[80] Insight into *this* problem, however, seems as yet impossible for many people.

With the help of the materials cited we have seen that demons can, for the most part, be viewed as projections of unconscious autonomous complexes but that definite limits to their integrability are set. Where they appear in archetypal forms it is only their *contents* that can (and must!) be integrated—that is, whatever in the symbolic images can be understood by the experiencing subject—but not the archetypal structure itself. To this structure one can only relate, ever and again, "religiously," by taking it carefully into account as long as one lives and awarding it respectful attention.

6

The Great
Mediating Daimons

Psyche and Eros in Apuleius

Among primitive peoples and also in the cultures of late antiquity, as we have seen, not all demons were regarded as evil;
whether they exerted a good or a malign influence on human
beings depended largely, if not entirely, on the behavior and
attitude of humans themselves. It was only during the first
stirrings of Christianity that the idea, coming by way of the

Orient, that there are purely destructive spirits began to spread (for example in Plutarch). But the majority of *daimons* are simply a part of nature, as good or as evil as human beings themselves. In what follows, therefore, I call the good-evil spirits "daimons" and the purely evil ones "demons."

The sharper ethical distinction that Christianity drew between good spirits and bad spirits indicates psychologically a growing consciousness of what Jung called the shadow: all those animal and otherwise inferior aspects of the conscious personality that tend to condense into an image of an enemy and that are unashamedly projected onto persons in the environment. This personal inimical image can be recognized, however, without too much difficulty, granted a little self-criticism; if one takes the trouble one can catch oneself *in flagranti,* in the very act of doing or saying just that thing one most dislikes in the other person. The shadow consists largely of laziness, greed, envy, jealousy, the desire for prestige, aggressions, and similar "tormenting spirits."

Among the daimons of antiquity, though, Plato also mentioned some that are the "great daimons," like the god Eros and the goddess Psyche. Psychologically interpreted, these "great daimons" are those contents of the unconscious that Jung called the anima and animus and that he described as *the* real projection-creating factors of the psyche.[1] He used the word *anima,* as we know, to indicate the feminine aspect of a man's psyche that is first embodied in the mother-imago and rejuvenated in the image of the beloved or the wife. *She* is *par excellence* the fate-spinning core of the unconscious psyche in a man, which is why in the East she is called Maya—the world-spinner, or the dancer who creates the illusion of the real world. Those projections woven not by the shadow but by *this* factor are much more difficult to recognize; without a close and living relationship with a countersexual partner one almost never picks up the trail. It is actually the power that stands behind all love entanglements and behind most marital conflicts. The anima appears as an irrational sort of temperament, or disposition, of which the man himself is deeply unconscious, or as a stimulus to life that drives him to this woman and not to that one and inclines him to this life-style and not to that one, that disposes his feelings to warmth and *joie de vivre* or to a cold and lackluster outlook, that fills him with enthusiasm or revulsion, seduces him to lust and "sin," and also finally brings him an awakening to himself.

One of the finest descriptions of the way in which a man can be guided through the chaos and entanglements of life produced by his anima, to awaken, finally, to the inner realization of this greatest of "daimons," is given in *The Metamorphoses, or The Golden Ass* of Apuleius of Madura, who wrote in late antiquity and whose theory of demons was referred to above. A philosopher and teacher of rhetoric who grew up in North Africa, Apuleius was an intellectual oriented toward Neoplatonism. As a great admirer of Plutarch, he became interested in occult phenomena. Because he tells his tale in a light and mannered, aestheticizing style, as was the fashion of the time, he has not always been taken seriously. This is, however, an injustice.[2] In my opinion, Karl Kerényi and, especially, Reinhold Merkelbach are correct in taking the hero's conversion at the end of the story as serious and genuine and in pointing out the threads that lead to this ending.[3] In particular they note that the tale of Amor and Psyche, which is inserted into the novel, refers in veiled allegory to the Isis cult in which, at the end of the book, the hero finds his inner goal. So far as I know, however, no one has as yet commented on the fact that *all* the parts of the novel are interconnected in their psychological meaning and that *all the various tales scattered throughout the main narrative are related to the latter in the same way that a person's dreams relate to his waking daily life.*[4] Here we shall consider only the roles played by the "daimons" Psyche and Eros (who are identical with Isis and Osiris).

The hero of the novel, Lucius (from *lux,* "light"), travels on a white horse, the sun god's animal, to Boeotia to study occult phenomena, out of simple curiosity and apparently without the slightest emotional involvement. He soon encounters two men, one of whom tells him a story about a wretched old man called Socrates, who is overpowered by two witches, humiliated, and finally murdered. The name Socrates is not chosen by accident; it is an allusion to the great philosopher who made a goal of complete *apatheia*—absence of all emotion and affect. In the early stages of his legend the talk of the populace had included a wife, Xantippe, who was forever after Socrates, nagging and making scenes. In our version the compensatory fantasy goes a step further. The figures of the dark witches—the mother-*imagines*—kill Socrates; that is, the Platonic philosopher in Lucius-Apuleius is overcome without his quite realizing it, because whenever a man comes close to occult phenomena rationally, these get under his skin and touch his primitive side.

Lucius, strangely bewitched and alienated by the Boeotian atmosphere, now finds lodging with an arch-witch, Pamphile (the All-loving, in the sense of the Great Whore), and at once begins to enjoy the sexual favors of her pretty servant, Photis (the light). This relationship, however, is one of "cold" sexual lust, since Lucius' ulterior motive in pursuing it is to discover Pamphile's secret. Photis unconsciously takes her revenge with all kinds of Freudian slips,[5] which harm Lucius, finally even transforming him into an ass. At this point calamity breaks in. Robbers storm the house, and Lucius, in the form of an ass and loaded with the robbers' booty, must continue on his way in their company. The robbers personify a brutal, vulger shadow side of Lucius that he obviously knows too little about and to which he will now be subjugated for some time to come. Throughout the whole "frame story" the ill-fated ass falls into the hands of criminals, usurers, homosexuals, sodomites, and sadists, and the reader accompanies him into the sordid depths of the ancient shadow-world with all its amoral unconsciousness and its social misery. It is an underworld that also opens up today in the psyche of every man who identifies with only the intellect and its false ideals and who represses his development of feeling. As he himself sees it, it is as if he were being inexplicably pursued by a negative fate, as if he were constantly running into cold and evil women, and as if the world's evil were intent on bringing all his ideals to nothing. In practice one sees this in still another form: namely, that this kind of man is always withdrawing from life into depression, into a superior or "lofty sense of injury"; in him the negative anima becomes a resentment that is inimical to life. The vulgar shadow — the robbers — is then neither lived nor integrated. Such a man seems to run into bad luck all the time. But seen from the point of view of psychic reality, he has fallen under the dominion of the negative mother archetype — in the language of Apuleius, into the power of the dark Isis-Nemesis, of Isis in the form of a punitive, vengeful daimon.

In the midst of these dark turns of fate, while Lucius is still in the company of the robbers, a beautiful young girl, Charite, is also abducted and forced to join their company. To console her the "mother" of the band of robbers, a toothless old woman, tells her the famous fairy tale of Amor and Psyche. This tale comes up like a dream from a deeper archetypal layer of the psyche and is like a brief gleam of light in the dark night of misery and suffering. Lucius misses its meaning but he is fascinated and somehow feels consoled by it. I shall remind the reader briefly of the salient features:

> A king's daughter by the name of Psyche is so beautiful that she excites the envy of the goddess Venus, who sends her son Eros to punish the girl. But Eros falls in love with her. They are married in a strange, otherworldly, enchanted palace, but Psyche is not permitted to see her husband, who visits her only at night. Urged on by her envious sisters and by her own curiosity, she takes a knife and a lamp into her room one night in order to kill the monster she suspects her husband to be. Instead of a monster, however, she gazes upon a most beauti-

ful divine youth. The knife falls from her hand, she trembles with love, and a drop of oil from the lamp falls on Eros and awakens him. He reproaches her for her curiosity and as punishment vanishes into Olympus: as he goes, however, he tells her how she might find him again, after wandering a great distance in search of him and after a trip to Hades. Psyche, after much suffering, does find Eros once more. Because she had yielded to her curiosity, she gives birth not to a divine boy but only to a girl, Voluptas (lust). The story ends with a jolly burlesque marriage celebration on Olympus, in which all the gods and goddesses take part.

While Lucius is swamped in moods of lust, egotism, fear, and stress and by ineradicable cynicism, the unconscious presents, in the form of this story, the secret, underlying meaning of his situation: the fate of his anima who suffers from her proximity to and separation from the god Eros. It is as if the unconscious were saying to him: "Behind your apparently meaningless and unhappy fate a deeper drama is being performed, a divine play of the daimons whose meaning is the redemption of the anima by the spirit of love." The story itself was not invented by Apuleius but belongs to a class of fairy tales that even today one finds all over the world;[6] the names Psyche and Eros (as well as those of most of the other characters), however, were invented by him. He has obviously projected his own conception of the daimons into these fairy-tale figures and has implied, with subtle psychological intuition, that the tale really concerns the fate of his own feeling-side, his daimon-anima, a spirit who mediates the experience of the divine. According to Jung, the anima is *the* projection-creating factor *par excellence:* she weaves the hidden pattern of a man's fate but she also builds a bridge to an experience of God within his own psyche. Reinhold Merkelbach has shown convincingly that the princess Psyche is really an anticipation of the goddess Isis, who appears in the great initiation ceremony at the end of the novel. Yet he is surprised by the duplication of Isis–Psyche and Isis–Charite, for, as he shows, the latter—the listener to whom the fairy tale is told—is also a parallel figure of Isis.[7]

Psychologically, however, this duplication, or in fact triplication, of Isis is easily understandable. In psychological practice we see again and again that the anima appears as a derivative or as a rejuvenated version of the mother-image in a man. She embodies, then, a fragment of inner psychic femininity that has come closer to the human, that is, to the man's ego-consciousness.[8] Charite, a human girl overpowered by the robbers just as Lucius is, would be, accordingly, the most human, as it were, aspect of his anima, the aspect closest to consciousness; Psyche, on the other hand, as a fairy-tale figure and the daughter of a king, is closer to the otherworldly kingdom of the gods. During the Alexandrine period, as the evidence of handicraft objects proves, Psyche was often ritually worshipped together with Eros. She was represented as a girl with butterfly wings, that is, as a spiritual being or as a being not of concrete reality but real enough psychologically.[9] In her journey to Hades she is at times identical with the Kore of the Eleusinian mysteries.[10] She represents an archetypal aspect of the feminine in Apuleius that is remote from consciousness. On the other hand, Isis, who appears at the end of the novel in all her cosmic majesty, personifies the archetypal collective aspect of the anima. There is no longer anything of Apuleius' personal wishes nor of his desire for her. She is the remote, lofty revelation of his deepest, transpersonal fate.

One motif of this journey has puzzled interpreters: Psyche must receive from Persephone a box containing a cosmetic, which she may not open. She again succumbs to curiosity and when she opens the box she is enveloped in a deathly sleep, like a cloud. It seems as if everything is lost, but just then Eros appears and calls her back by giving her a sip of the water of life. She is saved and at the same time she has finally fulfilled her task. Why a cosmetic at such a decisive point, and how is this supposed to work lethally?[11] Seen psychologically, this is connected with a familiar anima problem of men. The anima believes often enough, even today, in the pagan *kalon k'agathon,* in the idea that beauty and goodness go together; such a man cannot be convinced, for instance, that a really beautiful woman could also be stupid or totally unsatisfactory, and he will consequently have some unfortunate experiences with love. In the case of Apuleius himself, however, we see another destructive aspect of this "cosmetic": his literary aestheticizing, his addiction to a mannered, affected way of expressing himself,[12] which obscures the depth of the novel and robs it of its full emotional impact. Literary aestheticism and belletrism ultimately form a kind of block to genuine religious experience, because such experience comes from naïve, primitive ground levels of the psyche. That is why today the rather clumsy folk art of the early Christians moves us more than the affected, moribund ancient art of the Pompeiian wall paintings; it expresses simple, human, religious feeling. It is in the nature of the anima to produce aestheticism and vanity at a certain stage of development, and when these are not outgrown or overcome they stand in the way of the religious-spiritual deepening of inner experience; hence they are represented in our fairy tale as the danger of falling into a lethal sleep.

Although the fairy tale provides a happy ending for Psyche and Eros, when examined a bit more closely this ending is not as positive as one might think. The marriage takes place not on earth but on Olympus, Psyche is carried off to the realm of the gods, and Eros does not come down to earth. This means that both figures vanish into the collective unconscious. The motif of the holy marriage, the union of opposites, sinks once again into the unconscious; consequently both listeners, Lucius and Charite, get into serious trouble immediately afterward. Still another detail points to the fact that something remains unrealized. Instead of a boy, as foreseen by fate, Psyche gives birth to Voluptas, a girl. In all the great myths the "divine son" is the issue of the holy marriage; he is a symbol of new life and of the inner wholeness resulting from the union of opposites. Psyche is indeed rejuvenated in Voluptas but, as the name informs us, the process gets stuck in the realm of the anima, which is to say in the entanglements of desirousness, in the unconscious life-impulses in a man, instead of developing toward a realization of the Self. Still, Voluptas does represent the more *personal* anima of Apuleius; she is closer to consciousness than her mother, Psyche. It is only at the end of the novel, when Lucius-Apuleius, after his Isis ceremony, is initiated into the Osiris mysteries, that he finally attains to the experience of the "divine son," the Self.

The somewhat questionable end of the Amor and Psyche fairy tale anticipates the misfortune that follows shortly afterward. To be sure, Charite is saved from the robbers and finds her betrothed again, but her good fortune does not last long. Thrasyllos, an insolent youth who has fallen in love with her, mischievously murders her husband. She revenges herself on him by blinding him, then takes her own life in order to be united once again with her husband in the Beyond. Her life thus ends in a tragic "death-marriage";[13] seen from the point of view of human fate, the union of Psyche and Eros on Olympus has the same meaning. "Immortal mortal, mortal immortal, death is life for the one, and life is death for the other!"[14]

Lucius, the ass, escapes from the robbers and for a short time, thanks to Charite's solicitude, enjoys a better life. But then he falls once more into the hands of sadistic, evil men and his suffering begins all over again. The positive constellations in the unconscious do not reach the surface of consciousness. Cynicism, egotism, concupiscence are still uppermost in Lucius; but these features of the conscious attitude do again save him from death at the last minute. His soul, though, suffers deeply, without his realizing this consciously.

At the end of his wanderings, after escaping a final humiliation by flight, Lucius sinks down onto a beach, exhausted.

> Not long afterwards I awoke in sudden terror. A dazzling full moon was rising from the sea. It is at this secret hour that the Moon-goddess, sole sovereign of mankind, is possessed of her greatest power and majesty. She is the shining deity by whose divine influence not only all beasts, wild and tame, but all inanimate things as well, are invigorated. . . . Of this I was well aware and therefore resolved to address the visible image of the goddess, imploring her help; for Fortune seemed at last to have made up her mind I had suffered enough and to be offering me a hope of release. . . .
>
> "Blessed Queen of Heaven, whether you are pleased to be known as Ceres, the original harvest mother who . . . gave bread raised from the fertile soil of Eleusis; or whether as celestial Venus, now adored at sea-girt Paphos . . . or whether as Artemis, the physician sister of Phoebus Apollo, reliever of the birth pangs of women, and now adored in the ancient shrine at Ephesus; or whether as dread Proserpine . . . whose triple face is potent against the malice of ghosts, keeping them imprisoned below earth . . . I beseech you, by whatever name, in whatever aspect, with whatever ceremonies you deign to be invoked, have mercy on me in my extreme distress, restore my shattered fortune and . . . return me to my family, give me back to myself."[15]

Having finished his prayer, Lucius falls into a deep sleep. He has scarcely closed his eyes when the goddess appears to him in her most majestic form, in iridescent dress shimmering with color, now red, now yellow, and a mantle of deep black, a wreath, and a mirror-likeness of the moon over her brow. She tells him that she, the mother of creation and mistress of the elements, has been moved by his prayer and has come to him to prophesy that on the following day he will find redemption in the Isis procession by eating roses, the flower of Isis. In return he must commit himself to her forever, both in this life and in the life hereafter, and must serve her eternally.

The fairy tale of Eros and Psyche appeared and then vanished, like a treasure that rises to the surface of a pool and then, if not lifted out, sinks down again. This time, however, its content crosses the threshold. Isis and Osiris, who in the opinion of both Plutarch and Apuleius are the greatest of daimons,[16] represent the same primordial forms as Psyche and Eros.[17] They emerge again in this new form, and this time the genuine religious feeling that had been repressed breaks through in Lucius-Apuleius. His intellectualism falls away, his preoccupation with the trivialities of a purely materialistically oriented life-style ceases, and a deeper meaning is revealed to him in an overwhelming experience of the Egyptian *numina,* the gods of his ancient homeland. We can see that his conversion is real because he preserves the silence commanded in the mysteries; his intellect would for sure gladly have made a spiritual game of them, but now, having turned serious, he is committed and hence can give only a couple of hints about their meaning. Furthermore, the result of the development this time is not the birth of a girl but the encounter with Osiris, the husband and *son* of the goddess Isis, who is identical with Horus, Harpocrates, the divine boy, and who also symbolizes the philosopher's stone, the Self, in the alchemy of that day. The goddess Psyche-Isis is no longer the bearer and the bringer of suffering but has become a bridge to feeling and to a loyalty to the Self.

We are presented, then, in Apuleius' famous novel of late antiquity, with a step in the development of the anima that justified the greatest hopes; but this development was broken off by the spread of the Christian message. The spirit of masculine Logos prevailed one-sidedly against the feminine principle. It is not until the time of the medieval Minnedienst that we again find documents of anima experiences that move us as deeply; it is no accident that motifs of the Isis procession from *The Metamorphoses* appear in the literature of the Grail.

It seems to me, however, that we have only now come to the point where the daimon Psyche with the butterfly wings once again draws near to men and can finally be understood as the principle of a love that has no trace of egoistic motives and whose goal signifies the individuation of the man, with a liberation from all rationalistic one-sidedness.

In his *Amor and Psyche* Erich Neumann interprets the story as the development of a woman rather than as a description of the fate of the anima of Apuleius.[18] This can be justified inasmuch as the anima, as the feminine being in a man, is not of a structurally different nature from the feminine side of a woman; otherwise it would not be possible for men always to project their anima onto women.

The immaturity of the approach to the problem of love in Apuleius' tale of Amor and Psyche is evident in the fact that Eros behaves like a moody youngster; it is only in the nocturnal light-scene that he appears as the great and numinous god he really is. His "boyishness" (it is the equivalent of the immaturity of the Homunculus and of Euphorion in Goethe's *Faust*) indicates that the possibility of a realization of the Self is not yet present. The daimon is not yet integrable; he comes and goes, and the man who encounters him cannot understand the meaning of his appearance. But who, even today, can really grasp the meaning of a deep experience of love? A prayer to Eros from late antiquity comes close, perhaps, to expressing this incomprehensible experience:

> "I call to thee, the source of everything living, whose wings are outspread over the whole world, the unnameable and immeasurable, who breathes life-giving thoughts into every soul, who with his power has welded everything together. First-born, all-creator, golden-winged, dark mysterious one, who conceals discreet and crafty thoughts and inspires dark and ominous passion, thou hidden one who lives in stealth in every soul; thou kindlest the invisible fire in all that is animate by thy touch, tirelessly tormenting, with lust, through anguished rapture, since time began. . . . Thou youngest one,

> lawless, heartless, inexorable, invisible, bodiless, bringer of
> passion, archer, torch-bearer, thou master of every movement
> of the spirit, of all things hidden, giver of forgetfulness, father
> of silence, through whom and to whom the light shines forth,
> tender infant when you are born in the heart, ancient of days
> when you are quite completed. I call to thee, the inexorable,
> using thy great name. Thou hast been the first to appear, noc-
> turnal visitor, joyful by night, maker of night, thou who hears
> and answers . . . thou in the depths . . . thou hidden in the sea,
> thou eldest![19]

Seen from the point of view of woman's psychology, Eros
in Apuleius' fairy tale is also a pre-form of the god Osiris; in
woman he is the "spirit who shows the way," in the original
meaning of the word *(psychopompos),* that is, her positive
animus. One can study his destructive aspect in the very impressive medieval reports of possession by the devil, but here
he is the positive animus–daimon in the role of mediator to
the Self, which for a woman could be seen in the goddess Isis;
Isis was also officially invoked as "Isis of women" in Egyptian religious texts.

The Masculine Companion
in Woman's Psyche

Just as the anima derives from a man's mother-imago, so
the animus is a rejuvenated form of the father-image.[20] As
"father" he represents a traditional spirit which expresses itself in "sacred convictions" that the woman herself has never
really thought through. The animus as divine *puer aeternus,*
on the other hand, appears as a creative spirit who can inspire
a woman to undertake her own spiritual achievements. This
spirit is a spirit of love, that is, of her own living inner mystery, which comes into realization in the Eros between man
and woman. In the tale by Apuleius, therefore, Psyche can be
understood, as Neumann understands her, as a model of the

woman who frees herself from a hollow, exclusively female matriarchal way of life and attains a higher, individual femininity through much suffering and an experience of the masculine world. That Psyche in the story ends up on Olympus means that even here this way of individuation for a woman has not yet been reached in human reality. It appears to be in the nature of the animus to lure the woman away from reality now and again. Whereas the anima usually appears in the form of a fascination, an allurement that draws the man into life, the animus often appears as a spirit of death;[21] indeed there are even fairy tales in which a woman marries a handsome, unknown stranger who is revealed later on as death personified, a revelation that brings about the death of the woman herself. This is tied to the fact that, as a projection-making factor, a man's anima produces mainly passive, that is, empathetic, projections that bind the man to objects; the animus, on the other hand, produces more active, that is, more *judgmental,* projections that tend to cut the woman off from the world of objects. In both cases anima and animus effect an alienation from reality, because the empathetic projections of the anima are of an illusory nature and the judgments of the animus are very often simply beside the point.

We possess no document from late antiquity, so far as I know, that depicts the masculine daimon of woman in the context of a biography, but we do have one from the contemporary Christian sphere, namely, the tragic story of the martyr Perpetua of Carthage.[22] Perpetua was a proper twenty-two-year-old Roman woman who was condemned to death. While in prison awaiting execution she had various dream-visions in which she encountered figures of her personal animus in the forms of her fellow-martyr Saturus and the deacon Pomponius (these correspond to the figure of Charite in Apuleius' *Metamorphoses*) and in which, in particular, a white-clad divine shepherd and (in a later vision) a helpful fencing-master appeared. The former, in the first vision, gave her cheese as the "food of immortality," and the latter, in the last vision, a green bough with golden apples. Fortified by these dream daimons, Perpetua went without fear to her death. To her the two dream figures were appearances of Christ in disguised form, but the dream-visions themselves do not say that. These daimons, or better, this daimon (for the two are identical) is, rather, an archetypal figure that was constellated at that time in the collective unconscious of the whole world, including the non-Christian, a spirit of religious renewal whose special mark of distinction was *to appear directly to the single individual as a spirit who showed the way.* We shall meet him again as an inner figure in men;[23] in the *Passio Perpetuae,* however, he is to be understood unequivocally as an animus-figure—as a mediating spirit.

Just as in the case of Apuleius the mother-anima figure appears differentiated into a form close to the human (Charite) and two divine forms (Psyche and Isis), so Perpetua too is guided in her visions on the one hand by animus figures that are symbolized by men from her environment and on the other by the divine shepherd and fencing-master, who are wholly transpersonal. In the first vision a fellow-martyr, Saturus, takes her hand and guides her to the heavenly ladder that leads to the cosmic shepherd. Saturus in reality sought martyrdom intentionally and associated voluntarily with prisoners; in Perpetua he represents her personal animus, her courageous "absolute" conviction to which she committed herself. In the last vision a deacon, Pomponius, leads her to the amphitheater where she meets the fencing-master. Pomponius was the helper who in reality visited the prisoners and brought them spiritual comfort. Whereas Saturus embodies the qualities of courage and conviction, Pomponius is closer to the figure of a spiritual teacher; he personifies the gradually deepening Christian insights in Perpetua. She was only twenty-two years old and had received instruction for only a short time;[24] she was in every respect still a novice in the spiritual world of Christianity.[25] Corresponding to the goddess Isis in Apuleius, the sublime, wholly archetypal power appears here as the cosmic shepherd and the giant fencing-master, both of whom offer Perpetua symbols of eternal life. The "Shepherd of Men" (Poimandres), as he is called in a writing of about the same period, means a "Spirit of Truth" that "accompanies human beings wherever they are." In a gnostic Naassene writing, the god Attis is extolled as cosmic god-man and "shepherd of the shining stars," an epithet also applied to the Egyptian god Anubis and to the god Horus; the latter, for example, is called "the good shepherd who rules over the four races of men."[26]

Philo of Alexandria interprets the figure of the shepherd as follows:

> To be a shepherd is something so supremely good that it rightly applied not only to kings and to wise men and to souls purified by consecration but also to God Himself, Ruler of the Universe. Like a shepherd in a meadow or a pasture, God, the Shepherd and King, governs justly and by His law the earth and water, air and fire, and the plants and living beings in them, mortal and divine, and also the nature of heaven and the course of the sun and the moon and the paths of the other heavenly bodies and their harmonious rounds by delivering up to them for their guidance His true Logos, His first-born son, who will take over the cares of this sacred flock as a ruler sent by the Great King.[27]

Thus in this text the shepherd symbolizes the world-ordering understanding of God and of the Logos as "a *pneuma* that reaches from heaven to earth." In Christianity all the functions of this widespread shepherd symbol were assigned to Christ, as shown in Psalm 23:1: "The Lord is my shepherd, I shall not want." Early Christian art often therefore depicted Christ in the tradition of Hermes, with the lamb on his shoulder, the celestial bodies at his feet. As ruler of the cosmos he is everywhere, and at the same time he appears to the individual as personal guardian spirit, just as the shepherd/ fencing-master in Perpetua's visions concerns himself with her. In the final vision, when in the amphitheater Perpetua must fight a giant Egyptian—the spirit of heathendom—she is first disrobed by beautiful youths and rubbed with oil. In the process *she is transformed into a man* and as such, as a *miles Christi,* she then conquers the enemy. Clement of Alexandria quotes a contempory writing[28] which says that after death the male unites immediately with the world-spirit (Logos) in the Beyond, whereas the female enters the pleroma only after a process of masculinization.[29] The profoundly tragic fate of the Christian woman is here revealed: because the Christian god-image is exclusively masculine she can become one with God only through alienation from her own feminine nature.

This, however, is nothing other than a spiritual possession, a denial of her feminine consciousness and her physical reality. Thus even Augustine writes (*De anima,* IV, 18, 26): "In a dream I saw Perpetua, transformed into a man, wrestle with an Egyptian. Who can doubt that this masculine figure was her soul, not her actual body, which had remained completely feminine and which lay there, unconscious, while her soul was wrestling in the form of a masculine body?"

Perpetua changes her sex in an ecstatic state; her transformation is like that of the priests of the great Syrian mother-goddess Cybele, who in a state of ecstasy were transformed into females. In his novel, Apuleius depicts such a scene of ecstatic effeminization, which he calls a morbid frenzy, "exactly as if the men had been made weak and sick through the presence of the gods, and not much better than they were before."[30] Apuleius indeed condemned this kind of cult, but we know that the shaving of the head, the clothing, and the whole life of the "Galloi" (eunuchs), who castrated themselves, were meant as a kind of ecstatic dedication and sacrifice to the goddess. If we disregard Apuleius' moral evaluation, this is an exact parallel to Perpetua's masculinization: total religious possession.

It is understandable that the patriarchal one-sidedness of the early Christian god-image later called forth compensations that issued not least from women's psychic need: the proclamation in Ephesus of the Virgin Mary as *Theotokos* (god-bearer) and the development of a doctrine of Christ's androgyny may well be understood in this sense.[31]

In its practical effects Perpetua's masculinization symbolizes an ecstatic state of rapture; she is transported into the realm of the spiritual, just as Apuleius-Lucius dropped down into his hitherto split-off feeling-side in his encounter with Isis. Lucius, however, will be summoned after a while to a further, still deeper experience, to an encounter with the Self, which takes him through the encounter with the anima and beyond. Perpetua, on the other hand, perishes; a feminine divinity would have had to come to her aid had she been destined by fate to a longer life.

If we compare the two great daimons, Anima and Animus, as they are depicted in our two examples, it becomes clear that, for Apuleius, Isis would be the anima, whereas she would represent the Self for a woman, just as the cosmic shepherd appears as animus in Perpetua's visions but as the personification of the Self in texts that recount the inner experiences of men. The fully archetypal aspect of these two figures is therefore fundamentally beyond all differences of sex. They are inner images that are of concern to both men and women, if in rather different ways. They are thus symbols of far-reaching collective significance—scarcely daimons but almost gods, to speak the language of Apulieus.

We see here, too, as in the case of evil daimons, that the archetypal structure of these figures enters the realm of the personal only with its tip and that large areas of it are transpersonal. It is precisely these unintegrable parts that, as Jung has shown, are *the* projection-producing factors, that is, *the* secret wire-pullers of our destiny that are so uncannily difficult for us to track down. In "Psychology of the Transference" Jung tried to show what happens in the case of a strong love attraction between a man and a woman. It is a question of the six-fold relationship of *four* figures, namely, of the man and his anima and of the woman and her animus.

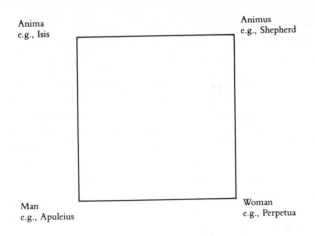

Anima and animus, as we have come to know them in the form of Isis and the shepherd (Hermes-Psychopompos) in the two examples discussed above, appear in the alchemistic tradition as king and queen. Jung used them as examples to illustrate his exposition.

These figures, king and queen or god and goddess, are the partners in the "sacred wedding," the union of the world-opposites that was the goal of the alchemists. In apparently "harmless" form this archetype of the *hieros gamos* (sacred wedding) stands behind the most frequent fairy-tale ending in which hero and heroine come together at last.

Love is such a fateful factor in the life of every human being because, more than anything else, it has the power to release the living from their ego-bound consciousness; it brings us a hint of a transcendental happening, making it possible for us to attend a divine play of the union of Shiva and Shakti, god and goddess, beyond the banality of this earthly life. It is a mystery which no human being has so far penetrated but which is at the same time the goal of life, born anew in each of us. All that we can say is that it is part of a process of reciprocal individuation, of becoming conscious and whole in the encounter. At the end of life this symbol occurs as a "marriage in death"; many dreams of older people who are not far from the end of life point to this. Something eternal, something with greater meaning, begins to shine through the dark veil of earthly existence. Thus a deaconess in her eighties dreamed that she received a bridal gown and wondered what use she might make of it. A year later she heard a voice in a dream telling her to prepare for the marriage. Such dreams are evidently a preparation for the experience of death. A doctor who was only fifty-four years old and did not suspect that the angel of death was drawing near had the following dream: He went to a burial, as he was often obliged to do professionally. The man being buried was unknown to him and he therefore felt indifferent toward him. The funeral cortege stopped in a square in the center of the city; men carried the coffin to the meadow in the center of the square and placed it on a prepared pile of wood. The pyre was lighted and flames began to lick the coffin. Then the lid of the coffin sprang open and a marvelously beautiful naked woman jumped out and ran to the dreamer with arms outspread— and he awoke with an indescribably blissful feeling of love. Two years later the dreamer died unexpectedly of heart failure. The man who was buried in the dream represents his bodily ego, which had become alien and indifferent to him; in death, however, his soul (anima) awakes and unites with his immortal part in the "sacred marriage."

When a man does not awaken to some awareness of the eternal element that is central to love, he may readily make a personal tragedy of it; in that case "a spark of the eternal fire hisses out in a puddle";[32] the "divine child" of the two transcendental factors, the symbol of completed individuation, cannot be born either.

If we compare the projections that issue from the shadow complex with those proceeding from the anima-animus complex, we may say that insight into one's own shadow projections means first of all a moral humiliation, intensive suffering. Insight into projections originating in the anima or the animus, on the other hand, demands not so much humility as level-headedness and commonsense self-observation and re-flection, which demand a certain wisdom and humaneness, because these figures always want to seduce us away from reality into rapture or pull us down into an inner world of fantasy. Whoever cannot surrender to this experience has never lived; whoever founders in it has understood nothing.

7

The Inner Companion

The Guardian Spirit

In the final initiation of Apuleius into the Egyptian mysteries he is called to the worship of Osiris, the son–husband of Isis. For the man of that day Osiris represented the immortal inner personality into which a man is transformed after death. In the alchemistic tradition, therefore, Osiris was the equivalent of the "stone," that is, the resurrected body. In Egypt the immortal nucleus of the soul was also called the Ba-soul. In his essay "The Dialogue of a World-Weary Man with His Ba," Helmuth Jacobsohn has shown that the Ba represented, on the one hand, something like the unconscious personality of a man and, on the other, what Jung has described as the Self, whereas the Ka embodied something resembling a man's vitality and those elements of his personality and constitution that are inherited.[1] The Ba was depicted as a *star* or as a bird with a human head. (We know that in the beliefs of many peoples human beings are supposed to have a number of different souls; the ancient Greeks also believed that people possess several souls—*psychai*.)

According to Plutarch, Isis and Osiris are very great "daimons" but they are not gods. Therefore they represent something which is transsubjective but which is closer to the human than are the gods, something which can be experienced inwardly in certain states of very strong emotion. Through initiation into the mysteries, a human being could become a special servitor of these daimons, could even be completely dissolved in them after death without losing his individuality; that is why in Egyptian coffin-texts the dead are evoked as "Osiris N.N." Apuleius does not tell us what happened to him during his encounter with Osiris, maintaining the silence imposed by the mysteries. We can only assume that in this experience he found an indestructible psychic ground for going ahead with his life.

We should be skeptical about attempts to relate some of these "souls" or "daimons" to the Jungian concepts of shadow, anima, animus, and Self. It would be a great mistake, as Jung himself often emphasized, to suppose that the shadow, the anima (or animus), and the Self appear separately in a person's unconscious, neatly timed and in definable order. In the reality of everyday practice it is much more likely that a person in depth psychological analysis will first meet with something psychically "absolutely other" in himself, a dark, chaotic something, appearing to him in complicated dream images in which, little by little, he begins to discover his alter ego. Some orientation begins to emerge from this chaos as certain inferior traits in this "other" begin to separate out, traits that are relatively easy to recognize as belonging to the particular person. As this process continues, the contrasexual aspects in this *massa confusa* gradually begin to be distinguishable. It is only after these, too, have drawn nearer to consciousness that it later becomes evident that a part of the great power and the divinity of these figures does not come from the person himself but originates in a still deeper and more embracing psychic center, the Self. In the series of dreams of a modern physicist, which Jung published in *Psychology and Alchemy,* there appears the image of a sublime and majestic woman whose head radiates light as the sun does. In this image the anima and the Self (sun) are still entirely one; this is rather like the appearance of Isis toward the end of *The Metamorphoses* of Apuleius. It becomes apparent only later that the anima may be distinguished from a power emanating from a still deeper level.

If we look for personifications of the Self among the daimons of antiquity, we see that certain daimons are more like a mixture of shadow and Self, or of animus–anima and Self, and that is, in fact, what they are. In other words, they represent the still undifferentiated "other," unconscious personality of the individual.

This is the case not only with the Egyptian Ba-Osiris but also with the ancient Roman idea of the *genius.* The *genii* of the ancient Romans were originally household gods of a kind. Their name is etymologically related to *gignere*—to "beget" or "engender"—so that the genius represented first of all the reproductive power of the father of a family and of the son and heir, much like the Egyptian Ka-soul of the Pharaoh. The marriage bed was called *genialis lectus;* this referred not only to sexual potency but also to the qualities that today we would call psychic vitality, temperament, resourcefulness, and a lively imagination. The genius rejoiced when those who honored him ate and drank well and when their sexual experience was good *(indulgere genio),* but homosexuality and sexual perversions put him out of humor. Miserly and dry people allow their genius to waste away. That the genius represented much more than the merely sexual is shown by the fact that for the Romans even places in a landscape or fields or groves could possess their genius, the *genius loci,* which assured the continuity of their existence. Used in this way the word *genius* referred more to the psychic atmosphere or to the mood that such a place can evoke. Here we have once again that original situation in which the objective psyche appears to live altogether in outer things, that is, is experienced by human beings only in complete projection.

For the Romans the house especially possessed several genii: Vesta guarded the hearth, the Penates protected provisions, the *Lar* guaranteed safety and good fortune, and, by no means the least important, the deceased members of the family lived on in the house with the living as anonymous *Dii Manes.*[2] The statuette of the genius of the father of the family usually stood by the hearth in the kitchen. It was the figure of a youth bearing a horn of plenty in which there were often phalli, or the genius was itself a phallus or a snake. (The *genius loci* was always represented as a snake.) It was not only the father of the house, however, who had his genius; the mistress also had such a guardian spirit, a feminine figure called "Juno," who embodied the power of giving birth and the maternal-feminine factors in woman.

Originally "genius" and "Juno" were quite impersonal "atmospheric" house gods, but by the third century before Christ they had become much more individualized. Not only the head of a family but every man had his own genius, every woman her Juno, and each person offered certain sacrifices to his genius at a small celebration on his birthday. It was thought that the genius was born with the particular person and was the arbiter of that individual's fortunes. Horace describes him: "Companion who rules the star of birth, god of human nature, mortal in each man, of changing countenance, white and black."[3] Later the genius was thought to be immortal. At the same time that the genius became more individualized, his image—probably as a result of the growing familiarity with the Greek spirit—was extended in the third century B.C.[4] The *genius loci* became the genius of the city, of schools, of the Senate. The genius of Jupiter, visualized as a phallus, protected the storehouses. The genius of a god, so employed, embodied at the same time his moral and psychic essence.[5]

The Italic ideas about the genius were altered in still another way through the encounter with the Greek spirit. They merged with the philosophic concepts of the Greek thinkers that centered on an immortal spiritual psychic nucleus. In the *Timaeus* (90B–90C), Plato sets forth his theory that every human being has a divine daimon that is the noblest component of his psyche. Whoever seeks wisdom and seriously concerns himself with divine and eternal things nourishes his daimon, whereas worldly trivialities abase and mortify him. A more intensive interest was thereby awakened in the Platonic school in those mysterious "voices" that, as we know, Socrates was in the habit of admonishing. This Socratic daimon[6] was regarded as an example of that divine daimon of which Plato writes. The extent to which this daimon or these daimons were thought of as endopsychic varies.

Some of the Stoics taught the existence of such a daimon in double form: one is a divine component of the psyche *(Nous),* but the other is a spark of the fiery world-soul that has migrated into human beings; this latter daimon—or this part of the daimon—guides a man from without through his whole life.[7] In the opinion of Plutarch (died A.D. 125), only a pure man can hear the voice of this daimon, a completely bodiless being[8] who is the mediator of supernatural, "parapsychological" knowledge[9] to the human being he watches over. The Neoplatonists thought of this genius-daimon as immortal, as one who becomes an actual divinity after his mortal sojourn. Whereas the Italic genius originally died with his bearer,[10] in the later view he lives on after death as a *Lar* (benign spirit).

As a result of the Stoa's spiritual-ascetic orientation in late antiquity, and of Neoplatonism, the Italic genius lost his earlier component of physical vitality, the pleasure principle, which originally had been innate to him. In *De genio Socratis,* a work by Apuleius, there is mention of two genii who live in human beings; one is the immortal ethical guardian and inner friend of a specific person, and the other (who lives in the *genua,* "knees") embodies sensual desire and covetousness and is evaluated negatively.[11]

The idea of the genius also merged quite early with the astrological idea of a personal *fate* shaped by the date of birth (hence Horace: " . . . who rules over the birth-star"), because sacrifices had always been made to the genius on one's birthday. In his *Saturnalia,* Macrobius describes this in detail.[12] In his view every human being is a combination of *four* daimons: of Eros, as we have become acquainted with him; of a particular destiny (a fate ordained by God); of a daimon whose nature is stamped by the position of the sun in his horoscope; and finally by a *Tyche* (fortune) that is dependent on the position of the moon. The daimon knows the future and is at all times in touch with the world-spirit, with the Logos or spermatic pneuma of the universe. *In him masculine and feminine are merged,*[13] so that he is thus an androgynous symbol of wholeness, no longer merely genius or Juno but an archetypal image that, like the *lapis* in alchemy, unites the opposites of masculine and feminine in *one* figure.

Apuleius describes Socrates' genius (*daimonion*) as follows: He is "a private patron and individual guide, an observer of what takes place in the inner person, guardian of one's welfare, he who knows one most intimately, one's most alert and constant observer, individual judge, irrefutable and inescapable witness, who frowns on evil and exalts what is good." If one "watches him in the right way, seeks ardently to know him, honors him religiously," then he shows himself to be "the one who can see to the bottom of uncertain situations and can give warning in desperate situations, can protect us in dangerous situations, and can come to our rescue when we are in need." He can intervene "now through a dream and now through a sign [synchronistic event], or he can even step in by appearing personally in order to fend off evil, to reinforce the good, to lift up the soul in defeat, to steady our inconstancy, to lighten our darkness, to direct what is favorable toward us and to compensate what is evil."[14] It is well known that in late antiquity a primitive element of religious experience in the philosophic-religious theories was much stronger than in the classic period, perhaps through contact with the more primitive outlying border areas of the Greco-Roman culture. I know of scarcely any account from antiquity that gives a better description of the experiences of the Self than this short summary by Apuleius.[15]

As in the case of the other daimons, this daimon, which embodies the individual's larger, more comprehensive personality, was in late antiquity also like a mountain the bulk of which lay in the transpersonal realm of the psyche, extending only a small tip into the human being's personal sphere. With the Christianization of the ancient cultural world, however, it was for the most part the transpersonal aspects that were retained,[16] his aspect as the messenger of the gods being assimilated to the idea of the angels; and the other aspects, that is, the parapsychological knowledge, the vitality, and lustfulness of the genius, were attributed to the devil and his tribe.[17] But a faint intimation of the individuality of this figure lived on in the idea that the individual may have a particular guardian angel or patron saint. The reason for this apparently regressive development lay in the fact that the figure of Christ had attracted to himself all the positive qualities of the genius figure. *He* was exalted to *one* symbol of the Self, in a form, however, in which the collective elements far outweighed the individual elements. Gradually, as the institutionalized ritual and the confession of faith increased in importance, less and less weight was given to the Pauline inner experience of the Christ and to the visions of the early Christian martyrs. Among those within the Church, only the mystics remained loyal to that line of tradition which put the central value on the inner *experience* of Christ.

The Inner Companion
in Hermetic Philosophy and in Alchemy

An attitude of mind lived on in the Hermetic philosophy of late antiquity and *in alchemy* which, in contrast to Christianity, sought an unprogrammed experience of the "inner companion" or of the daimon who showed the way. This daimon was usually honored in these traditions as Hermes-Psychopompos, as Poimandres (Shepherd of Men), and as *Agathos Daimon* (Good Spirit). Richard Reitzenstein has explicitly drawn attention to the existence of an actual Hermes religion in late antiquity, but so far his work has not been adequately recognized.[18] In my opinion this religion had a significance that should not be underestimated. In those circles a truly religious attention was paid to the "inner companion," an attention that in the language of today's psychology we would describe as relatedness to the inner "guru," or, in Jungian language, to the Self.

In an astrological document of the third century B.C., in which the priest Petosiris counsels King Nechopso, Hermes already appears as the teacher of all secret wisdom, which, however, can be experienced only in a state of ecstasy. This wisdom appears to the prophet as a "voice" wrapped in a dark garment. As the follower prays, this voice points out to him the paths of the celestial bodies in the universe and reveals to him the wisdom of the cosmos.[19] The same figure appears as Poimandres (Shepherd of Men) in the tractate of the

Corpus Hermeticum and is there described as *Nous tes authentias,* the "Spirit of Truth."[20] The alchemist Zosimos (third century A.D.) belonged to a community that worshipped this figure. The latter revealed himself to Zosimos as "spirit" *(pneuma)* and as "Lord of the Spirits" and instructed him in the transformations in the alchemistic *opus* by acting as his guide in a journey to the underworld of the kind with which we are familiar in Egyptian literature. In the *Poimandres* this spirit, who appears in the form of a human being of cosmic size, says to the praying man: " 'What will you hear and see and learn through reflection and experience?' I answer: 'Who are you?' 'I am the Poimandres, the Spirit of Truth (or of the Absolute). I know what is in your thoughts *and am with you everywhere.*' Then he changed his form and at once everything was opened up to me as in *one* blow, and I saw an unending vision—and a friendly, *joyous,* light illuminating everything . . . and I burned with love for him."[21]

This figure, according to another tractate of the *Corpus Hermeticum,*[22] had sent a mixing-bowl full of *Nous* (knowledge of God) down to men and had commanded that their hearts be baptized in it in order to come to God knowing wherefore it (the heart) had been born. But God can also appear to men in other forms: He, who imagines *(phantasion)* the whole world, "appears in all things and He appears especially to those to whom He wills to appear."[23] He delivers them in this way from *agnosia*—from unconsciousness.[24] The Nous in man, on the other hand, unites man and God; he is the "good spirit" *(agathodaimon)* in human beings.[25] "He will come to you everywhere on your way through life and will reveal himself everywhere, where and when you least expect him, waking, sleeping, at sea, in the street, at night, by day, when you speak or when you are silent, since there is nothing which he is not."[26] Nock refers to the similarity of this saying to that of the apocryphal Logion of Jesus: "Where one is alone, I say: I am with him. Lift a stone and you will find me there, split a log and I shall be there!"[27]

In the thirteenth tractate of the *Corpus Hermeticum,* Hermes gives to the pupil an account of his own awakening to a higher consciousness in the following words:[28] "After looking within and seeing a formless vision that came to me out of God's mercy, I was lifted out of myself and entered an immortal body, so that I am no longer he who I was but am reborn in the Nous. This experience cannot be taught. . . . Thus came the knowledge [Gnosis] of God to me and through this act of creation I have become divine."[29]

In a text that was also known to Zosimos it is said of this same Hermes-Thoth that he, the son of God, in order to save pious souls "became all things, god, angel, a human being capable of suffering. Because he is omnipotent and can become whatever he wills, he follows the will of his father (God) by permeating all bodies and illuminating the spirit of all humanity . . . and guiding it upward towards the light."[30]

One also comes across this god-daimon in similar form in the magic papyri of the period, except that in the papyri man makes the attempt, in accordance with the premises of magic, to master this god and manipulate him. Aside from this important difference we find the same archetypal-symbolic figure. There is a prayer to this power: "From out the four winds close to me, thou almighty who breathed into men the breath of life, bearer of the secret name and the unnamable . . . whose tireless eyes are the sun and the moon . . . whose head is the heaven, whose body the ether, whose feet the earth, thou art the ocean *(agathos daimon)* that gives birth to the good and nourishes the (inhabited) earth. . . . Thou, possessor of unerring truth, . . . enter into my heart and my thoughts for all the rest of my life and fulfill for me every wish of my soul. *For thou art I and I am thou.* . . . For I carry thy name in my heart as my sole protection (talisman)."[31]

Another prayer to Hermes runs as follows: "Hermes, ruler of worlds, cycle of the moon, round and square, who first taught the tongue to speak, goad to righteousness, wearer of the chlamys and the winged sandals, thou, whose way leads through the ether to the depths of the earth, the spirit's guide . . . who with light brings joy to those who inhabit the depths of the earth[32] and to the mortals who have come to the end of their life span. Foreseer of fate art thou called and the 'divine dream' that sends oracles by day and by night. Thou healest all mortal pains. . . . Come to me, bringer of bliss, Mneme,[33] who brings plans to fruition, greatest son."[34] Or: "Hear my greetings, dwelling-place of the spirit of air. O spirit who reaches from heaven down to earth, hear my greetings, who fills me and seizes me and departs from me in peace according to God's will."[35]

In all these texts the concern is with the one cosmic god (Hermes-Thoth) who can also become the personal "inhabiting" daimon of a man, an inner partner who appears now over and now under the man (that is, is dependent on him). He has the functions of an individual guardian-spirit and teacher that the Greeks and Romans attributed to Socrates' daimon and later in general to the genius of human beings; he is at the same time also a cosmic god of the universe who preserves and fulfills all of nature.[36] Thus an extreme paradox is contained in the symbol of the Self: it is at once that which is the most intimate, the most individual, and at the same time a mirror of total reality as well as a god-image, *the* Anthropos who embraces all human beings. Although this god can dwell in a human being, there is nevertheless a slight but perceptible difference in relation to the earlier examples: he comes and goes but he never really becomes human in the individual; he does not quite become a *subjective* mood or state of mind but, on the contrary, pulls the human being in his ecstasy right out of his ego-existence and into another divine and blissful state.

It is to be regretted that no documents from the literature of late antiquity and the early Christian period have, as far as I know, come down to us that reveal a similar or parallel development of the "Juno" in women. Apart from the *Interrogationes maiores Mariae,* in which Christ reveals his inner femininity to Mary,[37] I know of only one other report, that of the Montanist prophetess Prisca, according to which Christ appeared to her as a woman.[38] Apart from these we have no reports comparable to those by men in which this inner figure in women appears as a real psychological factor in an individual.

In the experience of modern women, this content appears most frequently as a kind of chthonic mother, the earth-mother goddess.[39] Perhaps the likeliest place to look for this missing figure might be in certain ancient prayers to the figure of the mother-virgin that was associated with Hermes and was even in part identified with him. In the magic papyri there has come down to us a prayer to her as moon-goddess, a prayer praising this great syncretistic goddess figure in, among others, the following words:

> Hail, mistress of Tartaus, which thou conquerest with light, hail, sacred brightness of light, coming out of the darkness where you confuse everything with ill-considered counsel . . . thou bitch in virgin's form! . . . Awake, thou needy Mene of the nourishing sun, warder of the subterranean ones . . . welcoming, shining one . . . rich in skills and high and swift . . . manly, courageous, healing one, providing and caring, blood-colored, ominous, Brimo.[40] Immortal answerer of prayers . . . belonging to the herd . . . time-honored radiant one, goddess of the sea, ghostly beauty . . . she-wolf . . . corrupter . . . savior with radiant embrace, fate-spinning, all-giver . . . pure, mild, undying . . . flowering one, all-holy . . . suffering one, crafty one, wanton one . . . thou who rescues us from terror—cast but a glance at yourself: just look, thou art as the beautiful Isis in the mirror, behold thyself, admire . . . I know thy great and beautiful and exalted names, Kore, through whom the heavens light up and the earth drinks and becomes pregnant, through whom the universe waxes and wanes, O mistress![41]

In another prayer the one who prays names the same figure: "Triple-headed nocturnal one, eater of excrement

. . . virgin with the gorgon's glance."[42] It is this goddess, "Isis, who is all things,"[43] the companion of Hermes, the universal god. In love-magic she is identified as Aphrodite and evoked as follows: "Foam-born Cythera, mother of the gods and of men, aerial and chthonic, all-mother Nature,[44] unvanquished, holding all things together, who drives the Great Fire in its course. . . . Thou sendest holy longing into the souls of men and women toward the men; and this makes the woman to yearn for the man all her days."[45] Another love-magic goes as follows: "Come, Hecate, thou giantess . . . Baubo, sender of arrows, unvanquished . . . of noble birth, torchbearer . . . exalted one . . . leader of the mob . . . goddess of the way . . . light-bringer, sublime virgin . . . underworldling full of cunning . . . fire-pacer, cow-eyed one, all-devourer . . . and breaker of barriers."[46]

The many names and symbols in praise of the great goddess are enumerated in the prayers in order to ward her off through the power of the word. However, they also show the profound emotion with which men and women of that day approached the mystery of the goddess Nature. A prayer to the moon-goddess piles up further significant images in a hesitant and stammering interpretation of her mystery: "Draw near to me, beloved Mistress, three-faced Selene[47] . . . Queen who brings light to us mortals . . . thou who calls out by night, bull-face, lover of solitude . . . goddess of the crossways . . . be merciful to me who calls upon you, listen kindly to my prayer, thou who rules by night over the all-embracing world, before whom the demons quake with fear . . . high-born . . . crowned one, all-mother Nature who bringest forth gods and men . . . beginning and end art thou, thou rulest over everything that is, for everything is from you, and in you, eternal one, everything has its end."[48]

In comparison with the figure of the cosmic Hermes, it is striking that in the case of the goddess many more dark, even quite sinister, unfathomable aspects are emphasized along with the light aspects. To aspire to perfection is, as Jung has pointed out, more characteristic of the masculine Logos principle, while the feminine ideal is more that of *completeness* in which everything is simply held together in one unified whole.[49] Consequently, this feminine goddess all-Nature also possesses cunning, cruelty, wickedness, unfathomable depths of passion and the uncanny gloom of death, the smell of corpses and putrefaction in equal measure with the potentiality of new life and rebirth. In practical reality every woman experiences the dark side of this power in herself when her erotic jealousy is aroused, when her children want to leave her, when she as a widow, abandoned, has to fight her own way alone through life. Then the tigress in her surfaces, the whimpering bitch, the intrigue-spinning goddess of fate, and no woman can become conscious of her larger, greater self without having lived *these* aspects of the goddess within herself.

In my opinion, it is no accident that the reports cited above, in which Christ appears as masculine-feminine or even as a woman, came from Montanist circles. The Montanists lived in a region where the great mother-goddess especially had been an object of worship.

If, at least in the pagan world, there is no lack of documents that report the worship of a great daimon-goddess alongside Hermes, we still have none in which a woman has experienced this figure as the inner center of her being. Whether the women of that time were less conscious of this inner figure and experienced her as quite outside themselves, or whether the relevant written reports are simply missing, I do not know. We possess reports exclusively from men, who were beginning to bring this projection back from the outside world into their own psyches.

As Henri Corbin has proven, the gnostic-hermetic Hermes figure lived on in Persian mysticism (for instance, Avicenna and Sohraward). There he is the emissary of the Oriental world, of the world of the sunrise, that is, of inner enlightenment, and he accompanies the visionary in his inner development and realization of the godhead.[50] In this mystical spot of the rising of the sun a *personal* figure takes shape, a figure embodying the visionary's innermost depths.[51] Normally this figure appears to men and women only after death, but it can be seen beforehand by the mystic in the state of ecstasy.[52] It was equated with the Metatron, with the original Anthropos, with the Nous,[53] and with the Holy Ghost and the archangel Gabriel.[54] It appears to the soul in order to lead it on an inner journey to God and to enlighten it with secret knowledge about God.[55] This angel symbolizes the individuality of the relation between God and each particular soul[56] and yet is at the same time only the *one* same figure in all souls. Here, too, as in the Hermetic philosophy, this personification of the Self is the most individual core of the individual person and simultaneously the human self, that is, the self of all humanity. Becoming conscious of this inner figure means for the soul that it becomes a *clear mirror* of this image and from that point on proceeds in its company as with an escort.[57] This image is, as Corbin writes, the *principium individuationis,* which is individualized "in solitude by the solitary" and which each person sees in the way in which by nature he is fitted to understand it[58]—*"Talem vidi qualem capere potui"* (I saw him as such, in the way in which I was able to understand him"), as it says in the *Acts of Peter.*[59]

The visionary journey guided by this psychic companion then leads, as Corbin explains, to a *continuing and progressive internalization* of the whole cosmos[60] and to a gradual transformation of the seer himself into the inner teacher.[61]

As to the attitude of consciousness needed to gain insight into *this* projection, the situation is differently modulated than that of the integration of the shadow and the animus or anima. In the case of the shadow it is largely a question of humility; in the case of the other two figures it is one of an at least partial insight into their individual qualities and simultaneously of a wise "live-and-let-live" attitude toward their overwhelming nature. When, on the other hand, personifications of the Self begin to appear, the ego is then confronted with the necessity of sacrificing itself; *it can never integrate the Self* but can only bow before it and try to relate to it in the right way. That does not mean a total renunciation of one's own freedom—even before God, man has to reserve the right to a last word,[62] remaining fully conscious, however, that the power he addresses is always the stronger one. The encounter with the Self means, therefore, a deep and far-reaching change in the conscious attitude. It is not for nothing that the above-described inner daimon is called, among other names, the "Angel of Metanoia":[63] he brings with him a *withdrawal* from the play of Maya, of the world's illusion, an absolute retreat from the world. No one can accomplish this by simply willing it. It is effected in him by the Self and in many cases takes place only shortly before death. Only a few thoughtful, reflective people experience it earlier. Insight into the nature, the essence, of the Self is purchased only at the price of great suffering that wipes out the worldly prejudices and preoccupations of the ego, thereby forcing it into a change of attitude. Every deep disappointment or disillusionment is, in this sense, a step forward along the way of individuation, if it is accepted with insight and not with resignation or bitterness.

In the encounter with the Self there emerges a goal that points to the conclusive ending of all projections, namely, to death. In his *Memories, Dreams, Reflections,* Jung reports a dream about this: He sees himself walking along a road through a sun-bathed landscape. He comes to a small roadside chapel and enters it. Instead of a statue of the Madonna or a crucifix, there is a beautiful flower arrangement on the altar. Before the altar sits a yogi in the lotus position and in deep meditation. "When I looked at him more closely, I realized he had my face. I started in profound fright, and awoke with the thought: 'Aha, so he is the one who is meditating me. He has a dream, and I am it.' I knew that when he awakened, I would no longer be."[64]

The yogi is the same archetypal figure as the inner Hermes-

Psychopompos described above, except that here he appears in Far Eastern dress. The dream points to the fact, as Jung himself also mentions, that there is a meaning here of which those in the East have always been much more conscious than we have: namely, that in the end the whole world is only a projection, a reality "arranged" with mysterious purpose and which, if the Arranger so wills it, can disappear again, to make place for a great awakening to another reality un-imaginable by us.

8

Consciousness
and Inner Wholeness

The Return

The fact that the Self appears as that aspect of the personality
which puts an end to all projections[1] is often expressed in the
symbolical products of the unconscious by no longer appearing in personified form. In the Poimandres vision we saw that
the soul's inner companion changed his form and then dissolved into pure light. This theme was also hinted at in the

Turkestan fairy tale "The Magic Steed," mentioned in Chapter 5. There the heroine escapes from the evil demon through the help of a magic pony, a creature we first interpreted as her healthy instinct. After the conquest of the demon, however, the little horse asks to be ritually slaughtered. His four legs become golden trees growing at the four points of the compass, his body becomes a paradisal land, and his head is transformed into a silver-bright spring. The slaughter means an "analysis" (dissolution) of instinct, which had hitherto functioned unconsciously. This corresponds to an act of reflection through which the genuine content, a spiritual urge that previously had been concealed within the instinct, comes to light. The psychological meaning of the partition into four parts, as Jung writes, is a "reduction to order, through reflection" and through becoming conscious,[2] the development of an inner readiness to accept the archetype of the Self. What comes out of the horse, in Jungian psychology, is a mandala.

Jung says repeatedly throughout his work that common sense, reflection, and self-knowledge are the only means of clearing away the clouds of projections of unconscious contents. In the long history of philosophy much has been written on the subject of reflection. Here my own comments on the subject will be limited to the context of actual experience and especially to the *preconscious* processes that make it possible for the ego to engage in reflection. The fact that the horse, instinct itself, asks for its own death contains the implication that the impulse to reflection comes finally from the unconscious, more precisely from the Self. When reflection occurs together with insight into the projection, it is very closely related to the phenomenon of deep moral change, of the Pauline *metanoia* (Galatians 6), of a mental and moral about-face toward a new goal, which for the most part is experienced as coming from within. *Metanoia*[3] is a change of character, even of mentality, through which the entire personality is renewed and altered in such a way that it is irreversible. It is for this reason that the soul-companion in the above-mentioned *Shepherd of Hermes* is also referred to as the "Angel of Metanoia."

The twenty-fourth chapter of the *I Ching,* the Chinese Book of Wisdom, bears the title "Return (The Turning Point)" and beautifully describes this act of coming-to-consciousness or transformation. It depicts the moment of the winter solstice: "The powerful light that has been banished returns" in a natural movement, arising spontaneously. "Everything comes of itself at the appointed time." Movement begins again. *"Return leads to self-knowledge."* In its beginnings the new light must be strengthened by rest. "The return of health after an illness, the return of understanding after an estrangement: everything must be treated tenderly and with care at the beginning." The single lines of the oracle then describe the kind of moral attitude a person must have at such a time: "Return always calls for a decision and is an act of self-mastery. . . . When the time for return has come, a man should not take shelter in trivial excuses, but should look within and examine himself. And if he has done something wrong he should make a noblehearted resolve to confess his fault." If one misses this moment in time, outer misfortune befalls one. "The misfortune has its inner cause in a wrong attitude toward the world."[4]

Here, too, we have a dual aspect of the "Return" as in the well-known question of works, or grace. On the one hand, the return occurs, as if spontaneously, at a particular moment in time (grace); on the other hand, one can fail to make the right moral resolution and then fall into disharmony with the meaning (Tao) and thus into misfortune. After a careful observation of oneself during such a process of return or about-face, one might come up with the following description of it: If one is caught in a projection that disturbs one's adaptation, whether it be an attraction full of fascination or hatred or obstinacy in clinging to a theory or an idea, at first one is carried along by a current of powerful affect as well as of desire or inner demand (to "devour" the beloved object, to "annihilate" the enemy, to force the idea onto other people). This leads to behavior that is constantly at odds with the outer world, and conflicts and disappointments result. Pride and defiance then seduce one into a further struggle to push ahead in the same direction. If the affect turns inward, it can also lead to suicide fantasies. When the suffering has lasted long enough, so long that the ego and its strength are worn down and one begins to feel oneself to be "small and ugly," then at last comes that merciful moment when reflection is possible, when there is a reversal of the stream of energy, which now flows away from the object or the idea and toward oneself or, better still, toward the Self. One becomes quiet, still, or rather "something in one becomes still." Insight into the projection itself is then usually a very simple matter; it is no longer a question of "yes, but . . ." even though injured pride may still go on grumbling a bit. The most painful part of this process is the recognition that through the previous wrong attitude or behavior one has lost valuable time or has even, through one's sacred convictions, been guilty of very serious misdeeds.

In his book *The Seven Days of Creation,* Maximov shows quite impressively how a painful insight of this kind dawns on an old Communist party commissar as he begins to see through the inhuman party ideology and to recognize that it is based on projections or illusions. Occasionally, however, the change proves to be just too difficult and the dawning insight is sacrificed for a regression to the old ways.

I remember an especially dramatic case of this kind in my own practice. A woman analysand who was psychically ill had made good progress in her treatment and in developing consciousness. While I was away for a time, however, she slipped back into her old erroneous attitudes and conceived the delusional fantasy that Professor Jung was going to be murdered by a group of conspirators. Seen symbolically, it was clear that the morbid tendencies, the "murderers," wanted to kill the germ of Jungian psychology in herself.[5]

She projected this content quite naïvely and called the criminal police, who pulled up at Jung's house, armed and with the blue light on their car blinking, only to discover that everything was completely in order. I returned from my trip and was able to give her an hour. During the first half of the session I succeeded in quietening her gradually and in reestablishing human contact with her. We began to converse quite reasonably. Then, suddenly turning pale, she said, "Yes, but if that's the way it is, then I would have to admit . . ." (She obviously meant that she would have to admit that she had "behaved like a fool.") She jumped up from the chair with an unnatural, wrenching motion; psychologically she was no longer there but back in the same psychic state as at the beginning of the hour. During the night her condition worsened to such an extent that she had to be hospitalized. She recovered quickly, however, and picked herself up. Some months later, as she showed signs of again becoming excited and I warned her with some concern, she said, smiling, "You've no need to be anxious; the hospital was so frightful I'll never let it go that far again." And for the last fifteen years she has been as good as her word. It can be seen here how this woman succeeded at first in recognizing that her delusion of murder had the character of a projection and how at the same time her injured pride (". . . then I would have to admit . . .") prevented her from following her insight through to its bitter conclusion. In my experience the ego's demand for prestige quite frequently does not admit the "better insight." If the insight nevertheless breaks through, this really is a greater or lesser act of grace on the part of Nature.

The return of the light is like a winter solstice, as the Chinese text so beautifully puts it. It is not by accident, it seems to me, that this text uses the metaphor of light, which is, after all, everywhere a symbol of consciousness. Reflection, however, is the very essence of every increase in consciousness.

In keeping with the Eastern attitude, the process and the

course of events are described in the *I Ching* from the unconscious side; *that* is where, in obedience to the laws of nature, the transformation takes place, in the return of the "new light," which man's ego-consciousness must then accept with the correct change of attitude. This description takes into account the quality of the time or of the moment in time. That this really is so is demonstrated over and over again in psychological practice. One cannot coerce a patient to insight into a projection; the time must be ripe. With the aid of dreams, however, one can estimate roughly at least when the time has come; but even then the ego is free to accept the required change, the "return," to reflect or to persist in the old attitude.

The Eye as Symbol of "Insight"

The moment at which the insight is "ripe" depends on the archetype of the Self, of inner wholeness, which controls the equilibrium of the *whole* psyche and corrects the ego attitude through dreams. Another, inner subject watches us in dreams; it sees us as too anxious, too reckless, too immoral, or too anything else that seems to be a deviation from the norm of wholeness.[6] This inner eye of self-recognition, which mediates a different view of ourselves than does the ego, was described long ago by Gerhard Dorn, a pupil of Paracelsus, as the real essence of the alchemical opus. He writes: "But no man can truly know himself unless first he see and know by zealous meditation . . . *what* rather than *who* he is, on whom he depends, and whose is he, and to what end he was made and created, and by whom and through whom."[7] With the word *what* (instead of *who*), Dorn stresses the objective reality of this vis-à-vis whom he is seeking and whom he regards as the image of god planted in the human psyche. Whoever looks upon him with attention, "little by little and from day to day will perceive with his mental eyes and with the greatest joy some sparks of divine illumination." He who knows God in himself in this way will also know his brother.[8] Paracelsus called this divine psychic center the light of nature that creates our dreams.[9] Other alchemists compared it to shining fish eyes or to the eyes of the Lord that range over the whole earth (Zachariah 3:9).

Whenever one understands a dream or some other spontaneous product of the unconscious, "one's eyes are opened" —hence the eye motif. Many authors of an earlier day have described how, after seeking this kind of self-knowledge in meditation for a long time, many lights or eyes gradually grow together into one great inner light or eye that is the image of God or of the light "which faith gives us."[10] I myself understand the words of Paul—"For now we see in a mirror dimly, but then face to face. Now I know in part; then I shall understand fully, *even as I have been fully understood*" (I Corinthians 13:12)—in this sense. At first this eye from the Beyond sees us; then through this eye we see ourselves and God or the unfalsified reality. Jung says: "The mandala is indeed an 'eye,' the structure of which symbolizes the centre of order in the unconscious. . . . The eye may well stand for consciousness . . . looking into its own background."[11] At the same time it is also the Self, looking at *us*.

The divine eye, which, so to speak, looks at us from within and in whose seeing lies the only nonsubjectively colored source of self-knowledge, is a very widely distributed archetypal motif.[12] It is described as an inner, noncorporeal eye, surrounded by light, which itself is also light.[13] Plato and many Christian mystics call it the eye of the soul,[14] others the eye of knowledge, of faith, of intuition. Jacob Böhme even says: "The soul is an Eye in the Eternal Abyss, a similitude of Eternity." Or: "The Soul is like a ball of fire or a fiery Eye."[15] Only through this eye can a human being really see himself and partake of the nature of God, who is himself all eye. Synesius even calls upon God as "Eye of thy self."[16] When this eye opens up in a mortal being, that being has a share in the light of God. When a man closes his outer, physical eyes in sleep, his soul "sees" the truth in his dreams.[17] This eye is also related to the phenomenon of conscience. A poem by Victor Hugo pictures this impressively.[18] After killing his brother Abel, Cain flees from God; with his family he stops to rest on a mountain but is unable to sleep; he sees "an eye, wide open, in the darkness," fixed upon him. "I have not gone far enough," he calls out, trembling, and continues his flight. For thirty days and nights he hurries on until he comes to the seacoast, but as he settles down there he sees the eye again, in the heavens. He cries out to his family to hide him from God! They build a tent for him but the eye is always there. Finally, at his request his family digs him a deep grave in the earth. He sits down in it, on a little seat, and his family pushes the heavy gravestone over him. As the grave closes and he sits there in the darkness, *"L'oeil était dans la tombe et regardait Cain."*[19]

Not only the highest godhead, however, but also single gods and demons of the most varied cultures sometimes have a single eye in their chest with which they can see everything happening on earth.[20] This motif is an allusion to the fact, which anyone in psychotherapeutic practice can experience again and again, that the unconscious gives utterance in dreams to a knowledge of things that we simply *cannot* know rationally and consciously. The word *telepathy* does not explain this phenomenon; it only describes it. The unconscious appears to have a sort of diffuse intuitive knowledge that reaches far out into the environment of the individual and that Jung has described as "absolute knowledge" (absolute in the sense of being detached from ego-consciousness), a luminosity of the unconscious or of its archetypal nuclei. Just as a demon's evil eye can cast a spell, so also an eye painted on a pot, a sign, and the like can ward off the evil eye. Seligmann has collected examples of this from all over the world, substantiating the extremely important apotropaic effect of the eye motif.[21] If the evil spirit is "seen," that is, reflected, he is overcome.

The fact that demon-figures often exhibit a conspicuous eye motif is connected with the curious fact that autonomous complexes themselves often possess a quasi-consciousness, hence also an apparent (but partial and not genuine) gift for reflection. The shadow or the animus and anima can infuse a person with curiously distorted thoughts about himself, but only that reflection which proceeds from the Self, the inner center, could be correctly described as genuine moral reflection.

The motif of the eye of God lends a personal nuance to our feeling of being "watched," whereas the related motif of the mirror underlines rather the impersonal aspect of this "knowledge" that, without intention, simply reflects our being. In the final analysis it is simply up to us to draw the right conclusions from our dreams; the unconscious often appears to be as "intentionless" as Nature herself.[22] When we have sugar in our urine, Nature does not tell us we have diabetes; we must draw this conclusion ourselves and take the necessary countermeasures. Jung interprets the motif of the observing eye in the unconscious, or more especially of the *one* eye (which is usually represented as a mandala), as a *"mirroring of our insight into ourselves."* It is only with the help of the inner center, of the Self, that we can know ourselves. Therefore Christ says to the Apostle in the apocryphal *Acts of John*: "A lamp am I to you that perceive me. Amen. A mirror am I to you that know me. Amen." As Jung explains in his beautiful interpretation of the complete text,[23] Christ in this connection is to be understood as a symbol of the Self, as the consciousness-transcending wholeness of the person, "the point of reference not only of the individual but of all those who are of like mind or who are bound together by fate."[24] Christ is here a mirror that "reflects the subjective consciousness of the disciple, making it visible to him," but, inversely, the human being thus "knows" Christ, that is, becomes conscious of the reality of the Self.

Re-Collection

The possibility of *integrating* projected contents instead of apotropaically casting them out into extrapsychic space does not arise until symbols of the Self begin to appear. From this center impulses proceed to a contemplative, thoughtful re-collection of the personality. The contents now seen to have been projected are at the same time recognized as belonging to one's own psychic wholeness. Consequently the psychic energy belonging to these contents now flows toward one's own inner center, strengthening it and heightening its intensity.[25]

Another depiction of the same process that appears spontaneously among the products of the unconscious is the image, or mythologem, of a "re-collection" of scattered units or sparks of light into an ordered, centered unity. This demands of the conscious side of the personality an attempt to form as objective an image of one's own nature as possible. "It is an act of self-recollection, a gathering together of what is scattered, of all the things in us that have never been properly related . . . with a view to achieving full consciousness."[26] The demand that we act thus comes from the Self.[27] The previously split-off contents of one's own psyche are made conscious and integrated. "Self-recollection," writes Jung, "is a gathering together of the self."[28]

"All the things in us that have never been properly related" refers to the phenomenon of so-called compartment psychology, that is, to the fact that in many people areas of the psyche are separated. For example, they have one kind of morality for Sundays and another kind for business; they believe in the commandment to "love thy neighbor" but not if the neighbor happens to be black; they make every effort to be honest and sincere but not in politics, and so on. These different areas did not "fall apart"; their separateness represents an original state or condition, because the field of ego-consciousness is a loose structure of originally separate single islands of consciousness that have gradually grown together. The seams are therefore still perceptible in many people.

If we try to look back on our own childhood, we see how at first we remember only single flashing moments of consciousness created by some deep impression. It is only at about the eighth or tenth year that most people begin to have a more continuous memory of their life. Phylogenetically, too, human consciousness seems to have grown out of such sudden flashes of consciousness. This psychological fact is pictured in the mythological motif of that psychic nucleus, or soul-particle, already mentioned.

In Stoic philosophy there is the theory that single human souls are sparks of the cosmic fiery ether, that is, of the world-soul, and, further, that even ethical inclinations, judgments, and concepts light up in them like little sparks (spin-theres, igniculi). These are the innate mental contents (notiones) that are common to all men and that constitute the better, more spiritual part of the psyche. When a human being really tries to lead a spiritual life, these "sparks" gradually grow together into *one* inner light of reason.[29]

This idea of sparks of the psyche, or light-nuclei of the soul, is also to be found in the systems of various Gnostics, although there it is formulated more mythologically-pictorially.[30] The Orphites, for example, taught that when God's feminine spirit was floating above the waters, "she" could not bear the brightness of the light of God and fell down into chaos with sparks of the Father's light still clinging to her.[31] With the help of these remaining sparks she tried to raise herself up again. When all the sparks are re-collected and have entered the eternal undying aeon, then creation will have come to its completion.[32] The Barbelo Gnostics taught that instead of sparks of light it was the seed of the godhead that was strewn throughout matter. When a man holds back his own procreative powers, he helps the godhead to regain its seed.[33] In one of their writings the prophetess sees a great man (God) and hears him say: "I am thou, and thou art I, and wherever thou art, there am I, and *I am scattered in all things,* and from wherever thou wilt thou canst gather me, but in gathering me thou gatherest thyself."[34]

The first tractate of the *Corpus Hermeticum* describes this dismemberment of the original man in a similar way.[35] The immortal Anthropos, likeness of the godhead, bent down through the strongholds of the celestial spheres and showed his beautiful godlike figure to the world of nether nature. Nature saw his image reflected in the water, his shadow over the earth. He, however, as he saw his image, so like himself, fell in love with it and wished to remain there. Then he descended into the reasonless form (body). But Nature took her beloved to herself, entwining herself around him, and they united, for their love for one another was passionate. Since then every human being has in himself a mortal physical human and an essential, immortal human who is a part of the cosmic Anthropos. Through self-knowledge this part can once again attain the light and eternal life.

The alchemist and Gnostic Zosimos of Panopolis (third century A.D.) supported a similar theory. According to it, the "great light-man" (Anthropos-Adam) abided in Paradise. There he was persuaded by the evil celestial powers to clothe himself in the earthly Adam and to take on a form capable of suffering in order to illuminate and save the light-men who were of his kind; afterward he returns to the kingdom of light. The alchemical work of Zosimos was devoted solely to achieving the liberation of the inner light-man.[36]

The teaching of the Manichaeans, influenced by the Gnostics, also holds that the man striving after immortality and perfection must liberate and save the seeds of light scattered throughout creation, even in stones and plants, as they are particles of the suffering soul of the Redeemer.[37] Similarly, according to the Gnostic Sethians, a small spark of the original light of God fell into matter and it is the task of mortal man to devote himself to helping the upper light to bring this spark back to itself.[38]

These Stoic and Gnostic texts reveal two trains of thought to the attentive reader. First, the individual human contains in itself various kinds of sparks, the sparks of collective representations, and must gather them into a unity (in variations it must even gather light sparks in the outer world). Second, the spiritual souls of men or of certain chosen men are themselves sparks that are gathered up by a god-man and redeemer figure and brought back into unity with God or with the divine world. Translated into psychological language, the first process depicts how a human being "gathers" or "collects" himself through meditation and, for example, with the aid of his dreams becomes conscious of his complexes and projections and in this way develops into a spiritually and morally more integrated and more whole personality.[39] As is well known, Jung named this the individuation process. The Self stands, says Jung, in a creative relation to the ego and at the same time the individual human being is the form in which the Self becomes manifest. The re-collecting, or gathering together, of the divine light-substance in the Gnosis and in Manichaeism corresponds psychologically to the integration of the Self through bringing split-off contents into consciousness.[40]

The mythologems cited above also, however, depict a process of re-collecting that proceeds from the god-man or the light-man or some similar Anthropos-Redeemer figure and that unites the many single human souls into a unity, that is, into a genuine community. Therefore not only does the individual become a whole in himself but a community comes into being that also represents a whole. In antiquity this whole was called the Anthropos. Psychologically it means that an organically united community becomes visible. A group of human beings of this kind is not organized by laws or by the instruments of power; to the extent that each individual relates to the Self in himself he will quite naturally assume his rightful place in a social order of a psychological kind. In the Middle Ages this thought was expressed by the belief that the *ecclesia spiritualis* was the body of Christ, the Anthropos. Hence Jung writes: "By appealing to the eternal rights of man, faith binds itself inalienably to a higher order, not only on account of the historical fact that Christ has proved to be an ordering factor for many hundreds of years, but also because the self effectively compensates chaotic conditions no matter by what name it is known: for the self is the Anthropos above and beyond this world, and in him is contained the freedom and dignity of the individual man."[41] The unification or integration of the individual and his integration into the higher unity of the many appears thus to be a *simultaneous process,* as it is so beautifully expressed in "The Gospel of Eve" when the great god-man says to the seeress: "And from wherever thou wilt thou canst gather me, but in gathering me thou gatherest thyself."

This dual motif of the process of gathering is found also in the Christian era. Once again it is Origen in particular who has been impressively explicit about this. In his Commentary on First Samuel, fourth homily, he says, *"There was one man.* We, who are still sinners, cannot obtain this title of praise, for each of us is not one but many. . . . See how he who thinks himself one is not one, but seems to have as many personalities as he has moods, as also the Scripture says: A fool is changed as the moon." And regarding Ezekiel 9:1, he puts it strongly: "Where there are sins, there is multitude . . . but where virtue is, there is singleness, there is union." In his sermon on Leviticus 5:2, he says: "Understand that thou hast within thyself herds of cattle . . . flocks of sheep and flocks of goats. . . . Understand that the fowls of the air are also within thee . . . understand that thou thyself art another world in little, and hast within thee the sun and the moon, and also the stars."[42] The individual human being must, through moral effort, bring this multiplicity together into *one* personality. As to the many individual souls in all humanity, these will each in its turn be gathered into a unit in Christ, alternatively united in his *corpus mysticum,* the Church.[43]

The first stage shows the process of the inner unification of the personality in the individuation process. The second stage, however, has reference to a special process that always accompanies individuation in the single person: namely, the development of relatedness to certain fellow human beings and to mankind as a whole, a relatedness that proceeds not from the ego but from a transcendental inner center, the Self.

Individuation and Relatedness

It happens again and again in psychological practice that when a person has been caught in blinding projections relating to his human environment and they are then withdrawn, in many cases this in no way annuls or sets aside the *relationship.* On the contrary, a genuine, "deeper" relation emerges, no longer rooted in egoistic moods, struggles, or illusions but rather in the feeling of being connected to one another via an absolute, objective principle. This is well expressed in the Brihadaranyaka-Upanishad: "Verily a husband is not dear, that you may love the husband, but that you may love the Self, therefore a husband is dear. Verily a wife is not dear, that you may love the wife, but that you may love the Self, therefore a wife is dear. . . . Verily the Self is to be seen, to be heard, to be recognized, to be marked. . . . Where the Self has been seen . . . then all is known."[44]

The following dream may illustrate the way in which a relationship that is guided from the "Beyond," that is, by the Self, was represented in the dreams of a man who was on the way toward individuation. The married dreamer had fallen deeply in love with another woman, also married, and after long and intense resistance had begun a sexual relation with her. At the time of the dream both were considering divorces from their present partners, in order to be able to marry each other. Then he dreamed:

I was with my teacher, an invisible presence, on the edge of a sphere which he described as "the ultimate reality," something timeless and spaceless, indescribable; only those who have seen it can describe this experience, an "all-nothing," an "everywhere-nowhere," an everybody-nobody, as "the word which has not yet been spoken." Somehow the teacher helped me to pull two beings or "somethings" out of this ultimate reality. I did not see them but I knew about them. In order to make them visible the teacher helped me to pull a silver-grey cloudlike material out of the space in which we were suspended. We clothed the two beings in it and a third something which separated the two. As soon as I saw them clothed a deep amazement fell over me. "Those are angels," I cried out. "Yes," he answered, "that's what you are." I saw the grey curtain which separated the two angels and the teacher explained, "That is the veil of illusion." It had many holes. I was deeply moved and called out, "Oh, it's going away, it's going away," and I felt that thousands of years that had been lived in the half-conscious hope that it could be broken through were now fulfilled. I went to the angel who was "I" and I saw a silver cord reaching down from him to a tiny little creature who was also "I" in the world of illusion. Another cord went down to a woman, down below; it was Alberta [the woman he loved]. The two angels appeared to be identical; they were sexless and they could "think together" in a kind of identity. (That has sometimes happened to Alberta and me in the reality "down below.") And we thought, "Such a small part of our consciousness lives in these little creatures and they worry so much about such little things. Poor little creatures." We saw that their union could only happen really rightly if the two little creatures met their obligations to their families and relatives and did not pursue their egoistic desires. And at once it was clear to us that it would be a sin against that "ultimate reality" (sin against the Holy Ghost?) if we did not go ahead in the process of reciprocal coming-to-consciousness.

The figure of the teacher in the dream is a personification of the drive to individuation by the dreamer's personality on its way toward wholeness, and it "knows" more than his ego. The two angel figures that emerge from the obscurity and indefiniteness of the unconscious are aspects of the two lovers themselves as they appear in the unconscious in their consciousness-transcending reality. As Jung explained in "The Psychology of the Transference"[45] and as we have already pointed out, *four* figures take part in every deeper confrontation of man and woman, the two conscious egos and the animus and the anima, the contra-sexual personifications of the unconscious in the two persons concerned. In this dream they are sexless beings—compensatory to the fact that sexuality was too much in the foreground of consciousness in both partners at the time. Angels are "God's messengers," emissaries from the deepest level of the unconscious where all distinctions are dissolved in one unknown. But it is precisely from that deepest level which transcends the ego-personality that the realization comes to the dreamer that he has to discharge his earthly obligations to his fellowmen. If it says anything at all, then, this dream states quite unambiguously that individuation is not an egocentric affair but demands and even rigorously necessitates human relatedness.

It is not only the relation between man and woman, however, that is contained in this union through the Self; it is also many other relations with one's fellow creatures. The Gnostic sect of the Perates taught that out of the divine original substance of the world, out of "the water which gives shape to the perfect man," that is, from the unconscious and its urge to individuation, "each creature selects that which is peculiar to it," that which characterizes it. What belongs to him is attracted to him "more than the iron to the magnet."[46] This means that bonds with other people are produced by the Self and these relations are very exactly regulated as to distance and closeness. One might describe this as *the social function of the Self*. Each person gathers around him his own "soul family," a group of people not created by accident or by mere egoistic motivation but rather through a deeper, more essential spiritual interest or concern: *reciprocal individuation*. Whereas relations based merely on projection are characterized by fascination and magical dependence, this kind of relationship, by way of the Self, has something strictly objective, strangely transpersonal about it. It gives rise to a feeling of immediate, timeless "being together." The usual bond of feeling, says Jung elsewhere, always contains projections that have to be withdrawn if one is to attain to oneself and to objectivity. "Objective cognition lies hidden behind the attraction of the emotional relationship; it seems to be the central secret."[47] In this world created by the Self we meet all those many to whom we belong, whose hearts we touch; here "there is no distance, but immediate presence."[48]

There exists no individuation process in any one individual that does not at the same time produce this relatedness to one's fellowmen.[49]

Along with the mythologem of the re-collecting of light sparks, there is another motif of archetypal images that refers to the coming together of certain people through the agency of the Self. It is the motif of the "Round Table" around which the individual persons are seated. The inner unification of the personality is often represented by this image in dreams, as is also the attachment to friends who are fellow members and finally to all of mankind. Arthur's Round Table, as it appears in the Grail legends, is the most famous. It is said of it in the *Queste del Saint Graal:*

> You know that since the advent of Jesus Christ there have been three most important tables in the world. The first was the Table of Jesus Christ, at which the Apostles ate on several occasions. This was the table that sustained bodies and souls

with food from heaven. . . . And the Lamb without blemish that was sacrificed for our redemption established this table.

After this table there was another *in the likeness and in remembrance of it.* This was the table of the Holy Grail, of which great miracles were once seen in that country, in the time of Joseph of Arimathea, when Christianity was first brought to this earth.

After this table the Round Table was set up, on the advice of Merlin; nor was it established without great symbolic significance. For what is meant by being called the Round Table is the roundness of the world and the condition of the planets and of the elements in the firmament . . . so that one could say that in the Round Table the whole universe is symbolized.[50]

In the fifth sura of the Koran (verses 112–115), God sends a table down from heaven to Jesus and his Apostles; on it lies a fish as a sign that he will feed them. As a result of humanity's sinfulness, however, this table is taken away again by God.[51] I suspect that the pleasures of the table, in which the dead, according to the belief of so many peoples, indulge in the paradise of the Beyond, refer to the same mythologem, to the image of a human community produced and governed by the Self. Since this is not yet, however, a realized goal of humanity, it appears in most myths as a postmortal goal, that is, one still in the Beyond, hidden in the unconscious.

9

Reflection

The Original Meanings of Reflection

The "momentary flashes of consciousness" we recall when we look back on our childhood have usually grown together in adults into a more or less continuous field of ego-consciousness.[1] But still earlier, before these momentary flashes were consciously recognized as inner experience, they existed as preconscious components of human existence and expressed themselves mainly in unconscious action. Jung surmised that the unconscious impulses to ritual actions, in comparison with the teachings and theories formulated in myths or in religious systems, were practiced at an earlier date and were the precursors of the latter.[2] He observed, for example, that the African natives on Mount Elgon spit on their hands at sunrise and held them out to the sun without "knowing" that this action has a meaning. "They had always done this." Seen in the light of today's psychological knowledge of symbols this gesture means: "Oh, God, I offer up my soul to Thee"—but, as we have just said, the deed precedes the word by a considerable period of time.[3]

The same law prevails in respect to the "momentary flashes of consciousness." They, too, were originally represented in symbolic form and given a ritual application in the shape of glittering small stones or other shiny, mirrorlike objects to which were ascribed the power to drive away spirits. The ethnologist Richard Gould reports a good example of this which he observed among the Australian aborigines.[4] He and his wife stayed for some time with a friendly family group of thirteen aborigines who, untouched by civilization, lived by hunting and by gathering plants and who had retained their original age-old outlook and way of living. Even when the heat was extreme a fire was lighted every evening and kept burning throughout the night to keep away the *mamu* (the evil spirits). But so far, no *mamu* appeared. One day Gould decided to go away for a couple of days with the oldest man, who was the spiritual leader of the group. His wife remained with the others. In the evening after this decision had been made, the children became restless and reported that they had seen two *mamu* skulking around in the twilight. Two men of the group who were versed in magic took two shiny fragments of mother-of-pearl they had found in a mission station and, pronouncing exorcistic formulas and making a great show of aiming, shot them from their bows in the direction of the two *mamu*. They then assured the others that the *mamu* had disappeared. It is likely that some of the men who were to remain with the white woman without the authority of the presence of the old man may have had some unorthodox thoughts, especially as these aborigines are not at all prudish in their views about sex. But evidently they did not experience these temptations as coming from within; their sudden restlessness was caused by two undefinable evil spirits. The glittering, reflecting pieces of mother-of-pearl acted as countermagic, as "apotropaic reflection" in the literally concrete sense.[5] The magicians asserted that the fragments came back to them at the right time—*re-flexio*! Thus even the phenomenon of "momentary flashes of consciousness" was originally experienced as projected onto an outer object.[6]

Whoever remembers these "momentary flashes of consciousness" from his own early childhood will know that they are always connected with strongly emotional states. This emotion is at its peak at the moment of the "flash" and usually subsides at the same time. It is as if the brief light of consciousness broke up the stifling obsessive emotion. Objects that "reflect" can therefore drive away spirits; the reflection calms the affect or the excited state. That is why when Perseus killed Medusa, the sight of whom turned people into stone, he did not look directly at her but instead took his aim with the help of a mirror. He could thereby protect himself from being overcome by emotion; rigidity is caused by an excess of strong emotion, as is shown in the catatonia of schizophrenics.

Perhaps it is worthwhile in this connection to take a look at the concept of reflection in physics. All light, as we know, is produced by the motion of electrons, either spontaneously, as when an electron changes its energy level in the atom, or when it is set in motion through the impact of a photon. In the second case reflection and transmission result. Neither of these events can take place, however, unless the electron has a certain freedom of motion and is not too firmly held in its atom. Normally, when light hits the electrons held at a certain energy level in a single atom, the energy of the light can be absorbed by the energy of the electron.[7] If, however, the atoms are held tightly together in a kind of crystalline lattice-structure, it can happen that electrons are able to move about freely inside the lattice and are no longer bound to *one* atom. In this situation the electron does not absorb the light energy but radiates it back.[8] Viewed as a physical phenomenon, therefore, reflection depends on the presence of certain atomic lattice-structures. The fact of the matter is that although the larger groupings, the atoms, are mathematically held together more tightly and with more force than usual, certain electrons have precisely for this reason more freedom of motion. Miraculously, as it would seem, the possibility of reflection in the unconscious area of the psyche is connected with an unknown factor that reveals itself on the threshold of consciousness, in dreams and in spontaneous fantasies, as a crystalline mathematical structure, namely, the symbol of the mandala. That psychic center which is represented by the mandala itself and which, as we know, Jung has called the Self is, when it represents *reflected* wholeness, very often symbolized by mathematical structures mostly of quaternary subdivisions and is often illustrated by the symbol of the crystal.

For primordial man the phenomenon of mirrors and mirroring had the quality of a miracle; for him the mirrored image was a reality in its own right. *Spiegel,* the German word for "mirror," is cognate with the Latin word *speculum* and goes back to Old High German *scukar,* "shadow-holder," from *skuwo,* "shadow," and *kar,* "vessel." In Old Indian, a mirror was thought of as "self-seer" or as "seer of Doppelgängers." The mirrored image was regarded as shadow or as Doppelgänger, that is, as an image of the soul, and the mirror therefore possessed great magical significance; it was an instrument for becoming objectively conscious of one's soul by means of reflection, in the literal sense of the word.

Mircea Eliade has collected abundant documentation on the part played by shiny or glittering objects as protection against psychic dissolution by evil spirits. In his book on shamanism, wherein he discusses the initiation rites of shamans and medicine men of innumerable peoples, he describes a ritual in which the novice's entrails are symbolically extracted, cleaned, and replaced by small shiny stones and glittering chips that give him magic power over the spirits.[9] Crystals themselves often have the same function of subservient spirits; they mirror events on earth or reveal what is going on in the soul of a sick person.[10]

In many places mirrors are used as a defense against the evil eye of both human beings and of spirits, because it was thought that mirrors throw the harmful "rays" back upon their source. In Spain, in Tripoli, and generally in China, mirrors are used for this purpose.[11] A similar purpose is served by "fear masks," that is, revoltingly evil-looking distorted faces that show the demon his own image, from which he flees in terror.[12]

Reflecting objects have thus had, from time immemorial, a numinous significance for human beings. The oldest experience of a reflecting object may well have been that of the surface of water. In what follows I am relying principally on the excellent book by Martin Ninck, *Die Bedeutung des Wassers im Kult und Leben der Alten*. Ninck shows that in the world of antiquity water was always thought of as chthonic, as having sprung from the earth, and that it was always associated with what he calls the "night conditions" or "night-states" of the soul: intoxication, dream, trance, unconsciousness, and death. These states were all connected with the mystery of watery depths.

Psychologically, water is one of the most frequent symbols

of the unconscious,[13] and hence the depths of the water were thought of in many places as the source of all prophecy and of use in seeing phenomena from the "Beyond."[14] The great gods with knowledge of the future—Nereus, Proteus, Thetis, and, in the Germanic tradition, Mimir—are all water divinities. In the water one can see one's own shadow, one's Doppelgänger, one's soul-image, separate and objective, and also the disembodied outlines of the dead and of gods. The custom of obtaining secret information by staring into a vessel of water, the so-called *hydromantia,* is therefore practiced throughout the world.[15] In the Middle Ages, in our own cultural tradition, burning candles were placed around a circular vessel filled with water and the demon was evoked; the spirit answered with images on the water's surface *(imagines aquae impressae).* In ancient Patras (Greece) a form of magic was practiced that combined both mirror and reflecting water. A mirror attached to a thread was lowered into a well to the water's surface and its reflection indicated whether a sick person would recover or die; in Lycian Kyenai, on the other hand, the same thing was seen directly in the reflecting surface of the water of the well.[16] In European folk magic the use of an "earth-mirror" was widespread.[17] A box was filled with earth, a glass disc was laid on it, and this disc reflected what was sought. In some places the magic power was imparted to the mirror by leaving the disc for three days and three nights on the face of the buried corpse of a woman who had died in childbirth. The association of earth and death with the prophetic powers of water and mirror is especially important in this connection. In Vergil, Aeneas receives the final prophecies just as he is about to descend through the lake of Avernus into the kingdom of the dead.[18] Closely related to the water-mirror is the dream oracle, which is also often sent by water divinities.[19] The unceasing transformation of the dream images is like a subterranean current, whose gods can likewise change without cease.[20]

The symbolization of the unconscious by water with its

mirrorlike surface is of course based in the final analysis on a projection. Nevertheless, the analogies are astonishingly meaningful. Just as we cannot "see" into the depths of the waters, so the deeper areas of the unconscious are also invisible to us; we can draw only indirect conclusions about them. But on the surface, on the threshold area between consciousness and the unconscious, dream images appear spontaneously, not only seeming to give us information about the depths but also *mirroring* our conscious personality, although not in identical form, but rather in a more or less altered form.[21] The mirroring is always by way of the symbolic *image* that has a place in both worlds.[22]

Even though during a dream we feel just as identical with the dream-ego as we do with our daytime ego, our dream-ego nevertheless has some features that astonish us when we are awake. We may, for example, perform bold deeds in a dream that we would never dare to undertake during the daytime, or our dream-ego may exhibit other qualities and attributes we have never seen in ourselves. In contrast to a physically normal mirror-image in an undisturbed and undistorted surface, the ego mirrored in dreams is sometimes greatly altered, as is indeed the case with all other dream images. Our dog can talk in dreams, objects blend into hermaphroditic forms, people who resemble overlapping photographs of two acquaintances appear, and so on. But as soon as we begin to interpret the dream according to the rules of the art,[23] an idea of what we are like begins to emerge from the symbolic dream images and it will astonish us again and again with its relentless objectivity. In his essay "A Psychological View of Conscience,"[24] Jung reports the dream of a businessman who on the previous day had been offered what appeared to be a perfectly honorable project, which he was inclined to undertake. During the night he had a dream in which he saw his hands and forearms covered with black dirt. The dream was advising him not to become involved in the matter, and in fact it turned out somewhat later to be "dirty business."

Fourfold Mirroring

The "mirroring" surface of the unconscious, manifested in dream images, shows us another, often compensatory image of ourselves that seems to have been perceived by another kind of sight or by another person.

What strikes us as strange or curious, however, is that the phenomenon of *consciousness,* which is to us almost completely mysterious, *likewise possesses a kind of mirroring quality;* one need only recall the above-mentioned theories and explanations of natural scientists on the nature of "material" phenomena in the external world. In the last analysis they are nothing but mirrorings, or imaginative, mental, ordered reconstructions of the external world in another medium, namely, the human mind. The roots and the basic structure of these imaginative ideas that reconstruct the external world indeed lie in the unconscious, as we saw in Chapter 4, but they are distilled, purified, altered, and given the form in which they are presented at any given moment by the observations, reflections, and formulations of the researcher's ego-consciousness. Even when we attempt, through indirect conclusions, to know not the external world but the nature of the objective psyche, that is, of the unconscious, we mirror it in our ego-consciousness. And, finally, a certain mirror-image relation seems to exist between the unconscious and matter, and this relation is today still filled with riddles.

In the case of these mirrorings there is no longer any question of a disturbance of adaptation to inner or outer realities. This question is contained only by implication, insofar as the suspicion exists that every psychic model–image we make of inner or outer facts or sets of facts *could* turn out, in the course of evolution, to be inadequate and merely "subjective," even though at first it serves as an adequate instrument in the attempt to grasp "objective" reality. For *this* aspect of projection, therefore, I use the term *mirroring,* which Jung also often used, for the sake of clarity.

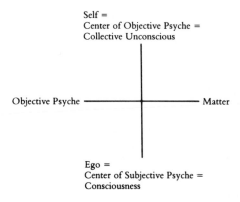

Self =
Center of Objective Psyche =
Collective Unconscious

Objective Psyche ———————————— Matter

Ego =
Center of Subjective Psyche =
Consciousness

We must therefore look more closely at *four* mirror relations: the mirroring of the ego by the Self, the mirroring of the Self by the ego, the mirroring of matter by the collective unconscious, and the possible mirroring of the latter in matter.

The mirroring of the ego by the Self, the center of the unconscious and of the whole psyche, has already been mentioned. We can discover in every dream how our conscious behavior is "objectively" mirrored and how a glimpse of the Self is thus mediated from an Archimedean point outside ego-consciousness, a glimpse that we could not otherwise have obtained. *What we see in the mirror held up to us by the Self is hence the only source of genuine self-knowledge;* everything else is only narcissistic rumination of the ego about itself.

Not only is the ego of the empirical human being mirrored in the act of self-knowledge, but also the Self is then first brought from its state of potentiality into realization by virtue of the fact that it is mirrored in the ego, that is, it is recognized. It is only from the standpoint of the Self that the ego can be seen as object and, vice versa, that the ego can obtain in every dream, for example, a clearer notion of the nature and existence of what it is looking at. Therefore when the ego follows the signals given in dreams, it is helping the Self attain realization in time and space. It is then "mirroring" the Self by lifting it out of its unconscious, merely potential existence into the clarity of ego-consciousness. So, in a certain sense, we can say that even the Self can become aware of itself only with the help of the ego, only in ego-consciousness, which is the mirror.

In his memoirs Jung has illustrated this mirror-image relation between ego and Self with two of his own dreams. In the first dream a kind of flying saucer appears in the heavens, flying directly toward him.[25] At the time of the dream Jung had interpreted UFOs as projections of the Self onto unknown external phenomena; but his dream turns the problem around, as he himself says, and suggests that the person, that is, his ego, is a projection coming from the Self. The fact that the flying saucer is a "machine" might indicate symbolically that behind this object is a power that devises and arranges our reality for us and whose goals and purposes are unknown to us.[26] The second dream is still plainer; it is the above-mentioned dream in which Jung discovers that he is imagined by a yogi. In that dream the Self (as meditating yogi) creates the dreamer's empirical ego; it projects the ego from itself outward, so to speak, and into the three-dimensional world. Here the word *projection* is understood in the technical sense as, for example, in the optical projection of an image. Therefore I prefer to use the word *mirroring*.[27] This relation between the ego and the Self is not only epistemologically but also in practice a delicate matter and a heavy responsibility.[28]

Paradoxically, the Self is the "other" in one's own inner world and yet again it is also only the ego. According to whether a person identifies too closely with the Self or regards it as too far away, as the "absolutely other," his dreams will emphasize one or the other aspect. In the *Acts of John,* cited above, it was the mysterious otherness of the Self that was stressed. In the following dream of a pastor's son who saw God as too outer and as the unknowable "other," the opposite was the case. The dream was an anxiety dream that had been recurrent for many years until the man's late forties. He dreamed that he was walking through a vast wasteland. He heard steps behind him. Anxiously he walked faster, but the steps too became more rapid. He began to run, the terror still behind him. Then he came to the edge of a deep abyss and had to stand still. He looked down: deep, deep down, thousands of miles below he saw hell-fire burning. He looked around him and saw—or rather sensed in the dark—a demonic face. Later on, the dream recurred exactly as before, except that instead of a demon the dreamer saw the face of God. And when he was almost fifty years old he had the same dream for the last time. But this time panicky fear drove him and he jumped over the edge of the abyss into the depths below. As he fell, thousands of little square white cards floated downward with him from above. On each card, in black and white, a different mandala had been drawn. The cards floated together into a kind of floor, so that he did not fall into hell but found a firm landing about halfway down. Then he looked back, upward to the edge of the abyss; there he saw—*his own face*! The pursuer in the dream is the Self, which appears first as "the uncanny," then as God, then as the dreamer himself. In the final dream, which evidently brought with it the solution, since it did not recur, the similarity of ego and Self, one the mirror-image of the other, is underscored.

Mirroring of Psyche and Matter (Synchronicity)

A further mirror-relation would be the one between psyche and matter. Every physicist today is aware that everything we know about matter in the external world is mental, thus psychic, mirroring. He devises hypothetical images in the form of mathematical structures that he hopes will coincide with the behavior of the material phenomena observed in the experiment.[29] To a large extent he in fact does the very thing that caused Eugene Wigner to speak of the "unreasonable effectiveness of mathematics in the natural sciences."[30]

As we saw in Chapter 3, all the great basic themes of the natural sciences are archetypal images whose content has varied and has in the course of history been defined with increasing precision. Our ego can therefore make explanatory statements only indirectly—with the help of the mirror provided by the objective psyche—about the external world and the aspect of matter perceptible by our senses.[31] That is why Jung emphasized that the collective unconscious is "a perpetual living mirror of the universe."[32] Our subject is "situated between two antithetical worlds—the so-called external world open to the senses, and the unconscious psychic substrate which alone enables us to grasp the world at all. This psychic substrate must necessarily be different from the so-called external world; otherwise there would be no possibility of grasping it, for like cannot cognize like."[33] Leibniz had already written of the human soul as an "active indivisible mirror," each soul or monad as "a perpetual living mirror of the universe."[34]

We are left with a big problem, namely, the question of the fourth mirror-relation: whether and how the material world can mirror the objective psyche. If the psychic mirrorings of the material world—in short, the natural sciences—really constitute valid statements about matter, then the reverse mirror-relation would also have to be valid. This would mean that *material events in the external world would have to be regarded as statements about conditions in the objective psyche.* This would indicate that a quite concrete event in the external world could be understood as a symbolic statement about an objective psychic process, which is conscious to an observer. Jung spent a good deal of time on this question. He emphasized that psychology has no Archimedean point outside the psyche and that there is therefore no possibility of measuring psychic conditions or states objectively. Indeed, atomic physics is in a similar position, inasmuch as the process observed is modified by being observed. The observation is carried out by the physicist's psyche.

> This strange encounter between atomic physics and psychology has the inestimable advantage of giving us at least a faint idea of a possible Archimedean point for psychology. The microphysical world of the atom exhibits certain features whose affinities with the psychic have impressed themselves even on the physicists. Here, it would seem, is at least a suggestion of how the psychic process could be "reconstructed" in another medium, in that, namely, of the microphysics of matter. Certainly no one at present could give the remotest indication of what such a "reconstruction" would look like. Obviously it can only be undertaken by nature herself, or rather, *we may suppose it to be happening continuously, all the time the psyche perceives the physical world.*[35]

The psyche creates consciousness or, better, the self-cognition of the universe.[36] Elsewhere Jung writes that in telepathy an "outer event *occurs simultaneously inside the psyche* and reaches consciousness by the usual pathways of inner perception. However, it is not always possible to determine whether a primary inner process is accompanied by an outer one or whether, conversely, a primary outer event is being reflected in a secondary inner process."[37] Jung is here alluding to the problem of synchronistic phenomena, events in the external world that have the same meaning as endopsychic events.

Before going into the problem of synchronicity in some detail, I would like to illustrate the practical side of this hypothetical mirroring of the psyche by matter. It is alien to our modern rational thinking and ideas, and occurrences that may serve as supporting evidence are generally dismissed as nonsense. That was not the case in primitive magical thinking, which played an important role in our own tradition down into the seventeenth century.[38]

In ancient China the principle of synchronicity was *the*

dominant way of understanding events in the environment and in history. As Liu Guan-ying has explained, it was believed that the behavior and the fate of man, the microcosm, had a clear connection with the macrocosm.[39] It was the emperor who was first of all responsible for harmony in nature and in society. If he or his government deviated from Tao, heaven expressed its anger in the form of unusual phenomena. These were appropriately interpreted, and the ruler then had to atone for his past behavior and change his ways. Sometimes, though, the interpretation of an event was disputed. On one occasion, after an earthquake, a mountain surrounded by a lake rose up out of the earth. The emperor's wife, Wu Tse-t'ien, took this to be a good augury and named the new creation "Happy Mountain." Whereupon a citizen sent the following petition to the palace: "I, your subject, have learned that cold and heat fall into disorder when the breathing of heaven loses its harmony, that an ulcer is formed when the breathing of men becomes disordered, and that heights and hills are raised up when the breathing of earth is confused. Now, your Majesty, a woman is taking the place of the original principle Yang, that is, the throne. This means exchanging the strong for the weak. . . . Your Majesty must cultivate repentance and fear in obedience to the warning from heaven. Otherwise I fear calamity will follow." The empress did not react with repentance but banned her outspoken subject from the court.

Translated into modern psychological language, the subject interprets the emergence of the mountain (*chen,* "mountain," is a masculine principle in Chinese) as a reflection of the fact that the empress was far too masculine in attitude and action (animus-possessed, in Jungian language). The masculine mountain, which towers over the feminine earth-symbol *(kun)* and the equally feminine image of the lake *(tui),* indicated this to him. All older Chinese thinking was oriented in this way to the principle of synchronicity. Whenever psychic and material occurrences with the same meaning coincided, they made visible what was happening in Tao, the meaning of the universe. Events in nature *mirrored* the psychological state of things at the emperor's court and provided information about psychic processes of which the rulers were not sufficiently conscious.[40]

Jung's above-mentioned view—expressed more or less incidentally—that matter might possibly mirror psychic processes *"as continuously as the psyche perceives the physical world,"* but that for the present it "lies beyond the scope of our understanding," was further clarified in one of his later works and in his later letters. The postulate was that a psychic process could be "reconstructed " as being at the same time a physical process. "One could also say that under certain conditions the physical process reflects itself in the psychic, just as the psychic does in the physical."[41] This idea led Jung in one of his later works, "Synchronicity: An Acausal Connecting Principle," to the formation of a new hypothesis, namely, the existence of an "absolute knowledge" in the unconscious.[42] This knowledge is directly connected with the archetypal structure of the unconscious. The archetypes appear to be connected with a knowledge of themselves that is independent of both external causal and conscious influences and at the same time stand in analogous or equivalent, that is, meaningful, relationship to objective external occurrences that have no recognizable or even conceivable causal relationship with them.[43]

What Jung describes as the "absolute knowledge" of the collective unconscious manifests itself, among other ways, in the extraordinary orientation to space and time of unicellular organisms,[44] which is at least partly rooted in an inner activity that functions independently of objective stimuli.[45] Absolute knowledge exists "in a space-time continuum in which space is no longer space, nor time time."[46] Inner and outer events that are parallel can be perceived only if they have some relation to the ego-consciousness of an observer.[47] So far we have been looking at the archetypes as psychic structures or psychic probabilities, but they have another aspect: they seem to be a structure that "also underlies psychophysical equivalences." The deepest and most clearly distinguishable archetypal factor, which forms the basis of psychophysical equivalences, is the archetypal patterns of natural numbers.[48]

All *a priori* factors as well as radioactive decay in the field of physics fall within this category.[49] In respect to *mathematical structure,* the acausal orderedness in matter is *of the same kind* as that in the psyche and each is *continually* reflected in the other.[50]

On the other hand, events like the appearance of the volcano in analogy with the psychic condition of the empress belong to those special cases, occurring only sporadically, in which an observer (in our case, the intelligent subject) is in a position to recognize the meaning of the equivalence of the two events.[51] But the empress, possessed by her power demon, misinterpreted the event—a problem to which we must return.

At first sight, "mirrorings" of psyche and matter that have the same meaning can be empirically established only in the relatively rare and irregularly occurring synchronistic events. It seems likely to me, however, that Jung's observation that the reconstruction of psychic processes in the microphysical world probably occurs as continuously as the psyche perceives the external world is to be understood in the sense that this mirror-relation exists *continuously* in the deeper layers of the unconscious but that we become aware of it only in certain exceptional situations in which synchronistic phenomena become observable. That would mean that in the deepest layer of the unconscious the psyche "knows" itself in the mirror of the cosmic world and that matter "knows" itself in the mirror of the objective psyche, but this "knowledge" is "absolute" in the sense that for our ego it is almost completely consciousness-transcending. Only in those rare moments when we are impressed by synchronistic phenomena do we become conscious of fragments or points of this mirror-relation.[52]

The fourth mirror-relation, that of psyche and matter, is based on the same element as the reflection of light in physics, *namely, an arithmetical order.* Number, as Jung wrote, "is the predestined instrument for creating order, or for apprehending an already existing, but still unknown, regular arrangement or 'orderedness.' *It may well be the most primitive element of order in the human mind,*"[53] that is, the most primitive manifestation of the spontaneous dynamics of the unconscious psyche.[54] In the deepest levels of the objective psyche there is probably an *acausal orderedness with a numerical structure* that is equally valid both for the psyche and for matter. There in the lattice patterns of the numerical field, psyche and matter, we may conjecture, are continuously mirroring each other, whereas in synchronistic events we become aware of this mirror-relation only exceptionally and then as specific happenings pregnant with meaning.[55] Synchronistic events are therefore characterized by the intrusion into our "normal" state of consciousness of a second psychic state, which usually remains below the threshold.[56] In our normal state of consciousness we are seldom aware of the fact that the unconscious psyche makes a substantial contribution to our perception of reality and that we never perceive reality as such. Moreover, we can apparently put our trust in our ideas of reality. If I reach for a box of matches, my hands reach out to the place where the box "is," the match lights, as expected, when the match is struck, and so on. Hence we are scarcely ever aware that even in this normal state of relation to the outer world we are moving in a field of images that deviates considerably from the "reality" that has been demonstrated by physics. That space-time and causality are modalities of apprehending our environment and are dependent upon the structure of our consciousness and perhaps do not even exist objectively is hardly ever conscious to us. These modalities build in us a kind of commonsense reality that makes it possible for us to communicate with one another fairly satisfactorily. When synchronistic phenomena occur, this normal psychic condition is interrupted by another state of mind during which one or more external events occur that are experienced as having a meaning parallel to the subjective state.[57] Using our example of the patient with a fear of outdoor stairways, this would mean that the patient perceives and knows or fears the danger of outdoor stairs as an inner image, although the event corresponding to the inner image has not yet occurred. A causal connection is not thinkable, because an event that has not yet taken place cannot produce effects. Nevertheless, one can hardly deny a meaningful connection between the anxiety-filled images and the external event. We have to understand "simultaneity" in a very broad sense in this example, since there is a distance in time between the beginning of the phobia and the corresponding event. For this reason Jung called such phenomena *synchronistic* and not *synchronous,* because the coincidence is not one in clock time. As long as the accident on the stairway had not yet taken place, the patient's phobia appeared to be a meaningless lack of adaptation and seemed to be a projection; the undeniable fact of his death on an open stairway, however, showed that the phobia was an example of telepathy or, alternatively, a synchronistic event.

The reverse of this case can, however, also appear in practice: that an event which should really be described as a synchronistic phenomenon is falsely interpreted and thus becomes a projection. A man who was on the point of slipping into a psychotic interval, more precisely into an attack of Messianic mania, did in fact attack his wife, who called in a doctor and the police. As they entered the house intending to remove the unfortunate man against his will to a clinic, the lamp in the corridor shattered with a bang, so that suddenly they were all standing in darkness in the midst of the broken glass. The patient saw clearly that what had happened was a supernatural sign: just as the sun grew dark when Christ was crucified, this event was to him a confirmation that he was a savior who was being unjustly arrested. We, on the other hand, would say that he had projected his delusion into the event. Thus the synchronistic phenomenon, in itself meaningful, was instead covered up by a projection. To a person with normal consciousness the "meaning" of the occurrence would be quite different. A lamp, in contrast to the sun, is not a cosmic principle but an appliance invented by man; it usually symbolizes ego-consciousness in dreams and fantasies. The meaning of the unusual event would then more probably be expressed thus: In the moment of intense agitation caused by his imminent arrest the patient's ego-consciousness was shattered and a "mental blackout" resulted. The patient, however, could not grasp this meaning.

When a synchronistic event takes place and *no* observer perceives its meaning, Jung speaks of *synchronous* (rather than of *synchronistic*) events;[58] in our case that would be the shattering of the light of ego-consciousness in the patient and of the lamp in the corridor. Nobody saw the "meaning" at the time; when the man's wife reported the occurrence to me I recognized it. I mention this because it is an example of a type of situation I have often observed in my psychological practice; at the time of dropping into a psychotic interval most patients are in a highly excited, emotional state, and an archetype in the unconscious or, indeed, the whole collective unconscious is violently activated. Hence synchronistic events occur with conspicuous frequency at such times (although they also occur with normal people when an archetype is activated). And at such times the patient will make a false interpretation of synchronistic phenomena in a way designed to confirm his morbid fantasies rather than to correct them. One of the old Church Fathers would have said in such a case that a demon or demons had worked a false miracle with the intention of misleading people with lying phantasmagoria. We have seen that the early Christian Fathers were much preoccupied with the problem of why demons, too, can work miracles and apparently speak the truth. Indeed, in the exorcisms of the six-teenth and seventeenth centuries what the devil spoke through the mouth of the one possessed was carefully writ-ten down, because it was thought that the demon often speaks the truth. Tragically enough, people were sometimes executed who had been accused of witchcraft by a devil speaking through a person in the state of possession.

If we want to grasp the differences between projection and synchronistic events more precisely, we shall have to look more closely at a point as yet mentioned only peripherally, namely, the flow of psychic energy. Jung pointed out that the aforementioned disturbance of adaptation that justifies our labeling subjective images as projections occurs only when the *psychic energy begins to regress,* the energy that before had flown toward the object and activated the psychic idea of it we had made for ourselves. The energy flows back to the subject, either because it is repelled by the object (unrequited love or an enemy unobligingly offering no opportunity for a quarrel) or because it simply flows back spontaneously, with-out any cause that we can discover. The inner self-regulation of the psyche sometimes causes this in order to "charge" another object or to raise the inner potential. In synchronistic events the situation is different. In this case an archetype in the unconscious is "explosively" constellated, which is often the case, as Jung emphasizes, when consciousness sees no way out of some life situation or when it sees no solution to a problem. In projection, therefore, the undisturbed flow of energy inward from ego to Self, that is, *re-flexio* (reflection), is blocked, whereas in the synchronistic event the flow of energy from the Self to the ego and daytime consciousness is thwarted, that is, a "realization" is blocked. In the case of projection the psychic energy recedes to the subject's uncon-scious; in synchronistic phenomena it flows from the uncon-scious toward the ego in order to guide it toward a creative discovery. That is why Jung also called synchronistic events *acts of creation* in time; they indicate that the experiencing subject should realize something which has been constellated in the unconscious, whether this be a new idea or a healing insight.

In Zen Buddhist meditation the master tries to teach his pupil how he can forever keep the inner mirror free of dust. To the extent that he lives in complete accord with the rhythm of psychic energy and with its regulator, the Self, he has no projections anymore; he looks at reality without illusion and more or less continuously reads the meaning of all the synchronistic events happening around him. He lives in the creative current or stream of the Self and has himself, indeed, become a part of this stream.

If he remains, so to speak, always in contact with the succeeding currents of psychic energy that are regulated by the Self, he no longer experiences disturbances of adaptation, no longer projects, in the stricter sense of the word, but remains at the center of the fourfold mirror relation. Obviously, only a person with the most highly reflected concentration can achieve this. We average human beings, by contrast, will hardly be able to avoid the necessity, for the rest of our lives, of again and again recognizing projections for what they are, or at least as mistaken judgments. It seems to me, therefore, to be extremely important to bear constantly in mind, at the very least, the possibility of projection. This would lead to much greater modesty on the part of our ego-consciousness and to a readiness to test our views and feelings thoughtfully and not to waste our psychic energy in pursuing illusionary goals.

Notes

Chapter 1

1. S. Freud, *Totem and Taboo,* pp. 61, 92ff. (For full references, see Bibliography.) For Freud, projection is a defense mechanism through which the neurotic person frees himself of a feeling of conflict (pp. 61–64). He displaces this feeling onto another as the intended object. Freud emphasizes, though, that projection also has a part in all our perceptions of the outer world because our attention is originally directed outward and tends to overlook endopsychic processes (pp. 63–64). The projection of the latter outward occurs under conditions that, as Freud emphasizes, are not yet satisfactorily established (p. 64). On the Freudian concept of projection, cf. the basic work by S. Ali, *La Projection.*

2. Jung, "Concerning the Archetypes, with Special Reference to the Anima Concept," *The Archetypes and the Collective Unconscious,* vol. 9, part 1, of *The Collected Works* (hereafter abbreviated as CW), pars. 121, 142; and *Aion,* CW 9(2), pars. 43ff. (The full title and number of each volume of CW cited are given at first mention; subsequent references appear as CW, followed by the volume number. See Bibliography for full details.)

3. Jung, "Concerning the Archetypes," CW 9(1), pars. 121f.

4. Ibid., pars. 121ff.

5. Jung defines paranoia as "identity of the ego-personality with a complex," as something similar to an extreme state of possession. "Concerning Rebirth," CW 9(1), par. 220.

6. E. H. Ackerknecht, *A Short History of Psychiatry.* See also W. M. Pfeiffer, "Politische Thematik im Wechsel der Zeit," *Transkulturelle Psychiatrie,* pp. 22f.

7. R. Bühlmann, *Die Entwicklung des tiefenpsychologischen Begriffs der Projektion.*

8. Ackerknecht, *Short History of Psychiatry,* pp. 3f.

9. Pfeiffer, *Transkulturelle Psychiatrie,* p. 4.

10. Ibid., p. 140.

11. Jung, "General Aspects of Dream Psychology," *The Structure and Dynamics of the Psyche,* CW 8, par. 507.

12. Ibid., citing L. Lévy-Bruhl, *How Natives Think;* also cited in Jung, "Transformation Symbolism in the Mass," *Psychology and Religion,* CW 11, par. 389.

13. Jung, *Letters,* I, p. 549 (italics added).

14. For example, in hatred against a person previously loved. (My footnote.)

15. Jung, "General Aspects of Dream Psychology," CW 8, par. 507.

16. Ibid., par. 516. See also Jung, "The Visions of Zosimos," *Alchemical Studies,* CW 13, par. 122.

17. Jung, *Psychological Types,* CW 6, "Definitions," par. 783.

18. For the following, see Jung, "The Spirit Mercurius," CW 13, pars. 247ff.

19. In other words, the *a priori* aspect of an outer object still appears to be identical with an unconsciously assumed image.

20. *Chinesische Märchen,* No. 66: "Die Geister der Erhängten" ("The Ghosts of Those Who Were Hanged").

21. Jung, "Concerning the Archetypes," CW 9(1), pars. 121ff, esp. n. 17.

22. Jung, CW 9(2), par. 44.

23. Jung, "The Philosophical Tree," CW 13, par. 437. Jung stresses that it is even dangerous to want to accommodate the whole archetypal content in consciousness; instead, it must be "religiously" taken into account as something autonomous.

24. Jung, CW 9(2), par. 47.

25. *Nordische Märchen II,* No. 7.

26. "Die verwünschte Prinzessin," *Deutsche Märchen seit Grimm I,* pp. 237ff.

27. Jung, CW 6, par. 784.

28. *Not* identification.

29. For example, the judgment that this or that person is "pursuing" or "persecuting" one.

30. Jung, CW 6, pars. 741, 784.

31. For details, see Jung, CW 9(2), pars. 17ff.

32. Jung, "Concerning the Archetypes," CW 9(1), pars. 120ff.

33. E. H. Ackerknecht, "Primitive Medicine and Culture Pattern"; also idem, "Natural Diseases and Rational Treatment in Primitive Medicine." Ackerknecht correctly emphasizes that primitive man often has rational explanations, although they generally are allied to magical-religious ideas. Cf. further Ackerknecht, *Problems of Primitive Medicine.*

34. For this reason the Eskimos do not scold their children, in order not to endanger their health through *Kränkung* ("offense," "wound").

35. L. Honko, *Krankheitsprojektile.* I am grateful to Dr. Alfred Ribi for calling this book to my attention.

36. See also Job 16:12f and 34:6.

37. *Rig-Vida,* 7:46, 1–3. See also *Atharva-Veda,* 11:2, 12; and Honko, *Krankheitsprojektile.*

38. Jung, "Concerning Mandala Symbolism," CW 9(1), pars. 696, 705.

39. Paracelsus once said: "It is possible that my spirit without the help of the body, and through ardent willing alone and without a sword, may pierce and wound another." S. Seligman, *Der böse Blick und Verwandtes,* II, p. 423.

40. *Sutta-Nipata,* trans. by V. Fausböll, p. 146, as cited in Jung, *Symbols of Transformation,* CW 5, par. 437; see also pars. 438ff for further literature. In the Old Testament, too, sexual passion is described as an arrow that bores through a person's liver (Proverbs 7:21ff).

41. Clement of Alexandria, *Stromata,* II, 20, 113, pp. 119ff.

42. Ibid., II, 112 and 114/116. See also Jung, CW 9(2), par. 370, n. 32.

43. This was also investigated with special attention by C. A.

Meier, *Projektion, Ubertragung und Subjekt-Objektrelation,* pp. 302ff.

44. Aetius, I, 7. 16, in H. Diels, *Die Fragmente der Vorsokratiker,* II, p. 102; also Plutarch, *Quaestiones Conviv.,* III, 10. 2, ibid., p. 103, and Cicero, *Epistulae,* XV, 16, ibid., p. 111.

45. Aetius, IV, 10. 4, ibid., p. 111.

46. Jung, "General Aspects of Dream Psychology," CW 8, par. 510.

47. Ibid., par. 519. "But the more subjective and emotional this impression is, the more likely it is that the property will be a projection."

48. Ibid.

49. Ibid.

50. See Meier, *Projektion,* pp. 302ff.

51. Jung, "General Aspects of Dream Psychology," CW 8, par. 521.

52. Ibid. Jung emphasizes in a footnote here (n. 17) that no imago comes "only from outside . . . its specific form is due just as much to the *a priori* disposition, namely the archetype."

53. Relative autonomy of the complex.

54. Jung, "General Aspects of Dream Psychology," CW 8, pars. 521f.

55. Ibid., par. 523. Therefore it is not always a disturbance in adaptation to society that necessitates the withdrawal of a projection; it is also often certain impulses toward development in the individual himself, in other words, the urge toward individuation.

56. "On the Nature of Dreams," CW 8, par. 242.

57. Honko, *Krankheitsprojektile,* pp. 75ff.

58. Cf. here the comprehensive treatment by T. K. Oesterreich, *Die Besessenheit.* Unfortunately, this work was available to me only in the French translation, *Les Possédés.*

59. A. Rodewyk, *Die dämonische Besessenheit in der Sicht des Rituale Romanum,* passim.

60. Honko, *Krankheitsprojektile,* pp. 27ff.

61. Ibid., p. 29.

62. Jung, "Concerning Rebirth," CW 9(1), par. 213.

63. A complex of this kind, which has not yet reached the surface, can be revealed by using the association test.

64. The pseudo–Platonic dialogue, "The Great Alcibiades."

65. On equating lightning with arrows sent by a god, cf. Honko, *Krankheitsprojektile,* p. 66.

66. "To a Passer-by" ("A une Passante," trans. by C. F. MacIntyre), *Flowers of Evil,* p. 118; original in French, p. 337.

67. For examples, cf. E. Benz, *Die Vision,* pp. 23ff. Many such visions, in any case, are visualizations of conscious contents rather than spontaneous products of the unconscious, or they can also possess a core arising from the unconscious, which is then consciously worked over. Jung, CW 9(1), par. 130, n. 19.

68. Benz, *Die Vision,* pp. 23ff.

69. Ibid., p. 31.

70. In G. Zacharias., ed., *Das Böse,* pp. 104ff.

71. "Concerning Possession," ibid., pp. 112ff. In his work *Die dämonische Besessenheit,* Rodewyk does attempt to make a diagnostic distinction between possession by the devil and psychogenic disturbance. His argument, though, is expressed in a vocabulary that is, to say the least, overcautious and not really convincing. What does emerge clearly is that the whole context of ideas of the Catholic faith must, in a case of possession by the devil, be present in the patient. That the conscious cultural context helps to condition the expression even of complexes is well known. Clearer and more detailed is J. de Tonquédec, *Les Maladies nerveuses ou mentales et les manifestations diaboliques.* Here, too, it comes out that the patient must have a Catholic background in order to be able fully to accept its distinctions. Some of the "signs" that the case is one of Satan's influence and not of mental illness seem to me, as an outsider, unconvincing (for example, unusual physical strength in the

one possessed; this has often been observed in schizophrenics). A balanced judgment is offered by W. Kasper and K. Lehmann, *Teufel, Dämonen, Besessenheit. Zur Wirklichkeit des Bösen.*

Chapter 2

1. Unfortunately, I cannot go into the highly significant Islamic hermeneutic here, but refer the reader to H. Corbin's essay, "Herméneutique spirituelle comparée."

2. Cf. Jung, "Archetypes of the Collective Unconscious," CW 9(1), par. 7.

3. Diels, *Die Fragmente der Vorsokratiker,* Fragment 14.

4. Cf. Scholion B of Porphyrios to Ilias, V, 67, cited after W. Capelle, *Die Vorsokratiker,* p. 53. Ancient and medieval hermeneutics will be discussed briefly below; for modern philosophical hermeneutics, see E. Palmer, *Hermeneutics.*

5. Fragment 3, in Capelle, *Die Vorsokratiker,* p. 311.

6. *Phaedrus,* 60 B.

7. Metaphysics, IV, 4 1091 b, in Capelle, *Die Vorsokratiker,* p. 49.

8. Cicero, *De natura deorum,* I, 29. That the images were thought of as concrete is implied in Democritus' assumption that they were "disturbed" by the falling of autumn leaves.

9. Fragment 81, Plutarch, *Symposium,* VIII, 10, 2.

10. Ibid.

11. Fragment 166, Sextus Empiricus, IX, 19.

12. Capelle, *Die Vorsokratiker,* pp. 465, 469, 420.

13. Fragment 168–170.

14. Fragment 121.

15. Cornutus, cap. 31.

16. Epiphanius, *Adversus Haereses,* III, 2.9 = Fragment 538.

17. Fragment 1094 (Plutarch).

18. Fragment 1027.

19. The Gnostic Justinus also interpreted certain Greek myths and related them to images in the Old Testament. Cf. Hippolytus, *Elenchos,* cited in H. Leisegang, *Die Gnosis,* p. 176: "Thus Justinus takes a myth related by Herodotus, raises it to the level of philosophical speculation by means of symbolic interpretation, and produces an intellectual homogeneity between it and the Old Testament." (Justinus interpreted the Hercules myth.)

20. J. Christiansen, *Die Technik der allegorischen Auslegungswissenschaft bei Philo von Alexandrien,* pp. 9f, 13.

21. Ibid., p. 51.

22. Ibid., p. 91.

23. Ibid., pp. 51ff.

24. Ibid., p. 133. In this procedure the synthetic function of the Logos became visible (p. 145). Two principles are at work in allegory, says Christiansen (p. 137); they are connected through the idea.

25. Ephrem the Syrian (d. 373), *Hymni et sermones,* II, col. 770 (*Hymnus de resurrectione Christi,* XXI, 6). Cf. Jung, CW 9(2), par. 216.

26. Ephrem the Syrian, *Hymni et Sermones,* p. 802. Cf. Jung, *Mysterium Coniunctionis,* CW 14, par. 29.

27. C. Andresen, *Logos und Nomos,* esp. pp. 144ff.

28. As Andresen brings out very clearly (ibid., p. 141), the Logos doctrine of Celsus represents "an interesting attempt at a religious interpretation of history by a non-Christian thinker."

29. Ibid., p. 141.

30. Ibid., p. 142.

31. Ibid.

32. Ibid., p. 143.

33. Cited in ibid., p. 145.

34. H. de Lubac, *Exégèse médiévale,* II, p. 373.

35. *Gegen Celsus,* I, 42, trans. by P. Koetschau, Part I, p. 57. What "empty tales" are remains the subject of the polemic. Cf. II, 58; IV, 49 and 50.

36. Cf. ibid., IV, 39; and IV, 49.

37. Cf. ibid., I, 42, 43; and IV, 15.

38. Ibid., III, 46. Cf. also F. H. Kettler, *Der ursprüngliche Sinn der Dogmatik des Origenes.*

39. *Contra Celsum,* I, 46–48.

40. Ibid., I, 48. Cf. also II, 69; III, 35.

41. Ibid., I, 48, esp. *Contra Celsum,* II, 48, where Origen characterizes this second reality as a psychic one. Cf. also Origen's conception of the resurrected body of Christ, ibid., II, 60.

42. Cf. esp., for example, *Contra Celsum,* III, 43, and IV, 17: "Or is it perhaps permitted to the Greeks to relate such things to teachings about the soul and to conceive them in images, while the door to an appropriate explanation remains closed to us, who begin with the idea that divine spirits inhabit pure souls?" Cf. also *Contra Celsum,* IV, 38.

43. Cf. ibid., esp. I, 67, on the greater force of the effectiveness of Jesus' life, ibid., II, 35. Cf. in this connection A. Miura-Stange, *Celsus und Origenes,* esp. pp. 54ff. Jesus is simply the stronger "daimon" when compared with the parallel pagan healer-images (p. 103).

44. *Contra Celsum,* II, 2.

45. R. Lobo, *Samkhya-yoga und spätantiker Geist,* pp. 58f. Cf. also H. Koch, *Pronoia und Paideusis,* passim.

46. De Lubac, *Exégèse médiévale,* II, p. 401.

47. *Contra Celsum,* II, 2 and 3.

48. "What shines dimly in the Old Testament, radiates with light in the New." Cf. de Lubac, *Exégèse médiévale,* I, p. 316, and esp. p. 338.

49. Like the godhead itself, Scripture has a threefold aspect: a literal (Father, as creator of being), a psychic or rational (Son), and a

pneumatic (Holy Ghost). *De Principiis,* IV, 2, 4. Cf. also *In Leviticum homilia,* V, 5.

50. De Lubac, *Exégèse médiévale,* II, pp. 397, 403.

51. Ibid., esp. vol. II.

52. Ibid., I, pp. 119ff.

53. Text of the thirteenth century, quoted in ibid., I, p. 117.

54. Ibid., I, p. 30.

55. There are also other classifications and arrangements of four such great masters. Cf. ibid., I, pp. 26–30. Cf. also E. von Döbschutz, "Vom vierfachen Schriftsinn," pp. 1ff.

56. Jung, CW 6, passim.

57. De Lubac, *Exégèse médiévale,* I, p. 39.

58. *De divisione naturae* 1, IV, c. 5: " . . . *est enim multiplex infinitus divinorum intellectus, si quidem in penna pavonis una eademque mirabiles ac pulchra innumerabilium colorum varietas conspicitur in uno eodemque loco eiusdem pennae portiunculae"* (749C, quoted in de Lubac, *Exégèse médiévale,* I, p. 123).

59. Reuter, *Die Geschichte der religiösen Aufklärung im Mittelalter,* I, pp. 8ff.

60. Ibid., p. 18.

61. Ibid., p. 25.

62. Ibid., p. 52. For John Scotus there are two sources of light: Holy Scripture and the creation. Scripture explains what creation makes manifest. Cf. de Lubac, *Exégèse médiévale,* I, pp. 121f, 125.

63. Reuter, *Geschichte der religiösen Aufklärung,* p. 61, Comment. in *Evangelium secundum Joannem,* Op. 345A. *"Mysteria itaque sunt quae in utroque Testamento et secundum historiam facta sunt et secundum literam narrata, symbola vero, quae solum modo non facta sed quasi facta sola doctrina dicuntur"* (Op. 348A). Reuter writes: "The mysteries break down, *to some extent,* in regard to what is sensory and temporal; only the invisible, spiritual, eternal remains valid" (ibid., p. 279).

64. Ibid., p. 63.

65. Ibid., p. 62. Insights of this kind must, however, be regarded rather as isolated cases before the year 1000, and at that time they had no widespread effect. The tenth century was, generally speaking, a century of barbarism; in France and Italy especially, paganism and superstition flowered; Pope John XII was even quite genuinely thought of as a heathen atheist. Gerbert of Rheims, on the other hand, began to lay the groundwork for free scientific inquiry, which was expected to develop *alongside* faith without encroaching upon it (p. 81).

66. Ibid., p. 211. Cf. also esp. p. 297. Abelard even went so far as to put reason above faith (p. 229).

67. C. Hahn, *Geschichte der Ketzer im Mittelalter*, I, pp. 31ff.

68. Ibid., I, p. 37.

69. Ibid., I, p. 45.

70. Ibid., I, pp. 93f.

71. Ibid., I, p. 157.

72. Ibid., II, pp. 472ff, 477ff.

73. Ibid., II, p. 779: " . . . *quod possit uniri Deo. . . . Item credunt se esse Deum per naturam sine distinctione . . . se esse aeternos et in aeternitate. Item dicunt se omnia creasse et plus creasse quam Deus. Item quod nullo indigent nec Deo nec Deitate.*"

74. Ibid.: "*Item dicunt se credere quod aliquis homo possit transcendere meritum Christi. Item quod homo perfectionis debet esse liber ab omni actione virtutis a Christo, ab eius passione cogitanda, et a Deo.*" The followers of Amalriche von Bena also brought many of the contents of the Credo into the inner psychic sphere: Heaven and Hell, according to them, were nothing other than inner knowledge of God or of sin; the resurrection of the dead meant illumination through the Holy Spirit.

75. Hahn, *Geschichte der Ketzer,* III, pp. 110, 125f.

76. 126 *Expos. in Apoc,* in ibid., III, pp. 84, 264.

77. Ibid., II, p. 139.

78. Ibid., III, pp. 299, 335. Cf. also de Lubac, *Exégèse médiévale,* III, pp. 462ff.

79. Dobschütz, "Vom vierfachen Schriftsinn," p. 13.

80. Cf. the Congress Report, *Exégèse et Herméneutique,* p. 13.

81. Ibid., p. 85.

82. Ibid., p. 287 (Ricoeur).

83. Ibid., p. 21.

84. L. Goppelt, in his *Typos,* attempts to revive the *typos* theory.

Chapter 3

1. Usually thought of as a world-soul, of which individual souls are parts.

2. Cf. Plutarch, Fragment I, quoted in Eusebius, *Praeparation evangelica,* III, 1. Cf. Andresen, *Logos und Nomos,* p. 257.

3. R. B. Onians, *The Origins of European Thought,* pp. 35ff.

4. Ibid., p. 13.

5. Ibid., p. 17. The idea comes from Stout.

6. Ibid., p. 37. Pneumonia was looked upon as love-sickness.

7. D. Mahnke, *Unendliche Sphäre und Allmittelpunkt,* p. 243.

8. Ibid., pp. 239f (not yet in Xenophanes, either).

9. Ibid., p. 240.

10. Ibid., p. 238.

11. Ibid., p. 236.

12. Ibid., pp. 229, 221.

13. Ibid., p. 220.

14. Ibid., p. 217.

15. Ibid., pp. 212ff. Cf. also p. 171.

16. Ibid., p. 214, and esp. p. 193.

17. Ibid., p. 192, citing *De divisione naturae,* I, 12, col. 455a.

18. Ibid., p. 193. Equally, God is also the monad that contains all other numbers in itself in a unity (p. 190).

19. Ibid., p. 164.

20. Ibid., p. 167.

21. Cited in ibid., p. 150.

22. Ibid., pp. 132ff. In contrast to Giordano Bruno, Kepler did not assume an infinitude of worlds but only one sphere which, though unbounded, was finite.

23. Ibid., pp. 135ff.

24. S. Samburski, *Das physikalische Weltbild der Antike,* p. 189. The stoic idea of a *tonos* that holds the world together corresponds, as Samburski points out, to the idea of a standing wave, or stationary oscillation.

25. Newton, Scholium Generale to the 2nd ed. of the *Principia,* quoted in M. Fierz, "Isaac Newton als Mathematiker."

26. M. Fierz, "Über den Ursprung und die Bedeutung der Lehre Isaac Newtons vom absoluten Raum," pp. 62ff, esp. pp. 67, 69ff.

27. Mahnke, *Unendliche Sphäre,* pp. 17/19. Henry Moore shared this view of Newton's. His work forms, among other things, the source for Leibniz, who likewise applies the figure of the sphere to the divine original monad. But all other monads are also, he says, *"des centres qui expriment une circonférence infinie."*

28. Fierz, "Über den Ursprung," pp. 100ff.

29. Ibid., p. 100.

30. A. Wheeler, *Einstein's Vision,* p. 1. Electric charge would then have to be defined as electric lines of force, which are everywhere without singularity but are bound together by the topology of a multiply connected space (pp. 10f).

31. Ibid., pp. 11, 43.

32. For further particulars on "gravitational collapse," cf. ibid., p. 28.

33. Ibid., p. 47.

34. Ibid., p. 63, and p. 95, n. 55. In an excellent article, Mary Gammon has attempted to relate the Einsteinian space-model to the Jungian *unus mundus* concept. The essential points of this at-

tempt are to be found in Gammon, "Window into Eternity: Archetype and Relativity," pp. 11ff.

35. Mahnke, *Unendliche Sphäre,* p. 12.

36. Ibid., pp. 8f.

37. Ibid., p. 3.

38. Cf. aso G. Holten, "Über die Hypothesen, welche den Naturwissenschaften zugrunde liegen," passim.

39. CW 9(1), par. 116.

40. Samburski, *Das physikalische Weltbild,* p. 228 (Leucippus). But the uncertainty relation, too, had long been suspected. Epicurus says that atoms are possessed of free will (p. 238). Cf. also p. 219, where it is recorded that the divine *pneuma* in Stoic philosophy anticipates the idea of the causal nexus.

41. Descartes, *Meditationes,* VI, and *Principia,* II, 36. 7. Cf. H. Stock, *The Method of Descartes in Natural Sciences,* pp. 11–15.

42. M.-L. von Franz, "The Dream of Descartes," p. 84, quoting Descartes, *Principia,* II, 37.

43. Ibid.

44. F. Capra, *The Tao of Physics,* pp. 274ff. Capra reckons with only three forms and includes singularities under the causality principle, which does not seem admissible to me, for which reason I count them a fourth. Another possibility is that the electromagnetic reactions are the fourth.

45. G. Holton, "The Roots of Complementarity," pp. 70ff.

46. Ibid., p. 73 (from "The Quantum Postulate and the Recent Development of Atomic Theory," in Niels Bohr, *Atomic Theory and the Description of Nature,* pp. 90f).

47. W. Pauli, "The Influence of Archetypal Ideas on the Scientific Theories of Kepler," p. 152 (italics added).

48. R. Carnap, *Einführung in die Philosophie der Naturwissenschaft,* p. 174.

49. Ibid., p. 175.

50. Ibid., pp. 177ff, 290.

51. *Physik und Philosophie,* pp. 52ff.

52. Ibid., p. 55.

53. Ibid., p. 56.

54. Ibid., p. 150.

55. Ibid., p. 159.

56. Ibid. Max Jammer ends his paper on the history of the concept of mass in physics *(in Der Begriff der Masse in der Physik)* with the following words: "Although it [the concept of mass] is of decisive importance for all branches of physics and represents an indispensable conceptual tool of scientific thinking, it seems to elude every attempt at a completely satisfactory explanation and a logical as well as scientifically unobjectionable definition" (p. 241).

57. M.-L. von Franz, *Number and Time,* passim.

58. On this and what follows, cf. Jung, "On Psychic Energy, CW 8, pars. 114ff.

59. For examples and references to the literature, cf. ibid., pars. 115ff.

60. Cf. ibid., par. 117.

61. Ibid., par. 126, citing A. O. Lovejoy, "The Fundamental Concept of the Primitive Philosophy."

62. Ibid., par. 127.

63. Ibid. Cf. Jung, "On the Psychology of the Unconscious," *Two Essays on Analytical Psychology,* CW 7, pars. 108f.

64. Capelle, *Die Vorsokratiker,* p. 133 (22 Fragment 76).

65. Ibid., p. 139 (45 Fragment 67).

66. Ibid., p. 142 (58 Fragment 30).

67. On the further development of this concept of energy, down to the most recent times, cf. C. G. Gillespie, *The Edge of Objectivity,* chaps. 6ff.

68. Samburski, *Das Physikalische Weltbild,* p. 219.

69. Ibid., pp. 219, 220, 225.

70. As Fierz has shown ("Über den Ursprung," pp. 74ff, 82ff), this idea of Newton's goes back to certain Italian Renaissance philosophers, especially Francesco Patrizzi (1529–1593), who postulated one absolute light-filled space, created by God, in which all motion took place (though still imagined as localized), and Giordano Bruno (1548–1600), who first postulated infinite space in the sense of contemporary physics; this infinite space contains the universes animated by God.

71. Ibid., pp. 89–91.

72. For further examples, see Jung, *Psychology and Alchemy,* CW 12, par. 473; and M.-L. von Franz, *Aurora Consurgens.*

73. Jung, CW 12, pp. 323ff.

74. Jung, CW 9(1), par. 68; and Gillespie, *Edge of Objectivity,* chap. 6.

75. *Das physikalische Weltbild,* p. 405.

76. Ibid., p. 619 (italics added).

77. R. Anschütz, *August Kekulé,* I, p. 625, and II, pp. 941f; see also I, p. 611.

78. Cited in ibid., II, pp. 941f.

79. Cited in ibid. The hypothesis concerned the ringlike structure of benzene.

80. Ibid., pp. 942f.

81. Cf. Jung, *Letters,* I, p. 412: Every explanation is, in the last analysis, projection.

82. CW 11, par. 279.

83. Cf. CW 13, par. 88.

84. Jung, CW 12, par. 346.

85. Ibid.

86. Ibid. (italics added).

87. Ibid., par. 380.

88. Ibid., par. 394.

89. Ibid., par. 394 (italics added). Cf. the contemporary work by R. Ruyer, *La Gnose de Princeton,* passim.

90. Cf. Capra, *Tao of Physics,* passim.

91. Cf. von Franz, *Number and Time.*

92. Max Jammer, in *Der Begriff der Masse in der Physik* and *Concepts of Space,* has described very well how baffling, even for modern physicists, concepts like space-time and mass, as well as matter, can be.

93. Jung, CW 9(1), pars. 151ff.

94. Jung, CW 11, par. 375.

Chapter 4

1. Jung, CW 9(1), par. 54.

2. Ibid., par. 21.

3. Ibid., par. 8.

4. Jung, *Letters,* I, pp. 199f.

5. G. Isler, *Die Sennenpuppe,* passim.

6. Jung, CW 11, par. 944.

7. The word comes, as we know, from the Greek *symballein,* "to lump together," "to join or connect or unite," and served at first as a sign of recognition. When guests separated from one another, a ring or a potsherd was broken in two, so that whoever was in possession of the one "symbol" could, by joining it to the other, show that he was an acquaintance of the other "guest."

8. The unconscious is not an epiphenomenon of consciousness; it is a *reality* of psychic dynamic and a carrier of meaning that cannot be reduced to anything else. Cf. Jung, CW 5, par. 670, and CW 9(1), pars. 7, 8.

9. Jung, *Letters,* I, p. 59. An idol, on the other hand, is a petrified symbol that causes "an impoverishment of consciousness" (pp. 59f).

10. Jung, CW 6, par. 816.

11. Ibid., par. 819.

12. Cf. ibid., pars. 823-824.

13. Ibid., par. 827.

14. Ibid., par. 828.

15. CW 11, par. 945.

16. Cf. Jung, *Letters,* I, pp. 393ff.

17. Ibid., p. 58.

18. Ibid., p. 395.

19. Ibid.

20. A. Jaffé, "Synchronizaität und Kausalität," pp. 1ff.

21. Which does not answer the question of what "light in itself" may be, any more than do those experiments that appear to show that light consists of particles.

22. CW 9(1), par. 155.

23. This presupposes that the method of observing psychic phenomena in general is based on the energetic principle, as it was postulated by Jung. Cf. Jung, "On Psychic Energy," CW 8, passim.

24. E. Benz, *Neue Religionen,* p. 168. Benz stresses that the development of religions occurs in unpredictable "spurts."

25. A method created by Jung for encountering inner fantasy images.

26. For more detail, cf. Jung, "On the Nature of the Psyche," CW 8, pars. 384 ff.

27. Ibid., pars. 398ff.

28. Ibid., par. 403.

29. Ibid., par. 405.

30. Ibid., par. 406.

31. One thinks of the conversion of St. Augustine from instinctuality to spirit. On the other hand, people with unusually high spiritual aspirations often become victims of their instincts unawares. Cf. also ibid., par. 414.

32. Jung, "Synchronicity: An Acausal Connecting Principle," CW 8, par. 855.

33. Jung, CW 9(2), par. 257.

34. Jung, "Synchronicity," CW 8, par. 840; cf. also CW 14, par. 661.

35. Latent, because it does not occur with regularity but only in its sporadic actualization in the form of synchronistic phenomena.

36. CW 12, par. 411.

37. Ibid., n. 29.

Chapter 5

1. Jung, CW 9(2), par. 62.

2. Jung, Letters, II, p. 276: " 'Devil' is a very apt name for certain autonomous powers in the structure of the human psyche. As such the devil seems to me to be a very real figure."

3. "The Magic Steed," Märchen aus Turkestan und Tibet, p. 126.

4. This is also true in the case of a negative mother-complex in a man or a woman.

5. Märchen aus Siberien, p. 81.

6. M.-L. von Franz, "Das Problem des Bösen im Märchen," pp. 91ff.

7. A. Friedrich and G. Buddruss, trans. Shamanengeschichten aus Sibirien, pp. 20, 26, 97.

8. Ibid., pp. 50f. For example, nine shaman maidens live in the heavens and their spirits spread madness among human beings.

9. Cf. the illustrations in H. Mode, Fabulous Beasts and Demons, passim.

10. Indianermärchen aus Südamerika, pp. 26ff.

11. Ibid., "Der Mond," pp. 232ff.

12. K. Preisendanz, Papyri Graecae magicae, I, pp. 83f, 119; and G. Soury, La Démonologie de Plutarque (Plutarch, De Deisideimonia), p. 47. Concerning the effects of the spirits of the dead on the living, cf. Jung, Letters, I, pp. 256f.

13. Or perhaps the deceased himself. On this, more detail below.

14. Jung, "The Psychological Foundations of Belief in Spirits," CW 8, par. 598.

15. Ibid., par. 600, n. 15. Cf. also Jung, *Letters,* I, p. 100.

16. Jung, "Psychological Foundations," CW 8, par. 597. Cf. also Jung, *Letters,* I, pp. 341f.

17. Jung, *Letters,* I, p. 344.

18. Ibid., p. 336 (italics added).

19. Cf. the tendency to mislead man into the idea that *machen* (to make, to perform) equals *Macht* (power). Cf. ibid., p. 352.

20. Ibid., II, pp. 81f.

21. Ibid., p. 82.

22. Ibid., pp. 82f.

23. Ibid., p. 81.

24. For examples, cf. Mode, *Fabulous Beasts.*

25. Cf. R. C. Thompson, *The Devils and Evil Spirits in Babylonia,* passim.

26. Cf. C. Colpe, "Dämonen," in *Reallexikon für Antike und Christentum.*

27. Ibid.

28. Plato, *Symposium,* 202e (Joyce translation, p. 555). Cf. F. Regen, *Apuleius philosophus Platonicus,* pp. 9f.

29. Plato, *Symposium,* 202e–203a. In Plato's *Epinomis,* whose authenticity is questioned, the demons are further subdivided: their home is the elements; there are visible and invisible demons, heavenly gods, gods of the ether, water demons, water demigods, and so on.

30. *De Deo Socratis,* cap. 12. Excerpted and translated from Apuleius, *Opuscules philosophiques et fragments,* I, pp. 31ff.

31. Cf. cap. 15, ibid., pp. 34ff.

32. Soury, *La Démonologie,* pp. 23–26.

33. Ibid., p. 30. Nymphs, for example, live for 9,720 years, according to Hesiod. Tree-nymphs live as long as their trees.

34. Ibid., pp. 43f.

35. Ibid., p. 49.

36. *De Divinatione*, 2. 58, 119.

37. Regen, *Apuleius*, pp. 16ff.

38. Ibid., p. 18.

39. There are naturally a number of variants; cf. Pseudo-Plutarch, *De fato*, 9, 572f, and Nemesios, *De natura hominum*, 44, 167.

40. They correspond to the spirits that are the "lords of nature" among the Yakut.

41. H. Wey, "Die Funktionen der bösen Geister bei den griechischen Apologeten des zweiten Jahrhunderts nach Christus," pp. 270–272.

42. Jung, "Psychological Aspects of the Mother Archetype," CW 9 (1), par. 189.

43. Wey, "Funktionen der bösen Geister," pp. 6ff.

44. Ibid., p. 10.

45. Ibid., p. 20.

46. Ibid., p. 28. Expressed in modern language, demons produce projections.

47. Jung, *Memories, Dreams, Reflections*, pp. 327f.

48. "Answer to Job," CW 11, par. 669.

49. Cf. Jung, *Letters*, I, pp. 336, 355–356, concerning the meaning of the *hieros gamos*.

50. Wey, "Funktionen der bösen Geister," pp. 35ff.

51. Ibid., pp. 41ff.

52. Ibid., pp. 47ff. Athenagoras's theory concerning angels recalls, in a number of points, Pseudo-Plutarch, *De fato*, 9, and Nemisios, *De natura hominis*, 44, 167.

53. *Metamelesas;* cf. ibid., p. 53.

54. Ibid., p. 58.

55. Ibid., pp. 63, 65.

56. Ibid., pp. 71ff.

57. Ibid., p. 72.

58. Ibid., pp. 73ff.

59. Ibid., pp. 97ff.

60. Ibid., pp. 109ff. The gods of the heathens were called *daimonia* (p. 121).

61. Ibid., p. 163.

62. Ibid., p. 165. For Justin Martyr the passion on the cross is "the greatest symbol of the fish and its (Christ's) *arche*."

63. Ibid., p. 221.

64. C. Ernst, *Teufelsaustreibungen*.

65. The same attitude comes out in Wunneberg's judgment of the girl exorcised by Father Jussel.

66. E. Niderberger, *Sagen, Märchen und Gebräuche aus Unterwalden*.

67. Officially, according to the *Rituale Romanum*, the innocent can also sometimes be possessed. Cf. Rodewyk, *Die dämonische Besessenheit*, p. 130. In this case their suffering serves the "glorification of God's power" (p. 131). It can also be caused by black magic or the magic of others used for the purpose of damaging or hurting; or the condition can be voluntarily taken on as expiation or as a penitential exercise (p. 135). God can give his consent to a case of possession; the possessed stand under his very special protection (p. 138).

68. Jung, "Concerning the Archetypes, with Special Reference to the Anima Concept," CW 9(1), par. 142.

69. Jung, *Letters*, I, pp. 82f, 108f.

70. CW 9(2), par. 19.

71. Ibid., pars. 209ff.

72. The doctrine of the fall.

73. In other words, an inflation.

74. CW 9(2), par. 114.

75. Ibid., pars. 209f. Cf. the fact that devils or demons often hide

behind mandala drawings. Jung, "Concerning Mandala Symbolism," CW 9(1), par. 689: "This shadow aspect of the mandala represented the disorderly, disruptive tendencies, the 'chaos' that hides behind the self and bursts out in a dangerous way as soon as the individuation process comes to a standstill or when the self is not realized and so remains unconscious."

76. Ibid., par. 209.

77. Ibid.

78. Ibid., p. 141. On the demonic nature of religions and ideologies, cf. also Jung, *Letters,* I, pp. 158f.

79. Jung, "The Undiscovered Self (Present and Future)," *Civilization in Transition,* CW 10, pp. 247ff.

80. Cf. Jung, *Letters,* II, pp. 163ff, esp. p. 168.

Chapter 6

1. Cf. esp. Jung, CW 9(2), par. 20.

2. Cf. the outstanding collection of earlier articles on The Metamorphoses in G. Binder and R. Merkelbach, eds., *Amor and Psyche.*

3. K. Kerényi, *Die griechisch-orientalische Romanliteratur in religionsgeschichtlicher Beleuchtung;* and in greater detail, R. Merkelbach, *Roman und Mysterium in der Antike.* B. Lavagnini offers an appraisal of the *literary* unity of the book in *Il significato e il valore del romanzo di Apuleo.*

4. I have dealt with this in more detail in my book *The Golden Ass of Apuleius.*

5. For example, in the Risus episode.

6. Cf. J. O. Swahn, *The Tale of Cupid and Psyche.*

7. For details, cf. Merkelbach, *Roman und Mysterium,* pp. 8ff, 47.

8. Cf. Jung, CW 9(2), pars. 24ff.

9. "Winged" equals "psychic." In Greek, butterfly, as we know, is one of the meanings of "psyche."

10. Merkelbach, *Roman und Mysterium,* pp. 47, 78.

11. It has been observed that the cosmetic is connected with the waters of Lethe in the Beyond (ibid., pp. 50f), but that does not explain why it is specifically a cosmetic preparation. What has beauty exactly to do with Lethe?

12. He has this in common with the style of the day, but this too originates in a (neurotic) attitude toward life that he also shares.

13. She equates her husband with Liber, that is, Dionysos, so that she herself thereby becomes Semele or Ariadne, partner in the divine marriage.

14. Heraclitus, cited in Capelle, *Die Vorsokratiker,* p. 133 (21 Fragment 62).

15. Apuleius, *The Metamorphoses,* translated by Robert Graves as *The Transformations of Lucius, Otherwise Known as The Golden Ass,* pp. 226–227.

16. Plutarch, *Über Isis und Osiris.*

17. Merkelbach, *Roman und Mysterium,* pp. 11ff, 67f, and passim.

18. In an appendix Neumann briefly touches on Apuleius' anima-problem but does not go into it in any detail.

19. Preisendanz, *Papyri,* I, p. 129.

20. Jung, CW 9(2), par. 28.

21. One thinks of stories of the Bluebeard type.

22. For an interpretation of the passion of Perpetua, cf. my work "Die *Passio Perpetuae.*"

23. Just as, in the case of Apuleius, Isis appears as anima but elsewhere can also be understood as "Isis of women."

24. Von Franz, "Die *Passio Perpetuae.*"

25. Ibid., p. 403

26. Ibid., pp. 433f.

27. *"De agricultura,"* 50, *Philonis Opera,* II, p. 105.

28. *"Excerpta ex Theodoto,"* c. 21, in J. P. Migne, ed., *Patrologia cursus completus, P. G.,* IX, col. 668.

29. Further in von Franz, "Die *Passio Perpetuae.*"

30. *Metamorphosen*, VIII, 27. The passage in Graves's version, p. 201, is too poorly translated.

31. Jung, CW 9(2), pars. 319f.

32. As Jung put it, in *Letters*, I, p. 73.

Chapter 7

1. H. Jacobsohn, "The Dialogue of a World-Weary Man with His Ba," pp. 5ff.

2. Nitzsche, *The Genius Figure in Antiquity and the Middle Ages*, chap. 1.

3. *Epistolae*, 2, 2, 187ff. ". . . *natal comes qui temperat astrum, naturae deus humanae, mortalis in unumquodque caput, vultu mutabilis, albus et ater.*"

4. The phallic form may have originated in the Etruscan god Mutinus Titinus.

5. Nitzsche, *Genius Figure*, p. 13.

6. The Romans translated *daimonion* as "genius."

7. Nitzsche, *Genius Figure*, pp. 31ff.

8. Some daimons have, as we know, a subtle body.

9. Nitzsche, *Genius Figure*, pp. 36ff. Cf. also E. Rohde, *Psyche*, for more general treatment.

10. Cf. Horace, *Deus mortalis*, etc.

11. Nitzsche, *Genius Figure*, pp. 32f.

12. Cited in ibid., pp. 23ff.

13. Cf. Valerius Soranus, chap. 133 (quoted by Augustine); cf. Nitzsche, *Genius Figure*, p. 25.

14. *De Deo Socratis*, chap. 16.

15. With the exception, naturally, of Apuleius' great teacher, Plutarch, who followed exactly the same line.

16. Certain magic papyri are an exception. Cf. Preisendanz, *Papyri*, II (Prayer to Christ).

17. For example, the case of Lactantius; cf. Nitzsche, *Genius Figure*, pp. 38f.

18. R. Reitzenstein, *Poimandres*.

19. Ibid., pp. 4–6.

20. I prefer the translation "Truth" to that of "Power" because it is less ambiguous. Truth *is* the kingdom of the Beyond and its "power."

21. Hermes Trismegistus, *Poimandres*, in *Corpus Hermeticum*, I, pp. 7ff, 11.

22. Ibid., I, pp. 50f.

23. Ibid., I, pp. 58f.

24. Tractate X, ibid., I, pp. 116f. The human psyche is *doisi-daimonia* when it is God-fearing.

25. Tractate X, ibid., I, pp. 124f. Here it is a case, as Nock remarks (p. 139), of a mixture of the idea of the Nous–daimon and of the Platonic Nous (as spiritual component of the human psyche). Cf. also p. 195.

26. Tractate XI, ibid., I, pp. 156f.

27. Ibid., I, p. 166.

28. Ibid., II, pp. 201f.

29. Tractate XI, ibid., II, pp. 204, 206.

30. Ibid., IV, pp. 118–121. That Hermes himself is this son of God. Cf. Reitzenstein, *Poimandres*, p. 104, n. 1. Cf. also Jung, CW 12, pars. 456ff.

31. Cited in Preisendanz, *Papyri*, II, pp. 122ff (ellipses added). Reitzenstein adduces relevant Egyptian parallels (*Poimandres*, pp. 19–21), as does Preisendanz (*Papyri*, II, p. 146).

32. The subterranean gods.

33. Recollection, memory.

34. Preisendanz, *Papyri*, I, p. 195. Cf. also the prayer to the same god, as Nous, quoted in Jung, CW 9(2), p. 184.

35. Preisendanz, *Papyri*, I, p. 111. Cf. also II, pp. 45ff: "Come to me, Hermes, as children into the womb of women. . . . Hear me,

Hermes, patron of the art of healing. . . . Protect me everywhere as long as I live. . . . For thou art I and I am thou, thy name is mine and mine is thine. *For I am thy image."*

36. Cf. also ibid., I, p. 238.

37. Cf. Jung's commentary on this in CW 9(2), pars. 314–323.

38. Cf. P. de Labriolle, *La Crise Montaniste;* and M. Y. van Beek, *Passio Sanctarum Perpetuae et Felicitatis.*

39. Jung, CW 9(2), par. 42.

40. A name of the goddess of the Eleusinian mysteries symbolizing strength.

41. Preisendanz, *Papyri,* I, pp. 141 ff. Cf. the evocation, "Subterranean Hermes and Subterranean Hecate," ibid., I, p. 121.

42. Ibid., I, p. 119.

43. Reitzenstein, *Die hellenistischen Mysterienreligionen,* p. 15.

44. In this text this is *physis.*

45. Preisendanz, *Papyri,* I, p. 167.

46. Ibid., I, p. 159.

47. Moon; cf. also ibid., I, p. 179.

48. Ibid., I, p. 161.

49. "Answer to Job," CW 11, par. 620.

50. H. Corbin, *Avicenne et le récit visionnaire,* I, pp. 19ff.

51. Ibid., p. 23 and esp. p. 25. It is the heavenly counterpart of the soul.

52. Ibid., p. 25.

53. *Intellectus activus.*

54. Corbin, *Avicenne,* p. 77, and the *natura perfecta,* p. 106.

55. Ibid., p. 12.

56. Ibid., p. 90.

57. Ibid., p. 106.

58. Ibid., p. 107.

59. Ibid., pp. 107f. Many saw the resurrected one there—an inde-

scribable light—and when those who looked on were later asked, some saw a child, some a youth, and still others an old man. Similarly, the Hermetic visionary, too, can see only *that* which is in him. Even at that time, therefore, there was a suspicion that it had to do with projection!

60. Ibid., I, p. 109. Cf. also the report of the first encounter of Hayg ibn Ygazan with the wise man, the "living one, son of the waking one," in Corbin, *Avicenne,* I, pp. 21f, and II (the whole report with commentary is given in vol. II).

61. Ibid., II, p. 75, n. 50. The teacher says: "Whenever you are alone and become a monad, I am your companion."

62. Jung, *Memories, Dreams, Reflections,* p. 220: "Man always has some mental reservation, even in the face of divine decrees."

63. Change of mind. In *The Shepherd of Hermes,* mandata 12.6.1, quoted in Reitzenstein, *Poimandres,* p. 13, n. 2.

64. Jung, *Memories,* pp. 323ff.

Chapter 8

1. Jung even equates the withdrawal of projections with individuation. Cf. CW 9(1), pars. 82ff.

2. "The Visions of Zosimos," CW 13, par. 111; cf. also "Transformation Symbolism in the Mass," CW 11, pars. 434ff.

3. The Lutheran translation of *metanoia* as "repentance" is no longer understandable to most people in its deeper meaning.

4. *I Ching,* II, chap. 24, pp. 145ff (italics added). The so-called *Acta Vercellenses* interprets the cross-beam of the cross symbol as "the return and change of meaning of a man's life." Cf. also Jung, "Transformation Symbolism in the Mass," CW 11, pars. 432ff.

5. In professional language, her native animi had won the upper hand.

6. On the personified aspect of the collective unconscious, cf. Jung, *Memories,* pp. 68ff, 87f.

7. Quoted by Jung, CW 14, par. 684.

8. Ibid., par. 685. The eye of self-knowledge is, so to speak, a counter-magic to the "evil eye," which operates in the same way as disease-projectiles (Seligmann, *Der böse Blick*).

9. Jung, "On the Nature of the Psyche," CW 8, par. 390.

10. Ibid., pars. 389 and 394, n. 68. Cf. also Jung, "Concerning Mandala Symbolism," CW 9(1), par. 704. Here the eye has the meaning of the Self.

11. "A Study in the Process of Individuation," CW 9(1), par. 593.

12. Jung, "On the Nature of the Psyche," CW 8, par. 394.

13. W. Deonna, *Le Symbolisme de l'oeil*, pp. 46ff.

14. Ibid., p. 47, n. 3.

15. Jung, "Concerning Mandala Symbolism," CW 9(1), par. 704.

16. Deonna, *Le Symbolisme de l'oeil*, p. 49.

17. Ibid., p. 51. Aeschylus *(Eumenides)* says that while we sleep the whole soul is lighted up by eyes; with these eyes it can see everything withheld from its sight during the day. A Hermetic philosopher acknowledges: "The body's sleep produced that illumination of the soul; my closed eyes saw the truth" (quoted in ibid., p. 51).

18. "La Conscience," from Henri Sens in *Chrestomathie française du XIX siècle,* pp. 99f (from *La Légende des siècles,* pp. 73, 83).

19. "The eye was in the grave and looked at Cain." On conscience as a manifestation of the Self (not of the superego), cf. Jung, "A Psychological View of Conscience," CW 10, pars. 825–827.

20. Deonna, *Le Symbolisme de l'oeil.*

21. Seligmann, *Der böse Blick,* II, passim.

22. A practical example in Jung, *Man and His Symbols:* An old patient who was too active dreamed that at the head of a band of riders he galloped over a grave. The unconscious shows here to what extent he behaves too youthfully. A young man who was too timid had the same dream. In his case it would be better to tell him that the unconscious was encouraging him to a more active attitude. In neither case, however, can we say that the

unconscious is "willing" anything—it simply *mirrors* what is constellated.

23. "Transformation Symbolism in the Mass," CW 11, par. 415.

24. Ibid., pars. 419, 427.

25. Jung, "Concerning Mandala Symbolism," CW 9(1), par. 682: " . . . in the individuation process what were originally projections 'stream' back 'inside' and are integrated into the personality again." Cf. also Jung, "Transformation Symbolism in the Mass," CW 11, pars. 398–402.

26. Jung, "Transformation Symbolism in the Mass," CW 11, par. 400.

27. Ibid., par. 400.

28. Ibid.

29. Cf. von Franz, "Dream of Descartes," p. 122, n. 257.

30. On this remythologizing of older thought in the Gnosis, cf. Leisegang, *Die Gnosis,* pp. 12ff.

31. That is a projection represented from the side of the unconscious.

32. Leisegang, *Die Gnosis,* pp. 183, 186ff (from Epiphanius, *Panarium,* chaps. 25–26).

33. Ibid., pp. 186, 189ff ("Gospel of Eve").

34. And at the same time, the Barbelo. Epiphanius, *Panarium,* XXVI, 3, from James, *The Apocryphal New Testament,* p. 12, cited in Jung, CW 14, par. 6, n. 26 (italics added).

35. Cf. Hermes Trismegistus, *Poimandres,* Tractate I-II, pp. 12ff. (Tractate I, chap. 14ff.)

36. For detail, see Jung, CW 12, pars. 456ff; and Reitzenstein, *Poimandres,* pp. 103ff.

37. H.-C. Puech, "Der Begriff der Erlösung im Manichäismus," esp. pp. 285ff.

38. Leisegang, *Die Gnosis,* pp. 151ff (from Hippolytus, *Elenchos,* V, 22).

39. Jung, "Transformation Symbolism in the Mass," CW 11, pars. 399, 400f.

40. Ibid., pars. 399–401.

41. Ibid., par. 444.

42. *In Librum Regnorum Homiliae* (Migne, *P. G.,* vols. 12, 13), cited by Jung, CW 14, par. 6, n. 26.

43. Cf. Jung, *Letters,* I, p. 395.

44. *The Upanishads,* trans. F. Max Müller, p. 182.

45. CW 16, pars. 437ff.

46. Cited in Jung, CW 9(2), pars. 288ff.

47. Jung, *Memories,* p. 297.

48. Jung, *Letters,* I, p. 298.

49. This is why group therapy and "self-experience" groups are so harmful. Composed artificially, they obscure the working of the Self in the individual and encourage in its place shameless projections, aggressions, egotism, and narcissistic self-mirroring.

50. E. Jung, and M.-L. von Franz, *The Grail Legend,* pp. 162f.

51. Ibid., p. 167.

Chapter 9

1. On the subject of consciousness conceived as a field, cf. Olde-meyer, "Überlegungen zum phänomenologisch-philoso-phischen und kybernetischen Bewusstseinsbegriff," pp. 83ff, and the literature cited there.

2. Gilbert Durand in *Le Symbole* makes the same surmise.

3. Jung, "On the Nature of the Psyche," CW 8, pars. 411f. Many modern people hide eggs at Easter-time "because people have always done it," without knowing what this means symboli-cally. The same is true of lighted trees at Christmas.

4. R. Gould, *Yiwara, Foragers of the Australian Desert,* pp. 199ff.

5. For further examples of the use of pieces of glass as defense against the evil eye and against evil spirits and persons, see Seligmann, *Der böse Blick,* II, pp. 41f.

6. Cf. Jung, "Archetypes of the Collective Unconscious," CW 9(1), par. 69: "Ultimately they [important ideas] are all founded

on primordial archetypal forms whose concreteness dates from a time when consciousness did not *think,* but only *perceived.* 'Thoughts' were objects of inner perception, not thought at all, but sensed as external phenomena—seen or heard, so to speak. . . . Thinking of this kind precedes ego-consciousness."

7. For example, when silver is finely pulverized, it no longer reflects but is black (that is, light-absorbent).

8. For the same reason it can also conduct electricity, which is why good reflectors are often good electric conductors. There are also crystalline formations in which the electrons are not free but are only loosely bound. Such materials are transparent to light but are electric insulators (for example, glass). I am grateful to Art Funkhouser for this information.

9. M. Eliade, *Shamanism,* pp. 49f, 153–154.

10. Cf. Jung, "The Visions of Zosimos," CW 13, par. 132.

11. Cf. Seligmann, *Der böse Blick,* II, pp. 176–178.

12. Ibid., II, pp. 310ff.

13. Cf. Jung, "Archetypes of the Collective Unconscious," CW 9(1), pars. 33f.

14. M. Ninck, *Die Bedeutung des Wassers im Kult und Leben der Alten,* p. 47.

15. Ibid., pp. 54f.

16. Ibid., citing Pausanius, 7th book, chap. 21, 12.

17. Ibid., pp. 71ff.

18. Ibid., p. 79.

19. Ibid., pp. 81ff.

20. Ibid., p. 136.

21. Cf. Jung, "Archetypes of the Collective Unconscious," CW 9(1), pars. 33ff.

22. Cf. Jung, *Letters,* I, p. 87.

23. Cf. Jung, "General Aspects of Dream Psychology," CW 10, par. 826, pars. 443f.

24. CW 10, par. 826.

25. Jung, *Memories,* p. 323.

26. Ibid., p. 324, n. 6; cf. also Jung, *Letters,* I, pp. 325ff.

27. This aspect of projection corresponds rather to the alchemistic concept of *proiectio,* which, as Fabricus shows, corresponds to a double perception by the subject of his Self after leaving his usual state of consciousness and his own bodily identity ("The Symbol of the Self in the Alchemical 'Proiectio,' " pp. 47ff).

28. In E. Edinger's excellent book *Ego and Archetype,* the casuistic handling of this is impressive, and I would refer the reader to this book.

29. W. Pauli, "The Influence of Archetypal Ideas on the Scientific Theories of Kepler," pp. 208ff.

30. E. Wigner, *Symmetries and Reflections,* pp. 222f.

31. Cf. Jung, "Transformation Symbolism in the Mass," CW 11, par. 442.

32. Leibniz on the soul as monad; cited in Jung, "Synchronicity," CW 8, par. 937.

33. Jung, *Letters,* I, p. 143.

34. Cited in Jung, "Synchronicity," CW 8, par. 937.

35. Jung, "Analytical Psychology and Education," *The Development of Personality,* CW 17, par. 164 (italics added).

36. Cf. ibid., par. 165. Cf. also Jung, *Letters,* I, pp. 255ff.

37. *Letters,* II, p. 539. See also Jung, CW 14, par. 662.

38. Cf. the summary of the doctrines of *correspondentia* or of the sympathy of all things and preestablished harmony in Leibniz and Schopenhauer, in Jung, "Synchronicity," CW 8, pars. 937ff, 828ff.

39. "Die ungewöhnlichen Naturerscheinungen in den T'ang Annalen und ihre Deutung," pp. 32ff.

40. In the West the astrologers of another day proceeded from premises similar to those of Chinese natural philosophy. The constellations of the stars in the heavens reflected psychic components of the fate of human beings. Jung therefore concluded that the starry heaven is in fact the open book of cosmic projec-

tions, of mirrored mythologems, that is, of the archetypes. The "truth" of astrological statements is probably to be explained on the basis of the principle of synchronicity, which, however, presupposes a qualitative aspect of time. ("On the Nature of the Psyche," CW 8, par. 392.)

41. Jung, *Letters,* I, p. 366. Dr. L. Bendit discovered such a "knowledge" independently of Jung and named it Paranormal Cognition. See Jung's letters to him, ibid., pp. 389, 420.

42. CW 8, pars. 856, 912.

43. For details I must refer the reader to ibid., pars. 856ff.

44. Ibid., par. 842.

45. Cf. also Jung, *Letters,* I, p. 249.

46. Jung, "Synchronicity," CW 8, par. 912; *Letters,* I, pp. 256f.

47. Cf. ibid.

48. Ibid., par. 870.

49. Jung, as is well known, calls this "acausal orderedness," ibid., par. 965.

50. Cf. also Jung, *Letters,* I, p. 87.

51. Cf. Jung, "Synchronicity," CW 8, par. 965.

52. Cf. also the excellent comments by Mary Gammon that point in a similar direction, in "Window into Eternity," pp. 11ff.

53. "Synchronicity," CW 8, par. 870 (italics added).

54. Jung defined "spirit" similarly in "The Phenomenology of the Spirit in Fairy Tales," CW 9(1), par. 393.

55. For a detailed discussion of this problem I must refer the reader to my book *Number and Time.*

56. Cf. Jung, "Synchronicity," CW 8, pars. 856ff; and Jung, *Letters,* I, pp. 176ff, 378f.

57. Cf. Jung, "Synchronicity," CW 8, pars. 849, 850f.

58. Ibid., par. 849.

Bibliography

Ackerknecht, E. H. "Natural Diseases and Rational Treatment in Primitive Medicine." *Bulletin of the History of Medicine,* vol. 19, May 1946.

————. "Primitive Medicine and Culture Pattern." *Bulletin of the History of Medicine,* vol. 12, no. 4, 1942.

————. *A Short History of Psychiatry.* New York and London, 1959.

Ali, S. *La Projection: Une étude psychoanalytique.* Paris, 1970.

Andresen, C. *Logos und Nomos: Die Polemik des Kelsos wider das Christentum.* Berlin, 1955.

Anschütz, R. *August Kekulé.* 2 vols. Berlin, 1929.

Apuleius. *Metamorphosen, oder der Goldene Essel.* Translated by R. Helm. Berlin, 1956. [English version: *The Transformations of Lucius, Otherwise Known as The Golden Ass.* Translated by Robert Graves. New York, 1951.]

————. *Opuscules philosophiques et fragments.* Edited by J. Beaujeu. Paris, 1973.

Atharva-Veda. See Bloomfield.

Baudelaire, C. *The Flowers of Evil.* Edited by M. and J. Mathews. Rev. ed. Norfolk, Conn., 1962.

Beek, M. Y. van. *Passio Sanctarum Perpetuae et Felicitatis.* Leipzig, 1936.

Benz, E. *Die Vision.* Stuttgart, 1971.

————. *Neue Religionen.* Stuttgart, 1971.

Binder, G., and Merkelbach, R., eds. *Amor and Psyche.* Darmstadt, 1968.

Bloomfield, M. *Hymns of the Atharva-Veda.* Sacred Books of the East, 42. Oxford, 1897.

Bohr, N. *Atomic Theory and the Description of Nature.* New York, 1934.

Bühlmann, R. *Die Entwicklung des tiefenpsychologischen Begriffs der Projektion.* Zurich, 1971.

Capelle, W. *Die Vorsokratiker.* Leipzig, 1935.

Capra, F. *The Tao of Physics.* Berkeley, 1975.

Carnap, R. *Einführung in die Philosophie der Naturwissenschaft.* Nymphenburg, 1969.

Christiansen, J. *Die Technik der allegorischen Auslegungswissenschaft bei Philo von Alexandrien.* Tübingen, 1969.

233

Clement of Alexandria. *Stromata.* Edited by von Camélot and Montdésert. Paris, 1954.

———. *Excerpta ex Theodoto.* See Migne, *P.G.,* vol. 9.

Colpe, C. "Damonen." In *Reallexikon für Antike und Christentum.* Stuttgart, 1974.

Corbin, H. "Herméneutique spirituelle comparée." *Eranosjahrbuch,* vol. 33. Zurich, 1965.

———. *Avicenne et le récit visionnaire.* 2 vols. Teheran and Paris, 1954.

Deonna, W. *Le Symbolisme de l'oeil.* Berne, 1965.

Diels, H. *Die Fragmente der Vorsokratiker.* 6th ed. 3 vols. Berlin, 1951–52. [English version: Freeman, Kathleen. *Ancilla to the Pre-Socratic Philosophers.* A Complete Translation of the Fragments in Diels, *Fragmente der Vorsokratiker.* Oxford and Cambridge, Mass., 1952.]

Dobschutz, E. von. "Vom vierfachen Schriftsinn." In *Beiträge zur Kirchengeschichte,* edited by A. Harnack. Leipzig, 1921.

Durand, G. See *Le Symbole.* Kongressbericht. Strasbourg, 1975.

Edinger, E. *Ego and Archetype.* New York, 1972.

Eliade, M. *Shamanism: Archaic Techniques of Ecstasy.* Translated by W. R. Trask. New York (Bollingen Series LXXVI) and London, 1964.

Ephrem the Syrian, Saint. *Hymni et sermones,* vol. 2. Edited by T. J. Lamy. Mechlin, 1886.

Ernst, C. *Teufelsaustreibungen: Die Praxis der katholischen Kirche in 16ten and 17ten Jahrhundert.* Berne, 1972.

Exégèse et herméneutique. Congress report. Edited by X. L. Dufour. Paris, 1971.

Fabricus, J. "The Symbol of the Self in the Alchemical 'Proiectio.' " *Journal of Analytical Psychology* (London), vol. 18, no. 1, 1973.

Fierz, M. "Isaac Newton als Mathematiker." *Neujahrsblatt der Naturforschenden Gesellschaft in Zürich,* 1972.

———. "Über den Ursprung und die Bedeutung der Lehre Isaac Newtons vom absoluten Raum." *Gesnerus* (Zurich), vol. 2, 1952.

Franz, M.-L. von. *Aurora Consurgens: A Document Attributed to Thomas Aquinas on the Problem of Opposites in Alchemy.* Vol. 3 of *Mysterium Coniunctionis.* Translated by R.F.C. Hull and A.S.B. Glover. New York (Bollingen Series LXXVII) and London, 1966.

————. *C. G. Jung: His Myth in Our Time*. Translated by W. H. Kennedy. New York, 1975.

————. "The Dream of Descartes." In *Timeless Documents of the Soul*. Studies in Jungian Thought. Evanston, 1968.

————. *The Feminine in Fairytales*. New York, 1972.

————. *The Golden Ass of Apuleius*. Zurich and New York, 1970.

————. *Interpretation of Fairytales*. New York, 1972.

————. *Jung's Typology*. New York, 1971.

————. *Number and Time: Reflections Leading toward a Unification of Depth Psychology and Physics*. Translated by A. Dykes. Studies in Jungian Thought. Evanston, 1974.

————. "Die *Passio Perpetuae*." In C. G. Jung, *Aion: Untersuchungen zur Symbolgeschichte*. Psychologische Abhandlungen, VIII. Zurich, 1951. [English version: "The *Passio Perpetuae*." *Spring* (New York), 1949.]

————. "Das Problem des Bösen im Märchen." In *Das Böse*. Studien aus dem C. G. Jung-Institut. Zurich, 1961.

————. *The Problem of the Puer Aeternus*. New York, 1970.

————. *Shadow and Evil in Fairytales*. New York, 1974.

————. *Time, Rhythm and Repose*. New York, 1978.

Freud, S. *Totem and Taboo*. London, 1975.

Friedrich, A., and Buddruss, G., trans. *Schamanengeschichten aus Siberien*. Munich, 1955.

Gammon, M. "Window into Eternity: Archetype and Relativity." *Journal of Analytical Psychology* (London), vol. 18, no. 1, 1973.

Gillespie, C. G. *The Edge of Objectivity*. Princeton, 1959.

Goppelt, L. *Typos: Die typologische Deutung des Alten Testaments im Neuen*. Darmstadt, 1973.

Gould, R. *Yiwara, Foragers of the Australian Desert*. New York, 1969.

Hahn, C. *Geschichte der Ketzer im Mittelalter*. Aalen, 1968.

Heisenberg, W. *Physics and Philosophy: The Revolution in Modern Science*. London, 1952.

Hermes Trismegistus. *Corpus Hermeticum*. Text established by A. Y. Nock and translated by E. Festugiere. 4 vols. Paris, 1960.

Hippolytos. *Elenchos (Refutatio Omnium Haeresium)*. In *Werke*, Vol. 3. Edited by P. Wendland. Leipzig, 1916. [English version: *The Refutation of All Heresies*. Translated by J. H. Macmahon. Edinburgh, 1911.]

Holton, G. "Über die Hypothesen, welche den Naturwissenschaften zugrunde liegen." *Eranosjahrbuch,* vol. 39. Zurich, 1970.

―――. "The Roots of Complementarity." *Eranosjahrbuch,* vol. 37. Zurich, 1968.

Honko, L. *Krankheitsprojektile.*

Horace. *Horace: Satires, Epistles and Ars Poetica.* With an English translation by H. R. Fairclough. Loeb Classical Library. London and New York, 1926.

Hugo, V. "La Conscience." In H. Sens, *Chrestomathie française du XIX siècle.* Lausanne, 1899.

I Ching, or Book of Changes. The German translation by R. Wilhelm, rendered into English by C. F. Baynes. 3rd ed. Princeton (Bollingen Series XIX) and London, 1967.

Isler, G. *Die Sennenpuppe.* Basel, 1971.

Jacobsohn, Helmuth. "The Dialogue of a World-Weary Man with His Ba." In *Timeless Documents of the Soul.* Studies in Jungian Thought. Evanston, 1968.

Jaffé, A. "Synchronizität und Kausalität." *Eranosjahrbuch,* vol. 42. Zurich, 1973.

Jammer, M. *Der Begriff der Masse in der Physik.* Darmstadt, 1974. [English version: *Concepts of Mass in Classical and Modern Physics.* Cambridge, Mass., 1961.]

―――. *Concepts of Space.*

Jung, C. G. *The Collected Works of C. G. Jung.* Edited by Sir H. Read, M. Fordham, G. Adler, and W. McGuire. Translated by R. F. C. Hull (except for vol. 2). New York/Princeton (Bollingen Series XX) and London, 1953–76. Volumes cited:

    5. *Symbols of Transformation.* 2nd ed. 1967.

    6. *Psychological Types.* 1971.

    7. *Two Essays on Analytical Psychology.* 2nd ed. 1966.

    8. *The Structure and Dynamics of the Psyche.* 2nd ed. 1969.

    9. Part 1. *The Archetypes and the Collective Unconscious.* 2nd ed. 1968.

    9. Part 2. *Aion: Researches into the Phenomenology of the Self.* 2nd ed. 1968.

    10. *Civilization in Transition.* 1964.

    11. *Psychology and Religion: West and East.* 2nd ed. 1969.

    12. *Psychology and Alchemy.* 2nd ed. 1968.

    13. *Alchemical Studies.* 1967.

14. *Mysterium Coniunctionis: An Inquiry into the Separation and Synthesis of Psychic Opposites in Alchemy.* 2nd ed. 1970.

17. *The Development of Personality.* 1954.

————. *Letters.* Selected and edited by G. Adler in collaboration with A. Jaffé. Bollingen Series XCV. 2 vols. Princeton and London, 1973 and 1975. ˇ

————. *Man and His Symbols.* (With M.-L. von Franz, J. L. Henderson, J. Jacobi, A. Jaffé.) New York and London, 1964.

————. *Memories, Dreams, Reflections.* Recorded and edited by A. Jaffé. Translated by R. and C. Winston. New York and London, 1961.

Jung, E., and Franz, M.-L. von. *The Grail Legend.* Translated by A. Dykes. New York and London, 1971.

Kasper, W., and Lehmen, K. *Teufel, Dämonen, Besessenheit: Zur Wirklichkeit des Bösen.*

Kerényi, K. *Die griechisch-orientalische Romanliteratur in religionsgeschichtlicher Beleuchtung.* Tübingen, 1927.

Kettler, F. H. *Der ursprüngliche Sinn der Dogmatik des Origenes.* Berlin, 1966.

Koch, H. *Pronoia und Paideusis: Studien über Origenes und sein Verhältnis zum Platonismus.* Berlin, 1932.

Labriolle, P. de. *La Crise Montaniste.* Paris, 1913.

Lavagnini, B. *Il significato il valore del romanzo di Apuleo.* Pisa, 1927.

Leisegang, H. *Die Gnosis.* Kröners Taschenausgabe. Leipzig, 1924.

Lévy-Bruhl, L. *How Natives Think.* Translated by L. A. Clare [from *Les Fonctions mentales dans les sociétés inférieures*]. London, 1926.

Liu Guan-ying. "Die ungewöhnlichen Naturerscheinungen in den T'ang Annalen under ihre Deutung." *Symbollon: Jahrbuch für Symbolforschung,* vol. 2. Basel, 1961.

Lobo, R. "Samkhya-yoga und spätantiker Geist: Eine Untersuchung der Allegorese des Origenes in Licht der indischen Philosophie." Dissertation. Munich, 1970.

Lubac, H. de. *Exégèse médiévale: Les quatre sens de l'Ecriture.* 4 vols. Aubier, 1959.

Mahnke, D. *Unendliche Sphäre und Allmittelpunkt: Beiträge zur Geneologie der mathematischen Mystik.* Stuttgart, 1966.

Märchen der Weltliteratur. Edited by J. van der Leyen and P. Zaunert. Jena-Cologne-Düsseldorf.

    Chinesische Märchen. Edited by R. Wilhelm. 1921.

Nordische Märchen II. 1922.

Deutsche Märchen seit Grimm I. 1922.

Märchen aus Turkestan und Tibet. 1923.

Märchen aus Sibirien. N.d.

Indianermärchen aus Südamerika. 1921.

Meier, C. A. "Projektion, Übertragung und Subjekt-Objekt-relation." *Dialectica* (Neuchâtel) 29, vol. 8, no. 4, 1954.

Merkelbach, R. *Roman und Mysterium in der Antike.* Munich and Berlin, 1962.

Migne, J. P., ed. *Patrologiae cursus completus.*

  P.L. Latin Series. 221 vols. Paris, 1844–64.

  P.G. Greek Series. 166 vols. Paris, 1857–66.

Miura-Stange, A. *Celsus und Origines: Das gemeinsame ihrer Weltanschauung.* Giessen, 1926.

Mode, H. *Fabulous Beasts and Demons.* New York, 1973.

Neumann, E. *Amor and Psyche: The Psychic Development of the Feminine.* A commentary on the tale by Apuleius. Translated by R. Manheim. New York (Bollingen Series LIV) and London, 1956.

Niderberger, F. *Sagen, Märchen und Gebräuche aus Unterwalden.* Stans, 1914.

Ninck, M. *Die Bedeutung des Wassers im Kult und Leben der Alten.* Darmstadt, 1960.

Nitzsche, J. C. *The Genius Figure in Antiquity and in the Middle Ages.* New York and London, 1975.

Oesterreich, T. K. *Les Possédés.* Paris, 1927. [English version: *Possession, Demonical and Other, among Primitive Races in Antiquity, the Middle Ages and Modern Times.* New York, 1966.]

Oldemeyer, E. "Überlegungen zum phänomenologisch-philosophischen und kybernetischen Bewusstseinsbegriff." In K. Steinbuch, *Philosophie und Kybernetik.* Munich, 1970.

Onians, R. B. *The Origins of European Thought.* Cambridge, Eng., 1954.

Origen, *Contra Celsus.* See Migne, *P.G.,* vol. 11, cols. 641-1632. [English version: *Contra Celsus.* Translated by G. W. Butterworth. London, 1936. German version: *Gegen Celsus.* Translated by P. Koetschau. Munich, 1926.]

Palmer, E. *Hermeneutics: Interpretation Theory in Schleiermacher, Dilthey, Heidegger and Gadamer.* Evanston, 1969.

Pauli, W. "The Influence of Archetypal Ideas on the Scientific Theories of Kepler." In C. G. Jung and W. Pauli, *Synchronicity: An Acausal Connecting Principle.* New York, 1959.

Pfeiffer, E. H. *Transkulturelle Psychiatrie.* Stuttgart, 1971.

Philo of Alexandria. *Philonis Opera,* vol. 2. Edited by P. Wendland. Berlin, 1897.

Plato. "Timaeus." *Platonis Opera,* vol. 4. Edited by J. Burnet. Oxford, 1955.

Plutarch. *Über Isis und Osiris.* Edited by T. Hopfner. 2 vols. Darmstadt, 1967.

Preisendanz, K. *Papyri Graecae Magicae.* 2 vols. Stuttgart and Leipzig, 1973.

Puech, H.-C. "Der Begriff der Erlösing im Manichäismus." *Eranosjahrbuch,* vol. 4. Zurich, 1936.

Regen, F. *Apuleius philosophus Platonicus.* Berlin and New York, 1971.

Reitzenstein, R. *Poimandres: Studien zur griechsch-ägyptischen und frühchristlichen Literatur.* Leipzig, 1904.

———. *Die hellenistischen Mysterienreligionen.* Leipzig, 1920.

Reuter. *Die Geschichte der religiösen Aufklarung in Mittelalter.*

Rig-Veda. Translated by Ralph T. H. Griffith. New rev. ed. Delhi, 1973.

Rodewyk, A. *Die dämonische Besessenheit in der Sicht des Rituale Romanum.* Zurich, 1963. [English version: *Possessed by Satan: The Church's Teaching on the Devil, Possession, and Exorcism.* New York, 1975.]

Rohde, E. *Psyche.* Translated from the 4th German ed. by W. B. Hillis. London, 1925.

Ruyer, R. *La Gnose de Princeton.* Paris, 1974.

Sam’bursky, S. *Physical Thought from the Presocratics to the Quantum Physicists.* New York, 1975.

———. *Das Physikalische Weltbild der Antike.* Zurich, 1965. [English version: *The Physical World of the Greeks.* London, 1956.]

Seligmann, S. *Der böse Blick und Verwandtes.* 2 vols. Berlin, 1910.

Soury, G. *La Démonologie de Plutarque.* Paris, 1942.

Steinbuch, K. *Philosophie und Kybernetik.* Munich, 1970.

Stock, H. *The Method of Descartes in Natural Sciences.* New York, 1931.

Swahn, J. O. *The Tale of Cupid and Psyche.* Lynd, 1955.

Symbole, Le. Congress report. Edited by J. Ménard. Strasbourg, 1975.

Thompson, R. C. *The Devils and Evil Spirits of Babylonia.* 2 vols. London, 1902.

Tonquédec, J. de. *Les Maladies nerveuses ou mentales et les manifestations diaboliques.* Paris, 1938.

Upanischaden. In *Indische Weisheit.* Düsseldorf-Cologne, 1975. [English version: *The Upanishads.* Parts 1 and 2. Translated by F. Max Müller. Sacred Books of the East, 1 and 15. Oxford, 1879 and 1884.]

Wey, H. "Die Funktionen der bösen Geister bei den griechischen Apologeten des zweiten Jahrhunderts nach Christus." Dissertation. Winterthur, 1957.

Wheeler, A. *Einsteins Vision.* Heidelberg, 1968. [English edition: *Einstein's Vision.* Heidelberg, 1968.]

Wigner, E. *Symmetries and Reflections.* Cambridge, Mass., 1970.

Zacharias, G., ed. *Das Böse: Dokumente und Interpretationen.* Munich, 1972.

Index